THE UPPER HOUSE IN REVOLUTIONARY AMERICA

JACKSON TURNER MAIN

The Upper House in Revolutionary America

1763-1788

1967

THE UNIVERSITY OF WISCONSIN PRESS

MADISON, MILWAUKEE, AND LONDON

Published by the University of Wisconsin Press
Madison, Milwaukee, and London
U.S.A.: Box 1379, Madison, Wisconsin 53701
U.K.: 26–28 Hallam Street, London, W. 1
Copyright © 1967 by the Regents of the
University of Wisconsin
All rights reserved
Printed in the United States of America
by the George Banta Company, Inc., Menasha, Wisconsin
Library of Congress Catalog Card
Number 67–20753

FOR

MERRILL JENSEN

IN ADMIRATION AND GRATITUDE

PREFACE

*T*HIS BOOK has three purposes; first, to examine the power structure of Revolutionary America through a study of a political elite; second, to investigate the effects of the Revolution as they are revealed by what happened to that elite; and third, to analyze the functions of the upper houses as they had evolved by the end of the colonial period and as they began to change after 1776.

In achieving these ends my first task was to determine the precise composition of the various upper houses. This meant gathering biographical data on the economic and social backgrounds of the more than eleven hundred men who served as councillors and senators during the years in question. Next, I examined the journals of the upper houses in order to determine the functions and contributions of those houses as well as their relations with the lower branches of legislature. Finally, I read through the letters and, more important, the pamphlets and newspaper essays of people living at the time, in an effort to discover their opinions and ideas about what the upper house should be and do.

Three significant conclusions emerge from this study. For one thing, the pre-Revolutionary councils did not consist merely of obstructive placemen, nor were the councillors simply rich men who defended their own economic and political interests. The councils, in other words, were not ciphers. On the contrary, their functions were extensive and often useful. In most colonies they had considerable power to formulate, amend, or reject laws, and their influence on the legislative process therefore was great. Secondly,

the view that the post-Revolutionary senates were nothing but aristocratic bodies appears to be entirely false. For the changes
wrought by the Revolution were enormous, beginning as early as
the Stamp Act disturbances and extending throughout the 1780's.
One major change was in personnel, for the senates, though still
composed mostly of well-to-do men, became much more nearly
democratic in their structure; they still favored the upper class,
but this was changing rapidly. Similarly, while the senators did
sometimes favor the larger property owners, other interests came
to be more important. And thus the senates could be and increasingly were justified on democratic grounds. Finally, the political
controversies of the 1780's turn out not to have involved primarily
a contest between an aristocratic upper house and a democratic
lower one, but a struggle between factions or parties which were
emerging in both. On vote after vote, in both houses and in most
states, one finds the same kind of alignment on the same kind of
issue. The significance of this development was not properly understood at the time, but it is clear in retrospect that political parties were beginning to form which would soon alter entirely both
the theory and practice of politics.

Two points need comment. The colonial councils had judicial
and executive functions which are not discussed here. They are important, but to examine them would require an entirely different
book, dealing fully with the controversy between the legislatures
and the executive—that is, with the causes of the Revolution. Secondly, a few words used in this study may require explanation. It
can be argued that, strictly speaking, the colonies did not develop an
"aristocracy." They did, however, develop an elite, an upper class,
a "better sort," and they did sometimes apply the word "aristocracy" to this colonial equivalent. It is this usage that is adopted
here. Also, the term "faction" is sometimes confined to men coop-
erating politically who share no particular ideology nor any social,
economic, or cultural interest, but only a desire for office; while
the word "party" sometimes assumes a particular degree of organization, and perhaps other specific qualities. Both are here used
loosely, however, as men of the eighteenth century employed them.

My major professional debt is acknowledged in the dedication. I
am also indebted to the American Philosophical Society for a
grant which helped me in the early stages of research. Of the many

libraries visited, those of the American Antiquarian Society and the State Historical Society of Wisconsin were of the greatest value for their extensive collections of published sources. The other materials used and depositories visited are indicated in the notes and in a bibliographical essay. And last but not least I am grateful to my wife for her forbearance and encouragement through months of research and writing.

JACKSON T. MAIN

Setauket, New York
March 1967

Contents

Part One

PRE-REVOLUTIONARY COUNCILS
1763–1776

$\mathcal{D}$URING THE PERIOD preceding the American Revolution eleven of the thirteen colonies that were to form the United States of America had bicameral legislatures.[1] Of these eleven colonies three were established by charters that either gave the voters the right to elect both houses (Connecticut and Rhode Island) or provided for the election of the upper house by the lower (Massachusetts). In the other eight colonies one branch, variously referred to as Burgesses, Commons, Delegates, Representatives, or Assembly, was elected by the voters and the other branch, always called the Council, was chosen by the king or, in Maryland, by the proprietor.

The royal and proprietary councils usually consisted of twelve members if all vacancies were filled.[2] Nominations in all of the royal colonies were made by the Board of Trade from a list of persons recommended by the governor. He was instructed to take care that they be men "of good life, well-affected to our government, of good estates and abilities, and not necessitous people."[3] The governors always tried to obtain the appointment of men upon whom they could rely, but they also had to placate powerful and prestigious colonials. The governor had the right to suspend a member, but he had to justify such a suspension and a rejoinder was permitted. This power was limited, moreover, because capricious or arbitrary action against a councillor might alienate the most influential colonials and vitiate any chance for future promotion. The governor's power was further reduced because the Board of Trade might ignore his recommendations in favor of a candidate who had been previously suggested.[4] Thus some councillors were chosen for their loyalty, others for their power; and although in theory a man served "at pleasure," which meant for as long as the king or proprietor wished, in practice he usually enjoyed tenure for life.

The council had various functions. In its executive capacity it advised the governor, who was required to obtain the council's consent in various matters including appointments. It also had judicial powers, being (in royal colonies) the highest court of appeals in all civil cases involving at least £300. Finally, the councils sat as the upper houses of the legislatures. A full history of the councils would therefore require an extensive account of political and judicial developments in the colonies. Naturally these functions could not be entirely separated, and indeed the governor and council sometimes met together discussing executive, legislative, and judicial matters concomitantly. In the later colonial period, however, the three roles were distinguished. Separate minutes were kept, and the governors eventually ceased to attend when the council sat as an upper house.[5]

The councillors can be divided into two general types. Some were primarily officials of the British government, economically dependent upon a major post other than that of councillor, which ordinarily was unremunerated. These men were usually, though not invariably, English or Scottish rather than colonial by birth. They were referred to derogatorily as "placemen." The placemen were concerned primarily with defending the authority and rights of the king. Most councillors, however, were colonials who either did not hold another high office or who were not economically dependent upon such an office.[6] These men, while not blind to the prerogative, represented primarily colonial society.

The role of the upper house in the pre-Revolutionary years varied from colony to colony depending upon the composition of the councils. Those that came to be dominated by placemen had histories quite unlike those controlled by local elites, while the elected upper houses differed even more markedly. Each of these three types requires separate treatment.

CHAPTER 1

THE PLACEMEN

*T*HE PLACEMAN, according to colonial invective, was one whose attitudes and allegiances were determined by the offices which he held, and who was, by implication, alien to colonial society. The epithet was often more useful for propaganda purposes than as an accurate description, for some high officials were native colonials who became ardent defenders of provincial rights, while many who were not colonial-born acquired extensive economic interests or intimate family ties which wedded them to the new society. A councillor became identified as a placeman when, as the contest between colonies and mother country intensified, he distinguished himself by his loyalty to king or proprietor.

To the colonials, the most obnoxious placeman was the English-, Scottish-, or Irish-born official. Such men formed a majority in only two councils; but in a total of four they became increasingly important after 1763, as the governors turned to them for support and as the native councillors refused to attend meetings or even resigned. The legislatures in which this process occurred had distinctive histories characterized by conflict between the two houses. Georgia, the Carolinas, and Maryland all experienced in varying degrees a determined struggle for supremacy between the council and the assembly.

GEORGIA

Georgia in 1763 was a relatively new colony. Founded only thirty years earlier, its youth had been turbulent, and despite a considerable increase in population it was essentially a frontier region. In 1760 there were fewer than ten thousand inhabitants, and on the eve of the Revolution the colony still contained fewer than twenty thousand whites. Georgians depended upon the Crown for protection from the Indians and even for financial aid,[1] and they never dared to challenge the governor until the Revolution was well under way.[2] The colony was weak, but it no longer was poor, for thousands of acres of good agricultural land were producing a profitable surplus. The number of slaves increased from 3,500 in 1760 to 15,000 in 1775. Although Georgia was so young that everyone in the colony was a recent immigrant either from another colony or from the mother country, a wealthy upper class had developed, consisting mainly of rice planters and merchants. Because so many of its members were newcomers to the colonies, this upper class had not yet transferred its allegiance from the old world to the new. The royal government was therefore able to rely upon the loyalty of many, if not most, wealthy* Georgians, and to select dependable councillors from among them. Their attachment to the Crown was strengthened by grants of land and profitable offices.

Georgia's Council contained a majority of placemen. They occupied most of the important posts: attorney general, receiver, surveyor general, treasurer, secretary, chief justice, and other judicial offices. Some of these officials drew large salaries: for example, the receiver earned £2,000.[3] Most of them were not colonials by birth. At least eight of the fifteen (not counting the Indian agent, who never attended) were natives of the British Isles, and one or possibly two others had immigrated from the West Indies.

---

* In the present work, the word "wealthy" is reserved for men owning property worth £5,000 or more. The word "rich" will be used synonymously. Later in the text it will become necessary to distinguish these men from those who are "well-to-do" (that is, who possess more than £2,000 but less than £5,000 in property) ; and from those who are of "moderate" means (owning property valued at less than £2,000).

The colonists used the English pound sterling as the basic monetary unit. Their common coin was, however, the Spanish silver dollar, worth four and one-half shillings sterling. Each colony adopted an imaginary money called "lawful money," which served as a unit of account, and the value of which was set by law: in South Carolina and Georgia 4s 8d, in New England and Virginia 6s, in New York and North Carolina 8s, elsewhere 7s 6d. But the actual as opposed to the legal value of colonial currency varied considerably. South Carolina's paper money, for example, circulated at £7 currency to £1 sterling. Figures in the text are lawful money unless otherwise identified.

Nevertheless the councillors, taken as a whole, were not alien to colonial society, and several of them belonged to prominent South Carolina families.[4] Others quickly established local connections. For example, Jonathan Bryan's father Joseph was a South Carolina planter, and Jonathan's daughter married the influential John Houstoun.[5] John Graham, the receiver, James Habersham, the secretary, and James Hume, the advocate general, all married Georgia girls, and Clement Martin's sister married a prominent colonial.[6] With few exceptions they could qualify as old residents. Four, indeed, had arrived in the colony within a decade of its founding; by 1755 all but two future councillors resided there and one of the exceptions was a native of South Carolina. The Council of 1763 consisted of men who had been Georgians, on the average, for a dozen years.

Not only were the councillors closely connected with the colonies by birth, marriage, or long residence, but they also had a significant economic interest in the future of the new land. Six had begun as merchants and had accumulated fortunes from the rapidly expanding economy. Two were lawyers and two had been doctors, though they no longer derived any significant income from medicine. The one great source of wealth in which all invested was land. Three depended entirely upon agriculture, and all of the others were actively engaged in acquiring plantations. As councillors they controlled land grants, and they took full advantage of their power. When James Read settled in 1755 he owned twelve slaves. By 1766 he had fifty slaves, had received 2,000 acres, and was applying for 1,750 more. When one 450-acre tract proved to be treeless, he asked for and was permitted an exchange. In the following years he added another 2,000 acres.[7] Land records are incomplete, but it seems that only one councillor owned less than 1,000 acres, the average being at least 5,000. Collectively they held at least 1,200 slaves. Obviously the members of the upper house had a very large economic stake in the community. It is evident, too, that they were not simply placemen. The councillors did occupy most of the important posts, some of which were remunerative, yet their other economic interests were equally significant. Graham's 262 slaves and over 20,000 acres were almost equal in value to his salary of £2,000. James Hume derived a considerable income as advocate general, but he was also a lawyer and planter of substantial means, with at least 1,500 acres and 100 slaves.[8]

The councillors' high economic rank was paralleled by their high social status. This was a consequence not only of their prestige as officeholders and men of property but also of their family backgrounds. Although the parentage of some is uncertain, the great majority came from families of repute or even distinction, and had made their mark before they arrived in Georgia. William Clifton's father was a baronet who had sent his son to the Inns of Court; Anthony Stokes came from the landed gentry and, like Clifton, had been a lawyer in London; Henry Yonge was also an English-trained lawyer whose father had been chief justice of South Carolina and a member of the colony's Council.[9] The social origins of the other men are not so clear, but in general they seem to have started with advantages.[10] The councillors therefore were part of the local upper class, a part which, to be sure, was favored by the government, profited from that favor, and supported the government in turn, but one which did not depend upon the government for its economic power or social position.[11]

Perhaps had Georgia been an older and stronger colony, the unrepresentative nature of the Council might have led to frequent attacks upon it. But so dependent was the colony upon the Crown that no such challenge could be made until the very end of the colonial period. The "Commons House of Assembly" always acknowledged the Council as an upper house, and most disagreements were settled amicably. The Council took an active part in the legislative process. In 1763, for example, it amended eight of the thirteen acts passed in that year; in the following year it originated two and amended five of the ten that became law. Indeed, until 1767 relations between the two houses were peaceful. They united in criticizing the Sugar Act, thereby bringing on a prorogation.[12] When the Commons, in a money bill, failed to allot the Council its customary proportion of nominations for commissioners to issue certificates, the upper house protested but passed the measure.[13] The Council did indeed take the governor's side in enforcing the Stamp Act (though by a split vote), but in general there were no serious differences.[14]

Beginning in 1767, however, the Council found itself obliged to defend its own rights as well as the royal prerogative. The first issue to arise was comparatively minor, but it marked a new era in the colony's political history. The Commons passed a bill which infringed upon an act of Parliament requiring that postmen be given free passage on ferries. The Council made the necessary amendments, but the lower house, far from automatically accepting them, rebelled, and a year went by before the changes were adopted. A few days later the Commons attempted to increase its influence over the colony's officials by nominating all of the commissioners of a pesthouse. The Council refused to be excluded, and when it insisted upon its right to share in making nominations, the lower house had to retreat.[15]

In the same session a major quarrel erupted. On March 18, 1767, the councillors sent a message to the lower house: an article or two in the tax bill required reconsideration, and a conference was needed. The Commons promptly replied that "such Request is contrary to the known Custom and Usage of Assembly." The Council then yielded and passed the bill by a vote of five to three.[16]

Two dissenting opinions from the Council's minority explained what was at stake. Grey Elliott, a wealthy planter and lawyer, surveyor general, auditor general, judge, and future Loyalist, argued that the Council should not allow payment for a service to which it had not agreed, for its assent was "necessary to make effectual every Vote of Credit of the lower House." James E. Powell, being a merchant rather than a lawyer, was more specific: the lower house had granted £154 for past and future services to Charles Garth, whose appointment as the colony's agent in England had not been confirmed by the Council.[17]

The case actually grew out of the Stamp Act crisis. When William Knox, Georgia's colonial agent, defended the Stamp Act, the Commons removed him and appointed Garth instead. The Council, however, had not agreed to the substitution, ostensibly because Garth was also the agent for South Carolina, with which Georgia was engaged in disputes.[18] For some months the upper house continued to support Knox, but in March a majority of councillors accepted the bill—not because they had decided to approve of Garth, but because they felt that since he was not the legal agent the clause could not take effect, and they did not want to reject the entire measure. Later in the month the Council was angered to discover that the Commons had chosen a committee to correspond with Garth as agent of the province. There was, the councillors insisted, no such agent, and the lower house had no right to act without the consent of the entire legislature. They then requested the governor to use his influence in England "to support the Just Rights and Priviledges of this House against the Encroachment of the Commons House of Assembly."[19] In the governor's view, the lower house was deliberately attempting "to thwart the Sovereignty of Great Britain, to destroy or weaken the weight of the Council as an Upper House, and to Endeavour to assume to themselves improper Powers."[20] Garth settled the matter by refusing to serve as the agent of only one house, and the Commons was forced to compromise. In April of 1768 the two houses agreed to appoint Benjamin Franklin as the colony's London agent.[21]

The next few years were uneventful. The Council continued to amend various bills, protecting its own rights together with the royal prerogative.[22] In the fall of 1773 the Commons again attempted to enhance its authority when it defined as a tax measure a bill establishing a watch company in Savannah. The upper house was not to be deceived, but resolved that the act, "blending together Matters of Legislation and Taxation and thereby tending to preclude this House from making Amendments thereto, is Unparliamentary, and in derogation of the Rights of this House." The bill was thereupon rejected, the Council resolving unanimously that "this House will Consider no Bill a Money Bill in which there is not the Usual and Necessary Clause of a Gift and Grant by the Commons to the Crown."[23]

The decisive conflict began in 1774 when the Commons at last took a strong stand. Once again the fundamental cause was the Council's determination to defend the rights of the Crown and the Commons' effort to augment its own power. This time the Council rejected an ordinance reappointing Franklin on the ground that he had not corresponded with the legislature. The facts were otherwise, and the real reason undoubtedly was the hostility of Governor Wright toward the agent. The lower house now acted independently: it chose Franklin as its own agent, insisting that this power "ought to be exclusively lodged in the Representatives of the People"; named a committee to correspond with him; and arranged for the payment of his salary. Such firm action for the first time rendered the Council powerless, and it could only complain that the proceeding constituted a "flagrent attack upon & high infringement of the clear & undoubted Rights of this House."[24]

As the Revolution approached, the Commons became increasingly bold. In the January session of 1775, the representatives refused to join with the Council in a conference to discuss conciliatory measures; and whereas the Council sent a respectful and pacific measure to the governor, the Commons' address was bellicose.[25] This event marked the end of the colonial period. The two houses had seldom or never disagreed concerning economic or social affairs, but only with regard to Empire relations. The lower house did not challenge the power of the upper until the very eve of independence. On the whole, during the decade prior to the outbreak of war, the Council had been "an effective check on the popularly elected Commons House of Assembly."[26]

South Carolina

South Carolina had existed for a century when the Revolutionary era began. A wealthy society had developed in the coastal parishes, characterized by rich indigo and rice planters, a flourishing merchant class, and many thousands of Negro slaves, who far outnumbered the whites. The inland districts, on the other hand, contained principally farmers of modest means who practiced mixed farming supplemented by household manufacturing. While a few wealthy planters with slaves did exist there, the overall social structure was democratic. However, the small landholders, though numerous, were of little political consequence prior to independence. Almost all of the men elected to the lower house came from near the coast rather than from the interior; moreover, representatives were required to own five hundred acres and ten slaves, or the equivalent property.[27] Therefore the eastern planter-merchant-lawyer upper class, centering in Charleston, protected its well-established economic and social position by its political power.

The same class controlled the Council. Theoretically that body consisted of fourteen persons, but in practice there were usually only ten or eleven members. Attendance was exceedingly irregular, for the surveyor general and the superintendent of Indian affairs rarely were present and others often were in England or on their plantations. Fortunately the colony's business did not suffer, because in royal colonies three constituted a quorum for legislative matters and five for executive affairs. However, as the Revolutionary movement progressed and the split between Loyalist and rebel widened, the uncommitted members of the Council, who might have moderated its stand, stayed at home, leaving the prerogative men in control. The Council therefore came to be increasingly Loyalist in sentiment, partly because of its basic composition and partly because the rebel element withdrew.

During the period from 1763 to 1776, a total of fifteen men served as councillors in South Carolina.[28] These were of two types: the native South Carolinians, and the British-born immigrants, most of whom held other offices and who eventually were accused of being placemen. A bare majority had been born in the colony. They had been chosen because of their loyalty, wealth, and influence. In addition, three others had resided in South Carolina for some years, married into the local elite, and become colonials. Therefore the Council, though it did uphold the prerogative, was not alien, but represented primarily a single element within colonial society: the wealthy merchant-planter upper class of the Charleston area.

The Bull family was an important part of that class. The first Bull, Stephen, was a lawyer who made a fortune in the Indian trade and became a councillor. His son William (1683–1755) continued the family business and the family office, adding a large amount of land and attaining the lieutenant governorship. William Jr. earned a medical degree at Leyden, succeeded his father in the Council, became lieutenant governor in 1759, and acted as governor intermittently after 1764.[29] One daughter of William Sr. married Councillor John Drayton (grandson of the immigrant), whose son William Henry Drayton also became a councillor.[30] Another councillor, Henry Middleton, took a daughter of William Bull, Jr., for his second wife, and Daniel Blake, great-grandson of a councillor, also married into the Bull family.[31] Finally, Othniel Beale, a former ship's captain who was born in Marblehead, Massachusetts, married a South Carolina girl in 1722, and had a daughter who became the wife of the second William Bull.[32]

Other councillors, though not related to the Bulls, came from the same social class,[33] and even some of the immigrant members were, like Beale, connected with the old established families. For example, Egerton Leigh, the Admiralty judge, was born in England, but his father had been chief justice of South Carolina and a councillor before him; Egerton himself came to the colony in 1753 and married Henry Laurens' niece.[34] Indeed, only two members of the Council had no local connections: Charles Shinner, the chief justice, who died in 1768, and Thomas Knox Gordon, who held the same office beginning in 1772. Only these two were entirely alien to the society in which they held power.

Commerce and commercial farming were the major occupations of the councillors. Two of the members were merchants themselves, and one, the younger William Bull, was the son of a merchant. Most of the rest were large landholders. The councillors were, with one or two exceptions, wealthy. Characteristically, they owned at least £10,000 worth of property, and, in addition, several of those who had smaller estates earned large incomes from their professions: Leigh seems to have owned only two thousand acres, though for some years he made over £1,000 sterling as a lawyer, while John Stuart's salary as superintendent of Indian affairs was £1,000 annually after 1768.[35]

Although the pre-Revolutionary councillors were described, both then and subsequently, as consisting largely of placemen, this description is obviously exaggerated.[36] It is true that the proportion of placemen had increased since earlier times; but only six of the fifteen, at most, can be reckoned in that category, including Thomas Skottowe and Leigh, both of whom had other interests. William Henry Drayton was a judge and Bull also was an officeholder, but neither was a placeman.

As a rule the two houses got on fairly well, and conflict developed only when relations with England became crucial. During the final decade of the colonial period the Council gradually became dominated by men determined to uphold British authority. Among those who were appointed after 1762, four out of seven held other offices. More important, these officials were particularly faithful in their attendance, whereas the native-born councillors absented themselves. In June of 1769, for example, a majority of the nine members were Carolina-born, but one of the natives embarked for London and another for Rhode Island, leaving the immigrants in control.[37] From that time on the antagonism between the Council and the lower house became very nearly irreconcilable.

In South Carolina most bills were originated by the Commons House of Assembly, and ordinarily were passed by the Council without change. Amendments were, however, made to a number of measures, including some of importance, and during the years 1763–1775 at least nine bills were rejected. Obviously the Commons always had to consider the attitude and probable action of the Council. The two bodies did not differ on domestic economic, social, or political matters, for they represented the same merchant-planter upper class. Therefore most such issues could easily be compromised. However on other questions the houses disagreed fundamentally. The Council was obliged to defend its role in the selection of the colonial agent and its power over money bills, to protect the prerogative, and to justify its very existence as an upper house. In all of these endeavors it ultimately failed.

The session that met during the summer of 1764 was enlivened by three such controversies, all of which were affairs of long standing. Early in July the lower house refused to accept a message of the Council because it had been sent by the "Speaker" instead of by the "President," on the ground that the Council was not a part of the legislature and therefore could not have a speaker. The Council, which had traditionally called itself "The Upper House of Assembly" when acting in its legislative capacity, replied that it was a branch of the legislature and therefore the word "speaker" was appropriate. The lower house thereupon addressed a bill to "his Majesty's Council." That body promptly returned a carefully phrased reply from "His Honor the Speaker," asserting "that as his Majesty's Council they would have no intercourse with the Commons house of Assembly, but were sitting as an Upper House and as such ready to receive the Bill."[38] The debate was not new: in 1756, for example, an article in the *South Carolina Gazette* had explained in detail the reasons for the Commons' objection.[39] Temporarily the matter was dropped, for the lower house continued to send resolutions to the "Council," while that body referred to itself as a "House" and its messages were signed by the "Speaker." The issue was only dormant, however, and would be revived in an acute form within a decade.[40]

The same session brought the re-emergence of another familiar dispute. The question of which house should control the colonial agent had originated in 1754–1755 when the Council tried to obtain power equal to that of the lower house. At that time the Commons had included an appropriation for the agent in a tax bill, which the Council rejected. The Commons had insisted that the agent represented the people and should be selected and paid by their representatives; the Council had finally been obliged to submit so that taxes could be collected.[41] The Council tried again in 1764. This time it attempted to establish a joint committee to instruct the agent and, when the lower house refused, rejected the whole bill.[42] After a brief prorogation, the upper house framed a measure similar to the one it had rejected (which technically was a bill to continue various acts). The lower house objected that the Council's version contained revenue provisions, and sent up its own bill. The Council protested that any money bills included in its measure must have originated with the lower house, and that merely to continue them did not constitute framing; it added parenthetically that "We have a right and We think a very good one, to frame, alter and amend money bills." To this the Commons merely replied that the house bill lay before the Council. The Council retorted that its measure lay before the Commons. The legislature was then adjourned.[43] When the assembly reconvened the following January, the lower house took the initiative. This time the upper house gave in: when one of the councillors introduced an amendment that would have required a joint committee to instruct the agent, a majority of the Council defeated it. The Commons was thus left in control, and the upper house did not renew the challenge.[44]

A more significant and prolonged debate concerned money bills. As early as 1725–1726 the Council had asserted its right to amend, though not to originate, money bills, and the ensuing dispute had never been settled.[45] In 1764 the Council inserted into a tax measure an amendment providing for the governor's salary, citing the royal instructions; but the Commons stood firm, and during the next session the upper house conceded the Commons' right to originate such appropriations.[46] Three years later the Council amended a bill concerning a watch company in Charleston. The Commons replied that this was a money bill and that "the many

Fruitless attempts you have made to wrestle from this House that valuable Priviledge of the sole framing of Money Bills ought to have discouraged you from so vain an Attack." The lower house resolved not even to read the amendments, and the bill died.[47]

The controversy was continued in the newspapers. "An Inhabitant" and Christopher Gadsden both denied the Council's right to amend money bills. They admitted that the royal instructions conferred such authority on the upper house, and that the Commons had previously "winked at" amendments; but they argued that there was no such power in England, and that colonials had all the rights of Englishmen. Instructions of the king were binding only on the governor; the Council, both writers asserted, had never possessed this authority.[48]

The Council was kept busy trying to defend its rights and dignity. In 1768, for example, it discovered that the Commons had drawn up a bill in accordance with a petition that had never been sent to the upper house. The Council thereupon resolved not to proceed until the petition had been presented in the usual manner, and only then to read the bill, "having received Satisfaction for the slight."[49] The prerogative also had to be guarded. The principle of permanent salaries was defended against the Commons' preference for periodic grants. The Council rejected an increase in the number of representatives in the assembly because the king had previously refused his assent, although in this case the upper house probably acted in accordance with its own opinions, as it did in delaying the establishment of courts in the west.[50]

The most important battle of the whole period began in 1769 when the Council rejected a tax bill because it contained a grant of money for the benefit of John Wilkes.[51] This incident, in which both the rights of the Council and the prerogative were at stake, inaugurated a lengthy interval during which no taxes were collected. John Wilkes, the idol of London, had become a popular hero in the colonies. In December of 1769, the Commons appropriated £10,500 currency (about £1,400) as a gift to a society that had been formed to pay Wilkes' debts. The Council denounced the grant. It was not "honorable, fit, or decent," and it was an insult to the king. A committee of the lower house presented a report which declared that this message was "conceived in terms Indecent and most Injurious to the Honor of this House," and that it was unparliamentary and unprecedented. The committee insisted upon the Commons' right to raise money for any purpose, and suggested that the king might be well advised "to bless this province, with an Upper House, distinct from the Privy Council, and composed of independent Men, and men of Property." The governor hastily prevented the Commons from communicating this invective by proroguing the legislature.

Time failed to settle the matter, which broadened to include the whole question of money bills. In August the lower house officially adopted the committee report. The Council in reply reiterated that it had been insulted, noted angrily that the money had already been sent to England, and declared that no funds could be appropriated without the Council's consent. It ended by rejecting the tax bill which included the charge of £10,500.[52] Moreover, the angry king issued additional instructions to the governor that were designed to halt the practice adopted by the Commons of paying out money without the consent of the governor and Council. No bill appropriating money was to pass unless the king requested it and unless it contained a clause guaranteeing that the money would be spent only for purposes specified in the bill. In that year, and almost annually thereafter, the Council vetoed tax bills because such clauses were omitted. The Commons stood firm, insisting that "we never shall regard any Ministerial Instruction in the framing of a Money Bill nor alter any part of the Schedule upon your requisition."[53] Thus the Wilkes incident openly pitted the will of the people against the king. The Council, by taking the royal side, suffered an irreparable loss of prestige.

An exchange of messages in 1773, after the Council had once again unanimously rejected a tax bill, found the two houses still unmoved. The councillors, in a long address to the governor, asserted that the treasury was in a critical condition. The duties that were supposed to be collected from import taxes had not been paid into the treasury, but had been left in the hands of merchants, who had given security and then used the funds in trade. Doubtless the security was adequate, but in the absence of a tax bill, the treasurers had available only £10,000 out of £127,674 due. The councillors absolved themselves of blame, for they could not have concurred in recent taxes without surrendering their rights. They recommended that taxes be collected by executive action. The lower house maintained that no such crisis existed: the conduct of the upper house was contemptuous, and dangerous to public credit.[54]

Not until the very end of the colonial period was the dispute resolved in favor of the Commons. In 1774, after the Council had rejected a money bill as usual, the lower house simply took over the government. Certificates were issued to the amount of some £200,000 for the payment of the public debt. The value of these certificates was guaranteed by the legislators themselves and by the merchants, who as creditors received most of the money; even the councillors accepted the bills. The Council was helpless, and the next year it acknowledged total defeat by passing, for the first time in five years, a one-year money bill.[55]

The final struggle between the two houses began in 1773 with a seemingly innocent bill to prevent counterfeiting the money of other colonies. Actually the Commons was trying to discover whether the Council still intended to block the passage of bills until the lower house submitted to the additional instructions of 1770. After the measure had lain for some days before the Council, the lower house requested that it be expedited. The upper house voted not to consider it that session, whereupon, in an unusual—though not unique—step, Councillor William Henry Drayton and his father, Councillor John Drayton, protested the decision.[56] A copy of the protest reached the hands of Thomas Powell, printer of the *South Carolina Gazette*, who published it. He was promptly arrested by the Council and jailed for breach of privilege. The Commons just as promptly bailed him out, acting through Speaker Rawlins Lowndes and Delegate George Gabriel Powell, both justices of the peace. Curiously, neither was a native of the province and Powell's father had been a colonial governor. The two judges asserted that the Council was "no Upper House of Assembly," and had therefore, as it were, no privileges to be breached. An irate Council found William Henry Drayton guilty of contempt, but he absolved himself by revealing that Edward Rutledge had sent the protest to the printer. The Council then turned its attention to Lowndes and Powell, demanding that they "wave" their privileges so that they could be found guilty of contempt. The Commons, on the contrary, unanimously defended the printer, thanked Lowndes and Powell, asked the colony's agent in London to seek the removal of the offending councillors, and requested the governor to suspend them at once. The indignant Council could do nothing but pass more resolutions.[57]

The ensuing trial brought to a focus the basic objections to the Council and completed its demise as an effective instrument. The printer's lawyer, Edward Rutledge (whose action had touched off the dispute), based his argument on the principle that the Council was not an upper house. No law made it one. There could be no "immemorial Usage," for "the Shortness of Time since the first Settlement of this Country, excludes the Idea." Nor was there an analogy with the House of Lords. The House of Lords was a permanent body whereas the councillors sat at pleasure. The Lords were not allowed to vote at elections because their influence might be too great; members of the Council could vote "because they are not looked upon to be of any Consequence at all." The House of Lords was a "balancing Power" between the king and the people, but the Council was a "dead weight."[58]

Rutledge's argument was accepted by Judge (and Speaker) Lowndes, who elaborated upon the dependent nature of the Council. Its lack of independence, he declared, prevented it from being a branch of the legislature. The people in England had nothing to fear from the Lords; but in South Carolina important matters were determined by three or four men, whose objective was primarily to defend the prerogative. Lowndes conceded that the Council could concur in the passage of laws, but it possessed that power only because the governor could not assent to laws until the Council had agreed to them. In general it was to be considered a Privy Council. Powell, in a concurring opinion, acknowledged that the people, "wishing also to have a Medium between the Crown and them, and willing to assimilate a Mode of Legislation, as near as may be to the Mode of the Mother Country," allowed the Privy Council to act as an upper house, but he, too, denied any analogy with the House of Lords.[59]

The Council had now nearly completed its own ruin. Its placemen members had consistently aligned themselves against the wishes of the Commons and of the province generally. There was increasing resentment in the colony against superior authority, and the defenders of governor and Council too often flouted colonial opinion. Thus, when in 1772 the members of the lower house quite understandably objected to the governor's calling a session at dis-

tant Beaufort, "A Freeman" informed them that the Commons had
no right "even to enquire into the Propriety of holding a General
Assembly in any Town"; their duty was only "TO OBEY."[60] William Henry Drayton, councillor and son of a councillor, though
defending the popular view in the affair of the printer, had previously refused to sign an agreement to halt importations from
England, and had insulted the butchers, cobblers, carpenters, and
those of little learning who, he said, had drawn up the agreement.[61]
Former councillor William Wragg had also refused to sign and defended himself in the newspapers, while Othniel Beale's wharf was
boycotted because he was a non-signer.[62] The whole Council might
well have been the target for the artisans' reply to Drayton, in
which they brilliantly defended themselves.[63]

The general character of the Council had indeed been attacked
for some years. As early as 1763 the Commons had denounced the
councillors as "placemen" who had "no natural tie or connection
whatever with the Province."[64] Christopher Gadsden, who was just
emerging as a popular leader, had written in 1764 that he was an
enemy of the Council unless it consisted of men "interested in, and
connected with, the province," and not "liable to be suspended, or
deprived of their seats, but by their own misconduct."[65] A few
years later the *South Carolina Gazette* had openly attacked John
Stuart.[66] Now, in 1774, "The Craftsman" called upon the Charles-
tonians to elect delegates who would act for the people, and contrasted the councillors, who assumed the right of imprisonment
and blocked tax bills, with men born in the province and educated
in the love of freedom.[67]

Finally, in 1775, even William Henry Drayton became too popular for the Council. A majority of that body petitioned successfully for his suspension, whereupon he, his father John, and the native-born Bernard Elliott declared that "a seat in this House, upon
a tenure of so arbitrary a nature, cannot be worth the attention of
an Independent American." At one time, William Drayton asserted, the Council had been composed "of the first Men in the Province, conspicuous for Family Connections, Influence, and Property. Their Personal Interests, and those of the Public were the
same; for their Fortunes could encrease only by the Prosperity of
the Colony. They were by no Means connected with the Crown but
by their Loyalty; neither did their Authority proceed from, or de-

pend upon the Crown." But now the Council was, and had been for several years, "actuated by the dictating Voices of Placemen, whose affluence has been acquired, and whose Power . . . exist[s] but by the Royal Pleasure."[68] After Lexington and Concord, as John Drayton later wrote in his *Memoirs,* "men could act under cover no longer; and the office of King's Counsellor for the Province, became incompatible, with the duties of a patriot."[69] Thus on the eve of the Revolution even the most conservative South Carolinians refused to serve in the upper house, which had become entirely alienated from the colony's leaders.

North Carolina

Whereas South Carolina possessed a fairly homogeneous upper class, which occupied a limited geographical area along the coast, participated in the same social life concentrated in the capital city, and agreed on most political and economic matters, North Carolina was in almost every respect heterogeneous. Its upper class, not nearly as wealthy or as stable as South Carolina's, was scattered along a coast which lacked a good harbor, so that, instead of there being a Charleston to serve as the social, economic, cultural, and political center, several small towns competed with one another. Indeed, there long had been rivalry between the northern and southern sections. Moreover, the interior of the colony, which was more populous and elected more representatives than the South Carolina upcountry, was at odds with the coastal area, the dispute finally exploding into armed conflict. This lack of cohesion put the colony at a disadvantage in its quarrel with the royal authority and indeed, as is well known, North Carolina was to be badly divided throughout the Revolutionary era.

Perhaps because the indigenous upper class was not unified and powerful enough to force the appointment of its members—it produced no Bull family, for example—the royal government looked elsewhere for its officials. The North Carolina Council was unique in containing not a single prominent and trusted leader of the community, and scarcely a man of greater than mediocre ability. Even more than in South Carolina and Georgia it consisted of placemen, men new to the province, who identified with the small group of royal officials rather than with the colonists.

This alien majority is typified by Thomas McGuire, John Rutherford, and Martin Howard. McGuire, who was appointed in 1775, was an Admiralty officer, a graduate of the Inns of Court, and a Loyalist. Otherwise his record is a blank. He was not a Carolinian, so he must have been Scottish or Irish, and must have come from a family of some means, judging from his education. Certainly he had no local roots or connections.[70] John Rutherford was born in Scotland, where his father and a cousin both had "estates"—but they were the kind of estates that nearly bankrupted him in 1772. He was a cousin of James Murray, a Boston merchant who moved to North Carolina and became a councillor. Rutherford clerked in Murray's store, became head of a firm, prospered, and married Governor Gabriel Johnston's widow. He also bought several thousand acres of land. He was popular, perhaps because he was an inefficient collector of quitrents. Rutherford was the lieutenant general in command of the campaign against the Regulators, a group of westerners who had revolted against domination by the east. He ultimately became a Loyalist.[71] Martin Howard was born in England, the son of a Martin Howard about whom nothing is known. He immigrated to Newport where he studied law, becoming learned and prominent. Howard chose the ministry's side in 1765 and his house was destroyed during a Stamp Act riot. He fled to England, where he obtained appointment to the office of chief justice in North Carolina. Once there he acquired property valued at £3,329 and consistently sided with the governor. It is hard to imagine an appointment less likely to win popularity for the Council.[72]

The Council did include a few native-born Carolinians. For example, William Dry, the only member to become a rebel, was the grandson of an immigrant, the son of a councillor, and the possessor of important family connections and nearly twenty thousand acres.[73] Other councillors also had local interests, such as Alexander and Henry E. McCulloh, whose fortune derived from a wealthy merchant with extensive landholdings in the colony.[74] A majority of the councillors, however, were entirely alien to the society in which they lived. As a group they were merchants, lawyers, and officials rather than planters. They lived in the eastern towns such as Wilmington, New Hanover, and Bath rather than in the country or in the west. Most of them occupied some high office.

No more than half were wealthy, for many of the officials had little income other than that of their offices. Although a majority were new to North Carolina, few were *nouveaux riches.* Characteristically they had important connections or possessed independent fortunes. In general these connections and interests were with the Old World rather than with the New, and the councillors usually identified with the governor and the prerogative rather than with the Assembly and local rights.

The composition of the Council made conflicts with the Assembly inevitable. As in South Carolina, the upper house had to defend its rights and even its existence. In March of 1764—a few months before the South Carolina Commons issued a similar challenge—the North Carolina Assembly deleted the word "House" as applied to the Council and substituted "Board," a term used when the Council met in its executive capacity. The Council protested the change, whereupon the Assembly suggested the use of "Council." The Council replied that "a dispute about Words would be frivolous, were it not introductive of a dispute about Things and Powers." It insisted that in any bill, resolution, or message the term "House" must be used, and if it were not, the Council would refuse its assent. This threat was sufficient. The representatives might still protest and call the message "inflammatory" and "obstructive," but in the same breath they referred to "each branch of the Legislature" and agreed, in the interest of peace and harmony, to reinstate "House." The councillors clinched their victory by having the last word. They insisted on being addressed in their different capacities by the appropriate titles, and demanded respect in all of their roles.[75] The Assembly was momentarily silenced, but renewed its attack on somewhat different grounds later in the year, passing a resolution in which it declared that the right of the upper house to reject bills was "of considerable prejudice."[76]

The Council in other ways, and with varying degrees of success, defended its authority. Especially important was the power of appointment. The Assembly on a number of occasions tried to get its own men into office or to prevent the Council from participating in the appointment process. Naming and instructing the colony's London agent occasioned a dispute as it did in Georgia and South Carolina. The Board of Trade had acknowledged that the lower house should nominate the agent, but the committee to correspond with him was to include members of both houses. But the Assembly on the one hand had been trying for some years to obtain complete control, while the governor and the Council on the other hand wanted the agent to represent them rather than the lower house. An acrimonious dispute had terminated in 1761 with the appointment of the Assembly's candidate, Couchet Jouvencal, who was the secretary of William Pitt. In 1764 the Council amended a bill providing for the continuation of Jouvencal as agent so as to include a member of the Council on the committee of correspondence. The Assembly replied that it had always appointed the committee from its own membership and would not surrender the right, whereupon the Council rejected the entire measure.[77] Later in the year the Assembly passed a resolution in favor of a new agent, but the Council would not confer on the subject at all.[78]

Two years later the debate was renewed. The Assembly argued that in North Carolina, as in other colonies, the representatives of the people ought to have the power of naming the agent: the Council might only concur. The upper house insisted that it had an equal voice in the nomination.[79] In 1768 the Assembly resolved that Henry E. McCulloh, a councillor, be appointed agent. The Council was not to be bribed, and another year elapsed before an appointment was made, after the Council had been assured the right to share in the selection and in the correspondence. Although in practice the Assembly conducted most of the business with the agent, the upper house had the better of the controversy.[80]

Sometimes the Council acted to protect not only its rights but its own members. In 1765, for example, the upper house named Councillor Lewis De Rosset as public treasurer for the southern district, but the Assembly determined upon Richard Caswell and neither house would yield.[81] The next year the Council again nominated De Rosset while the Assembly backed John Ashe, who, like Caswell, was a representative. The lower house insisted that it had the right of appointment, but informed the Council that if Ashe were accepted, his selection would not be regarded as a precedent relinquishing any right which the Council might think it possessed. The Council argued that since it had the right to amend any bill, it had a joint right of appointment. The Assembly assured the Council that its rights were not infringed by the bill, which then passed.[82] On another occasion the Council was able to name Councillor William Dry as commissioner of pilotage instead of the Assembly's nominee.[83]

A similar case concerning the appointment of the official printer led to a general attack on the authority of the upper house. The dispute began in 1764 when the Council objected to paying the printer chosen by the Assembly, James Davis, because no resolution had been sent up for its concurrence. Such a resolution was duly sent and accepted.[84] Later in the year, however, a new Assembly resolution reappointing Davis was rejected; the Council, acting in its executive capacity with the governor, chose a different man. The lower house was informed of this decision by the governor. The Assembly protested that this was an "extraordinary and unparliamentary" procedure by "that body who hath hitherto Denominated themselves an *Upper House.*" The Council, instead of being an *"Intermediate Body* of the Legislature," seemed now to have become "a *mere property* of his Excellency."[85] The representatives thus vented their feelings but for the moment accomplished nothing else. Ultimately, however, the Council surrendered and Davis received his money.[86]

The Assembly continued to question the rights of the Council as a part of the legislature,[87] but in practice those rights had to be acknowledged. The upper house did function as an intermediate branch. Indeed, Governor Martin complained that the councillors "discriminated between their duty in the Upper House of Assembly and at the Council Board," and that they were willing in their legislative capacity to pass a bill that violated royal instructions, while in their counseling capacity they advised its rejection.[88]

The two houses also fought for control over finances. In general the Assembly's right to initiate money bills was not disputed, and ordinarily it was able to appropriate funds without interference. Occasional objections of the Council were repulsed.[89] However, disagreements did arise over the payment of the colony's officials. On one occasion the Assembly failed to provide for several persons, among them the governor, so the Council promptly rejected the bill. The Assembly tried to reduce salaries, sometimes with success, as in the case of the superior court clerk.[90] Especially annoying to the Council was the lower house's refusal to pay the clerk of the Council as much as the councillors wished. This was, they wrote, "highly derogatory to the dignity of this House."[91] The

Council did, however, obtain a higher salary for the chief justice.[92] This grant was connected with the general question of control over the judiciary. The Council tried to support the judges with high salaries granted permanently.[93] Since the judges held office at pleasure they would in this way be entirely free from local control. The representatives therefore used the only weapon they had: the power to dispose of money, they reminded the councillors, was the "undoubted privilege of the people," and for the Council to interfere was "an open infraction of a fundamental principle in our Constitution." They admitted that a permanent and substantial salary, independent of fees or the number of cases, was desirable, but it could not be granted unless the judges served during good behavior.[94] In this dispute the Assembly was partially successful. The judges were made to depend upon the lower house for their salaries, though appointees still served at pleasure.[95]

Controversy over the court system involved both the prerogative and economic policy. The Council defended the prerogative by safeguarding the governor's fees deriving from the judicial process.[96] It protected the special interest of aliens, as might be supposed, by rejecting clauses that permitted the attachment of property belonging to nonresidents.[97] The upper house insisted that trials for riot be held in a district other than that in which the crime was committed, and rejected a bill when the Assembly did not agree.[98] The representatives, many of whom were justices of the peace and county clerks, tried to retain as much legal power as possible in the inferior courts, whereas the governor and Council sought to create a powerful superior court which would hear appeals.[99] The bill that finally became law contained several provisions that the councillors opposed, yet they passed it, and then split four to four on whether the governor ought to sign it. The governor refused to do so and dispatched a letter to England describing in uncomplimentary terms the councillors who had sided with the Assembly.[100]

Occasional disagreements arose over taxation and monetary policy. In 1768 the Council tried to amend one such measure so as to retain a poll tax, but the Assembly quickly denied the Council's right to do anything but concur or reject, and the latter gave in.[101] Later in the session the Council objected to a tax bill because it might be construed as a paper money bill; but it did accept the measure (which the governor later vetoed).[102] A few years later the Council approved a bill that reduced taxes and left in circulation paper money that was scheduled for redemption.[103] Martin again vetoed it, explaining in a letter that the bill had passed the Council "when some Members who would have made a Majority against it were absent."[104]

The Council's position on social and humanitarian matters was inconsistent. It favored the Church of England over other religious groups, striking out a clause which permitted Presbyterian ministers to perform marriages, and insisting that the master of an Edenton school be an Anglican.[105] When the Assembly prohibited persons of mixed Negro blood to the third generation from testifying in the superior court, the Council changed it to the fourth generation.[106] On the other hand, the Council objected to a clause levying a fine of twenty shillings on freeholders who failed to attend the election of vestries, on the ground that justices could then harass poor people and those who lived far from a church; it supported a hospital when the Assembly did not; and it tried unsuccessfully to increase the sum paid to a widow for her husband's work.[107]

The Council rejected a large number of measures that probably had popular support. On a number of occasions it refused assent to the creation of new counties; the inhabitants of Rowan and Orange were especially disappointed.[108] Bills for triennial assemblies twice were vetoed.[109] Another important measure would have discontinued the taxes that had been levied to retire the paper money, thereby leaving the money in circulation. The bill pleased taxpayers by reducing taxes and it pleased debtors by keeping the money in circulation; but the Council rejected it.[110] The assemblymen must have been annoyed when a bill furnishing them with adequate allowances failed of passage.[111] The upper house also rejected bills that would have permitted payment of taxes in commodities, relieved insolvent debtors, pardoned certain Regulators, and exempted several persons from payment of taxes.[112] Many other debates between the appointive and elective bodies occurred, most of which ended in victory for the former, and some of which resulted in the rejection of important measures.[113] Indeed, the Council rejected a very large number of bills—three dozen, in addition to those already mentioned, in a dozen years.[114] The governors kept pace. Martin at one point vetoed eighteen bills in a day! When one considers that for every bill that was rejected several were amended, it is evident that the councillors earned their keep. Neither the Assembly nor the people appear to have been grateful. Although the lower house did win some important disputes, it failed to achieve the dominant position that the South Carolina Commons secured. Some of the Council's amendments may have been wise, but on the whole its activity seems obstructive, and so it was considered in North Carolina as long as it was chosen by the king instead of by the people.

MARYLAND

The economy of Maryland, with its rich commercial farm land and extensive overseas trade, resembled that of South rather than North Carolina. The merchant-planter class, fully developed and self-confident after several generations of maturation, was as well prepared to defend its power as was the Charleston-based aristocracy far to the south. It was confronted, however, with an opposition that derived its strength not only from the distant royal authority but also from the immediate, pervasive influence of the proprietor. This influence was exerted most powerfully through the appointed officials and the upper house, but was felt in the House of Delegates and, to a lesser extent, throughout the colony.

Maryland's Council contained three nearly equal elements, all of which included high-ranking officials. One group consisted of men related either to the Calvert family or to the proprietary governors. Several of these men had been born in England, and almost all lived in the capital city of Annapolis. As might be expected, this group received the highest and most profitable offices at the proprietor's command. Such offices were not their sole source of income, however, for, with one or two exceptions, they were great landowners and often had other economic interests as well. The governor, of course, could rely upon their active support, and, when revolution threatened, so could the king. As a consequence this element played an increasingly important role in the government after 1763. Because of their Loyalism, their offices, their connections, and in some instances their place of birth, they were vulnerable to the epithet "placemen." They made up the core of the "proprietary" or "court" party.[115]

The second group was almost the opposite of the first. This was the extensive Lloyd family of native Marylanders. Its members were usually associated with the "country" as opposed to the "court" party, the latter centering in the rural areas of the lower Chesapeake, especially in the counties of the Eastern Shore; the former located farther north and west (though the Lloyds themselves lived on the Eastern Shore). The central figure was Edward Lloyd III, whose father and great-grandfather, Edwards I and II, had been councillors before him. Through his mother, a Rousby, he was related to three fellow councillors, and four others had married cousins of various degrees. These men also held offices, but usually not the most profitable ones; and they were increasingly out of favor with the proprietor as the Revolutionary movement progressed and the Lloyds took the popular side. At the end only three retained their seats, all of whom became rebels; and indeed the extended family produced a remarkable number of Whig leaders, including nine state senators. The members of this group had, in a way, earned their promotion by service in the lower house, whereas the proprietary party characteristically had not held elective office. The elevation of members of the country party was not a reward for loyalty but an attempt on the part of the Calverts to conciliate these powerful and wealthy men.[116]

The third element was not cohesive. It consisted of native Marylanders from the western shore of the Chesapeake, principally from the Potomac River counties. With the exception of two former Virginians, these members previously had served in the lower house. Like the other councillors, they held high office and were independently wealthy. The group—if it can be so called—gained strength at the expense of the Lloyds as the period closed. They were on the whole inclined toward the court party, but were divided in their allegiance during the Revolution.

The division between the proprietary and Lloyd groups was significant, but still more important were the unifying elements within the Council. Maryland's upper house was homogeneous in a number of respects. All but five councillors had been born in the colonies. Among the exceptions, Philip Key[117] and Samuel Chamberlain arrived early in the century and became rich and important men a generation before the Revolution, while Benedict Calvert was, shall we say, descended from large landowners of the province. Nearly all came from wealthy and prominent families. Indeed, half of the councillors owed their fortunes and status to grandfathers or even more remote ancestors: Lloyd and Charles Hammond were great-grandsons of founders.[118]

The councillors were therefore among the wealthiest men of the colony. Only one or two were well-to-do rather than rich. The others were without exception great landholders who owned an average of nearly eight thousand acres each in 1771.[119] Most of them had other income as well. Four were merchants, two were doctors, and seven were lawyers, all but one of whom had been trained in London.[120] Two, Walter and Daniel Dulany, owned an ironworks. The councillors also profited financially from their marriages: Benedict Calvert received £3,000 as a dowry; Walter Dulany married the daughter of a wealthy Newcastle merchant; Samuel Chamberlain's first wife was the only child of Talbot County's leading businessman; William Fitzhugh's first wife was the daughter of Richard Lee, London merchant, and the widow of George Turberville, a wealthy Virginia planter; John Ridout married Governor Ogle's daughter; Benjamin Tasker married Governor Bladen's sister, who brought with her a considerable dowry; and the men who married Lloyd girls chose wisely.

Finally, many councillors profited from the offices they held. Every member of the upper house except Benjamin Ogle held a position other than that of councillor, and several had more than one. Some of these posts were not remunerative, but the average office, in 1754, returned about £372 currency (£223 sterling). The receiver general was paid £450 annually, and seven councillors received over £600 as judges. The commissary general, attorney general, and treasurer were also well rewarded. The councillors did not depend upon such income, and were not simply placemen, but they were careful to keep in their own hands these lucrative and, it seems, undemanding offices.[121]

The councillors, then, while not alike in all characteristics, conformed to a pattern. Most of them were native colonials, who inherited wealth, married well, owned large amounts of land, and derived income from still other sources. They were better educated than the average planter, belonged to the Anglican Church, served several terms in the lower house, and finally attained the highest offices. The attributes of this composite did not materially change between 1763 and 1776.[122]

Of crucial importance to the relations between Maryland's two houses was their differing composition. The House of Delegates certainly was not a truly representative body; nor did it always bow to the will of the majority. But it was much more responsive to public opinion than was the Council, and was less antithetical to the colony's social structure. Whereas the councillors were wealthy, the delegates were well-to-do. Half of the councillors had economic interests other than agriculture, but farmers dominated the lower house. The councillors were descended from Maryland's most prominent old families—they belonged to the aristocracy; whereas the House of Delegates, though it did contain such men, contained even more whose ancestry was undistinguished. Few of the delegates held other offices. Above all, the court party, which naturally dominated the Council, was even before 1763 being challenged in the lower house by the country or anti-proprietary party. The gradual progress of the Revolutionary movement was accompanied by the increasing strength and ultimate triumph of the latter. The contest between the two houses probably should be attributed less to any social or economic differences in their composition than to the dominance in one of the court party, and in the other of the country party.[123] The fact that the councillors held other offices was not a cause of this conflict but rather it was a symptom of their loyalty to the proprietor, to the prerogative, and ultimately to the king. At the same time the fact that the delegates were elected made them subject to the influence, if not of Marylanders generally, then of that dominant minority which finally chose rebellion.

Relations between the two houses in Maryland were characterized by almost continuous conflict. The Council, of course, defended the prerogative and the economic rights of the proprietor. It also defended its own legislative and economic interests and generally favored the creditor class. The two houses clashed not only on economic and political issues but also on a variety of social and cultural matters. The extent, if not the intensity, of the disagreement is suggested by the fact that in the single session of November–December, 1766, the Council rejected seventeen bills.

Whereas in South Carolina the very existence of the Council as an upper house was being openly challenged as the Revolution approached, in Maryland the question arose before 1763 but was not important thereafter. In 1757 the lower house asserted, "What are the Rights and Privileges of those Gentlemen, that are said to constitute another Branch, we know nothing about; as it is a Branch undevised in our Charter, and unknown in it's Original."[124] Five years later the delegates again declared that the Council had become an upper house only by "inadvertency . . . little short of infatuation."[125] Nevertheless the existence of the upper house was thereafter acknowledged, and subsequent attacks upon it were designed not to eliminate it but rather to restrict its power.

The attitude of the two branches toward each other was expressed by an exchange of messages and pamphlets in 1762. The delegates contended that the Council owed its existence entirely to the proprietor and could be dismissed by him, and that he dispensed favors among the members to secure them to his interest; therefore the Council was not the guardian of the people's rights. There was much truth to the charge. At that very time Governor Sharpe was writing to Lord Calvert that the members of the legislature were going to find "that opposition is no longer to be the Road to Preferment." A few months later he wrote, "I do not doubt but when the principal ones in the opposition find that those who act a different part are the only persons thought worthy of Favour their pretended Zeal for the people's Good will become cool. . . ."[126] The councillors, however, insisted that they were interested in the welfare of the whole colony and would protect it even against the proprietor. They unquestionably did play an essential role in the system of checks and balances so widely accepted at the time by American leaders. The Council, its members claimed, was able to "oppose any wicked measure of an oppressive governor on one hand, and to check the violence of a levelling, popular assembly, or tyranny of a few demogogues on the other, or to prevent the evil consequences of a collusion between a corrupt governor, and a few leading men in the Lower House."[127]

Convinced that they were necessary to good government, the councillors jealously defended their power. The result was a long contest for supremacy between the two houses. The period opened with a controversy concerning payment of the Council's clerk. The Journal of Accounts, the bill appropriating the colony's funds, was sent up by the delegates in 1763 without an allowance for the clerk. When the Council returned the bill it noted the omission. The delegates replied that the clerk ought to be paid by the proprietor, thus implying that the Council served the Baltimores rather than the colony in general. The upper house suggested that a bill might be drawn to pay all officers except the legislators. The delegates parried this bid for public favor and counterattacked. "The situation of the Members of our House is very different from that of your Honours," they wrote,

for besides the Superiority in point of private fortune, the very lucrative Offices you hold &[c] would make the delay of payment in this Case a trifling inconvenience to you, but as it is otherwise with us you cannot expect our acquiescence in your proposition, and therefore we hope you will excuse us when we Say it rather appears to us an Ostentation than a real mark of Disinterestedness or of your Equity and tender concern for the Publick Creditors.[128]

The lower house continued to insist that the clerk should be supported by the proprietor. If he performed services according to the laws of Maryland, then he should duly account for them and receive payment as did other creditors of the government. The Council maintained that he should draw his salary as clerk of the upper house, and, until 1766, refused to accept any Journal of Accounts that omitted him. The clerk finally was paid in 1773, when the Council gave in, but even then he was paid not as clerk of the Council but as clerk of the upper house.[129] To be sure, the delegates thereby recognized the Council's claim to legislative power as an "upper house," but this had ceased to be an issue by that time.

The two houses also struggled for control over the raising and spending of money. In 1766 the lower house passed a resolution thanking Pitt, Camden, Garth, and others for their aid in repealing the Stamp Act, and appropriating funds for a statue of Pitt and a portrait of Camden. The Council promptly rejected the resolution because it authorized the expenditure of money without the approval of the upper house.[130] In the same year, when the Council amended a bill paying public claims, the delegates denied that the Council possessed such a right, claiming that the lower house had exclusive power over money bills. The upper house cited precedents in its favor dating as far back as 1732, but then yielded, not on the principle but, it asserted, out of compassion for the public creditors and the people.[131] Again in 1770 the upper house amended a bill appropriating money, urging that the recipients be paid on the general Journal of Accounts. The delegates protested that:

this House will ever claim, as their inherent, undoubted and fundamental Right, the sole and exclusive formation of all Money Bills, as well for the Application and Disposition, as for the granting and raising of all publick Money: a Right so essential to the Liberties and Properties of those we represent, that we are determined never to give it up, or wave or weaken it in any Manner....[132]

To this message the Council replied:

The many Instances in which this House have from Time to Time exercised their Right to Amend Bills for the Appropriation of Public Money are too well known to make it necessary for us to point out Precedents. ... We shall therefore only Say ... that, disregarding the exclusive Claim you are now Pleased to Set up, this House will, as freely as they have heretofore done, continue to exercise their Judgment whenever Bills for the Application of Public Money come before them, and either refuse Absolutely, give their Assent to, or propose Amendments to such Bills in the manner they may think most expedient or reasonable.[133]

The bill thereupon died. However the lower house accepted amendments to a similar bill the following year.[134]

The dispute over money bills was revived in a somewhat different form during 1771. This time the Council amended a bill that provided for emitting bills of credit. The lower house again claimed "their inherent undoubted and fundamental Right" to raise, grant, and spend all public money. The upper house repeated that it had in the past amended and even originated such laws. The bill finally passed during the session of March–April, 1774; but the basic disagreement remained unsettled down to the Revolution.[135] In general the outcome was a draw. The lower house ordinarily did control money bills, but the Council's power to reject them forced the delegates to propose only such bills as would be accepted; moreover, the Council did succeed in making amendments even though the delegates never admitted that it possessed the right to do so.

In addition to defending its own authority, the Council protected Maryland's equivalent of the royal prerogative—the proprietary interest. During the whole period 1763–1776 the lower house tried to reduce the power of the Baltimores, whereas the upper house was determined, as it assured Governor Sharpe in 1763, never to assent to a bill "which might be deemed repugnant to an Act of Parliament or likely to expose your Excellency to the displeasure of his Majesty or the Lord Proprietary."[136] The Council was obliged to defend both the political and the economic rights of the proprietor against the attacks of the lower house: the delegates attempted to control the colony's agent, the induction of clergymen, and appointments generally; they also endeavored to wrest from the proprietors certain revenues, and manipulation of the currency supply.

The controversy concerning the colonial agent began in 1765 when the delegates attempted to gain complete authority over him. A bill was introduced appropriating money for an agent who would represent the people rather than the colony as a whole. The proprietor, who had previously opposed the appointment of any agent at all, objected to the measure, and the Council therefore prevented passage on the ground that the agent should be chosen by both houses.[137] The lower house then selected Charles Garth as its own agent, and he did in fact serve, though the upper house consistently vetoed appropriations for his support.

A bill to regulate the clergy touched off a debate over whether vestries or the proprietor had the right to induct clergymen. The Council defended the proprietor's right, and was strongly supported by a writer in the *Pennsylvania Chronicle*, who asserted that the councillors had the duty to protect the proprietor against the people in the same degree that the delegates supported popular rights. Only in this way could a "due equilibrium" be preserved. "An affection of popularity," the article declared, was dangerous to the state. Mobs and riots demonstrated that the executive power was already too weak, so the upper house was obligated to defend the executive and thereby to protect property and order against the "bad disposition of the people."[138] On other occasions, also, the

Council protected the right of the proprietor to make appointments, as when it vetoed a bill for the independence of justices.[139]

The councillors also shared in some of the specific economic interests the Baltimores had to defend. The lower house as early as 1754 attempted to control the money obtained from licensing peddlers. In 1766 the delegates tried unsuccessfully to win the approval of the Council by designating the use of the fees for the establishment of public schools.[140] A similar dispute persisted for several years over the money from "ordinary" (tavern or inn) licenses. For example, in 1763 a bill was introduced to support troops on the frontier by using license fees. As a rule, all of the colony's expenditures were provided for in the annual Journal of Accounts, but the delegates argued that the soldiers and those who had advanced money to the government had a particular claim. The soldiers, and presumably the public creditors, were restlessly demanding justice. The revenue from tavern licenses had always been claimed by the Baltimores, and the Council therefore vetoed the bill, ostensibly because it felt that the soldiers and those supplying them should be treated like any other creditors.[141] The proprietor finally surrendered the right when Daniel Dulany submitted an adverse legal opinion.[142]

In defending the economic interests of the Baltimores, the councillors also defended their own interests and those of the wealthy classes in general. Often these coincided. When, in 1773 and 1774, they rejected a bill for the regulation of officers' fees on the ground that the officers were not given "competent" support, the councillors obviously were looking out for the proprietor's appointees, themselves included.[143] The issue of fees had arisen as early as 1754 when the lower house tried to tax the incomes of government officials.[144] In 1770, when the delegates attempted to reduce the fees, several officials declared their willingness to give up their fees for a salary of £600 sterling, and the Council approved of the change. The lower house refused, objecting that the proposed salary was too high and that salaried officers might neglect their duties.[145] The delegates pointed out that members of the upper house held the major posts, remarked that they had "manifested an unreasonable attachment to the emoluments of office," and referred to "those schemes of Wealth and Power which it is to be much apprehended are formed by some of the great Officers of this Government, and which, if carried into execution, will tend to the oppression of the People, and, in the end, greatly endanger their Liberties."[146] In this case the delegates lost. They lost again when they tried to regulate the fees of lawyers.[147]

A prolonged and bitter controversy, which involved the power of appointment, the right to establish fees, and monetary policy, grew out of the "Act for amending the Staple of Tobacco, for preventing Frauds in his Majestys Customs, and for the Regulation of Officers Fees," which had first been passed in 1747, and in 1763 had to be renewed. There were several specific points of disagreement. One was the question of who was to inspect the tobacco and what the inspectors were to charge. The lower house hoped to appoint the officers and to pay them at a rate lower than that previously established, preferably in tobacco or paper money. The Council preferred that the law be enforced by justices of the peace, who were chosen by the proprietor, and that the justices be paid in sterling or an equivalent (such as tobacco), but not in paper. The whole currency question was therefore raised. One part of the bill fixed the value of various coins, and provided for the payment in paper not only of the officers' fees but also of other fees, allowances for the clergy, public dues, and charges of inspection. The delegates were convinced that payment in sterling would be prejudicial to the people because sufficient money did not exist. Payment in tobacco, they asserted, was no advantage for those who did not raise it, and would stimulate the culture of that crop, of which there was already a surplus. The delegates also hoped to establish such valuations for the various media of exchange as would lower the costs to the people. The Council was opposed on every point, its position dictated in part by the fact that the bill was certain to be vetoed by the governor or the proprietor. It reminded the lower house that "our Measures must be adapted to our Circumstances, where we have no Power to Controul these."

To this the delegates replied that they were "totally unacquainted with the connection between the Governor and one Branch of the Legislature."[148] But besides upholding the prerogative, of course, the councillors, as officeholders, were personally concerned in the question of fees. Indeed, it was at this very time that the upper house was suggesting salaries of £600 for certain officials. The revelation that these posts were so lucrative helped to stiffen the determination of the delegates that the fees be reduced.

The dispute, which also involved some lesser matters, mushroomed into a serious struggle for supremacy during 1770–1771, and led to an acrimonious exchange in which the upper house received what it called a "wanton insult," and declaimed that "the want of Decency is as little proof of superior Probity as it is of superiour Sense." To this the lower house replied "that a particular Answer to your illeberal Language cannot be productive of any Publick Good; and not being disposed to attempt a Rivalship with your Honours in the Talents for petulance and impertinent invective the Lower House have ordered an End to be put to this conference." Not until November of 1773 did the measure finally pass, after the lower house agreed to eliminate from the bill those clauses that were most offensive to the Council. The Council succeeded in retaining the old fees, but the dispute further alienated the two houses and, what is more important, contributed to the rising strength of the anti-proprietary party.[149]

Another economic issue concerned the relations between debtors and creditors. A protracted dispute occurred over prisoners jailed for debt. In general the Council supported the creditors, and rejected or amended bills relieving the prisoners.[150] It at first insisted that no relief should be granted to debtors of the proprietor or of the loan office, but later gave in on these points. It also wanted to sell into servitude for five years all debtors without dependent families. The lower house obtained a modification whereby anyone would be relieved who had been in prison for five years, or whose creditor rejected an offer that he be sold.[151] The delegates also sought to provide more rapid and inexpensive court suits for debt, which the Council opposed.[152] Location of trials, too, was an issue, the lower house preferring local courts, which, it maintained, were essential to liberty and property, the upper house favoring trials in Annapolis.[153]

Social and cultural questions also caused disagreement. The Council was friendly to religious minorities, aiding the Quakers and others by allowing them to "affirm,"[154] and on several occasions trying to protect the property and rights of Catholics, who had been disfranchised.[155] When the Canadians in Montreal suffered a heavy loss by fire, the upper house declared that it would gladly contribute assistance, but the lower house first postponed action until the final day of the session, then voted against sums of £600 and £500, and finally deferred action on the whole matter.[156] On educational affairs, too, the Council seemed more liberal. When, in 1769, the governor suggested state aid to schools, the upper house promised to cooperate but the lower house pleaded lack of sufficient time to consider the bill.[157] On the other hand a bill to establish a college was blocked by the Council. It took this position, however, not because the councillors opposed higher education, but because the building to be used was one that the governor wanted himself, and because the necessary money was to be raised from ordinary licenses, which the proprietor regarded as his own.[158] The upper house also rejected a bill that levied an import duty on slaves for the support of schools. Here again its action was owing not to a disapproval of state support for education but to the fact that England opposed duties on goods imported by British merchants.[159] The Council appeared to good advantage in amending a bill that made apprentices of children who were public charges, so that if the mother or father could furnish security, apprenticeship would be nullified.[160] The councillors attempted to raise the salaries of ministers, and especially to reward those who were of superior ability. To establish all on an equal level, they maintained, "would if admitted, impose an unequal Tax on the People, and [be] oppressive on such as reside in some of the small Parishes, as well as damp the emulous Exertions of Merit, which the hopes of Preferment are wont to animate."[161]

This long catalogue of disagreements, many of them bitter, is far from exhaustive. The upper house rejected several bills concerning the court system, and amended others, sometimes so extensively that the lower house then rejected them.[162] When a bill was introduced "to preserve the independence of Members of the House" (evidently an early corrupt practices act) the Council added a series of amendments, some of which were surely calculated to annoy: a delegate had to swear that he had not bought votes or deceived electors; he had to support bills conscientiously, and no member was hereafter to receive any emolument for attendance or travel. Action on the measure was postponed by the lower house.[163] The delegates also deliberately aggravated the councillors, passing many bills that were certain to be defeated and the rejection of which would then make the upper house unpopular. As a rule the actions of the upper house were enough to render it unpopular without assistance; for example, it blocked the sale of Maryland's capital bank stock. Many of these bills rejected or amended out of existence by the Council were desired not merely by the lower house but by the general populace.

It is true that the Council sometimes had the better of the debate. Moreover it did not entirely lack defenders outside of the legislature. Daniel Dulany, writing in the *Pennsylvania Chronicle* of February 17, 1772, asserted that Baltimore would never rival Philadelphia because Maryland's lower house had favored rival towns and had discriminated against non-Anglicans. However, he continued,

it is still alledged, that whatever may be the opinion and conduct of the *Lower* House of Maryland, respecting these matters, yet, that an impartial spirit of freedom, unbiased by party, place, or connexions, characterizes the Honourable Members of the *Upper* House—That they are friends to the unalienable right of private judgment and equitable taxation—are, what indeed no one would have supposed them not to have been, Gentlemen of liberal education, well acquainted with the systems of foreign states, and fully sensible of the immense advantages, resulting from freedom of trade—and of thought.—I have not the honour of an acquaintance with any of those Gentlemen, but have collected these sentiments of them from among the people, with whom I conversed in *Maryland*. Nor am I disposed to doubt the justice of this predilection of the people in favour of the Upper House, when I consider that their councils *are* animated by that firm and independent spirit, which so uniformly actuates the patriotic author of the most excellent *Considerations*.

And a writer refuting him, though defending the delegates, admitted that "he has done justice to the virtues of our Upper House."[164]

Virtuous the Council may have been, but popular it surely was not. Because it had to defend the royal and proprietary prerogative, and because it did defend its own power and the private interests of its members, it consistently opposed, and often thwarted, the desires of a majority of Marylanders. That it did so may have been due in part to the weakness of the Lloyd element. Although that group was as numerous in the Council as was the court party, its members were often absent at crucial times. Edward Lloyd himself did not attend after 1765. He, Chamberlain, and Henry were all absent during the exciting session of November, 1766; and again in 1771 the Lloyds were outnumbered from the beginning and had only one member present when the dispute reached its climax. At the close of the colonial period the placemen in the Council, few though they were, dominated the upper house. Perhaps had the Lloyd group obtained control, the Council might have won the approval of many Marylanders as a defender of the rights of large property holders and as a body which, economic interest aside, might have proved more humanitarian and conceivably more wise than the popular branch. Unfortunately the Council came to be considered primarily as the instrument of an increasingly unpopular external power, controlled by officeholders who protected their own narrow interests; and appointment to it was rejected by truly patriotic Marylanders.[165]

The history of the councils in which placemen were prominent invariably was stormy. Although they were criticized on many counts, what distinguished these councillors was not wealth, occupation, or social standing: members of the upper house everywhere were men of property and status, engaged in commerce, the law, or plantation farming. Rather, their characteristic qualities were place of birth and attachment to the prerogative. Of course, many were born in the colonies, and some took the popular side even to the extent of becoming rebels. But the dominant minority (which on the eve of independence became a majority of the active members) was foreign-born. The typical placeman was a Britisher, sometimes of prominent family, who, though he often acquired local attachments and interests, never really transferred his loyalty. He was supported by influential colonials who had the same loyalties and—whether as cause or as result—also held the same offices. These were prerogative men. The council which they controlled usually agreed with the lower house on economic and social matters and on domestic policies. Thus, except when the prerogative was involved or some special interest of the council was at stake, the two houses seldom quarreled over monetary policy, the protection of agriculture and commerce, and the rights of creditors, and never over the collection of taxes, the preservation of the social order, and slavery. The issue that did generate almost continuous conflict was the relationship between colony and Empire. The course of the struggle varied, depending upon circumstances: in Georgia the Council was more powerful during most of the colonial period, while in South Carolina the Commons gradually established its superiority; but everywhere the lower house prevailed in the end, as the movement for self-government reached its climax. The functions performed by the placemen-dominated councils were always extensive and useful, and in ordinary times their existence was accepted, if not applauded; but by the end of the colonial period they had become not a check but a clog. The colonials then prepared to purge the councils of placemen—to separate them from the executive and subordinate them to the electorate. The servants of the king were to become the servants of the people.

CHAPTER 2

THE ELITE

*T*HE COUNCILS in which placemen were important invariably clashed with the lower houses when the latter challenged the royal prerogative and the former vigorously defended it. Councillors who were members of the colonial elite rather than placemen, however, were less inclined to uphold royal authority; some, like the Lloyds of Maryland, even became patriots. What happened, then, when the councils were controlled by the provincial aristocracy? For the answer to this question we turn to those councils in which placemen played a relatively minor role. In Virginia, New Jersey, New York, and New Hampshire, officeholders were comparatively unimportant. Instead, the upper houses consisted of members of the colony's most prominent and wealthy old families, whose fortunes and status in no way depended upon office but derived from inherited property and prestige.

VIRGINIA

Virginia's Council differed from those of the other southern colonies in precisely this crucial respect: the absence of placemen. Whereas in South Carolina seven councillors out of fifteen, in Georgia nine out of fifteen, in North Carolina nine out of eighteen, and in Maryland sixteen out of twenty-two occupied major posts of profit, in Virginia there were, at most, three such men; and whereas in the other colonies many of the incumbents were motivated to defend their own interests in conjunction with those of the governor, in Virginia the councillors did not at all depend upon the governor's favor. On the contrary, it might be more accurate to say that the governors relied upon them, for they represented the politically most powerful families of the colony, and were selected, not because they were attached to the executive by British birth or by the offices which they held, but because the executive could not function without their support. The Virginia councillors are to be compared, then, not with the Leighs, Skottowes, and Ridouts, but with the Lloyds of Maryland. One need know but little of the Old Dominion's history in order to recognize the names of Blair, Burwell, Byrd, Carter, Corbin, Fairfax, Lee, Nelson, Page, Randolph, Tayloe, Thornton, and Wormeley. Yet, with only one exception, this is the complete roster of the Virginia Council between 1763 and 1776. Only the Reverend John Camm, appointed in 1774, had no connection with the Virginia elite.[1]

The group was indeed extraordinary. Most of its members had fathers, grandfathers, or even (in two cases) great-grandfathers who had been councillors before them. They were interrelated in a complex way, and were also kin to many other families of importance who had furnished councillors in the past.[2] Other than Camm only two members did not entirely fit into the intricate pattern of family relationships. George William Fairfax inherited some fifty thousand acres of the huge Fairfax grant in the Northern Neck. His father, William, cousin of the grantee, was born in England, and rose through various offices to become chief justice of the Bahamas. He finally moved to Virginia as agent of the estate, and there was appointed president of the Council. George William Fairfax solidified the Virginia ties by marrying the daughter of Colonel Wilson Miles Cary.[3] Cary, of an old Virginia family, himself had married the daughter of Councillor John Blair. Blair, who was the only other possible exception, perhaps did not belong to the elite originally, though his father had been a member of the House of Burgesses for many years. His uncle left him £10,000 and thereafter he and his family were considered members of the upper class.[4] Among all the councillors, then, Camm was the only one who owed his advancement entirely to the governor rather than to his own connections and prestige.

These circumstances suggest that the councillors would identify their interests with those of the colonists in general. But the councillors also possessed some attributes that dictated otherwise. They were certainly not typical colonials. Eight had been educated in England, and three more had matriculated at William and Mary College.[5] Although all but Camm were very large landowners, they frequently had other interests as well: five were lawyers and one was a merchant. Their wealth was exceptional. Camm was evidently of modest means, but the others were not merely rich but (by American standards) very rich indeed. The typical councillor owned about ten thousand acres and over a hundred slaves. As we have seen, they almost always married extremely well, which somewhat counteracted the dispersal of wealth through inheritance. The largest estate was perhaps that of Robert Carter, which must have been worth about £80,000; but at least nine other councillors each owned property worth in excess of £20,000. These men possessed some of the greatest fortunes in the colony, and their land extended far into the west.[6] They were atypical too in that most of them lived near the coast. The lesser planters and Virginians of the Piedmont had no representation on the Council. Neither did the dissenting religious sects, for most, if not all, of the councillors were Anglicans. Therefore, although on the one hand they were not attached by birth, experience, or economic interest to the Crown, on the other hand neither were they representative of the ordinary people of Virginia.

There were certain obvious differences between the upper and the lower house, deriving in part from the fact that the burgesses were elected. Geographically, a slight majority of the lower house lived west of the fall line.[7] A considerable number were well-to-do rather than rich, and there were even a few burgesses who had only moderate property. Their social origins were much less eminent than the councillors' family backgrounds. About a fourth were of humble families, and others belonged to the respectable middle class and had shared, during their youth at least, the general experiences of middle-class colonials. Finally, as an elected body, the House of Burgesses had to pay some attention to public opinion.

These differences might have resulted in frequent contests between the Council and the House of Burgesses had they not been effectively offset by important similarities. Many of the burgesses who lived west of the fall line came from the Northern Neck (between the Potomac and the Rappahannock) or the valley of the upper James, areas that socially, economically, and politically were extensions of the Tidewater.[8] They represented, in other words, planter-dominated constituencies. Therefore a large proportion of the House of Burgesses represented essentially the same sections as did the councillors. Large landowners dominated both houses. About half of the burgesses were wealthy. If those of lesser property had been united, a slight addition from the ranks of the wealthy members would have given them a majority; but in practice it seems to have worked the other way, namely, that the wealthy men were joined by enough lesser planters to assure them control.[9]

Thus, economically and socially the two houses were on the whole similar. The burgesses derived their leadership from men who came from the same families, and who enjoyed the same wealth, social advantages, and education, as did the councillors. Indeed, among those who held the most powerful posts in the lower house, at least two-thirds were related to members of the other branch. Moreover, although the councillors owed their offices to the governor, they owed little else to him: their property and power came not from him but from their parents or forebears. They might uphold the prerogative against encroachment from below, or they might on the contrary actually join in that encroachment. Although the two houses did at times differ on matters of importance, there never developed the bitter, evenly matched, and perhaps irresolvable conflicts that characterized the legislative history of the other southern colonies.

Many of the issues that caused protracted controversy in other colonial legislatures did not exist in Virginia after 1763. The role of the Council as an upper house was never challenged. The burgesses' power over raising and spending money was never questioned. Control over the colonial agent had ceased to be an issue. As a result, many sessions passed peacefully. In May of 1763 the Council accepted everything passed by the burgesses; in 1768 (when no governor was present) the two branches agreed on every measure except one; in 1773 the upper house accepted twenty-two bills and resolutions without change, amended five, and rejected none; again in 1775 no measure was rejected and only two out of thirty-two were amended. When in 1764 the burgesses drew up an address to the king, a memorial to the House of Lords, and a remonstrance to the House of Commons concerning taxes, the upper house made some amendments but agreement was reached without trouble.[10] In 1768 a petition, a memorial, and a remonstrance were agreed to without alteration.[11] Although six of the councillors opposed the Revolution, only three did so openly and only one became an aggressive Loyalist.[12]

The two houses did, of course, have their disagreements. Virginia's Council, like the others, was required to and did defend the prerogative; but this was seldom necessary, and the Council did not make too great an effort. On several occasions the upper house added suspending clauses.[13] Usually the lower house agreed to them; but when it did not, the Council gave in. On one occasion the Council tried to protect the executive authority of the governor, but when the lower house rejected the amendment the upper house did not press the matter.[14] The Council also defended the king's right to grant the privilege of holding fairs.[15] But incidents so rare demonstrate harmony rather than discord. The act concerning the inspection of tobacco, which caused so prolonged a controversy in Maryland, occasioned no debate in Virginia except for a brief dispute over the location of warehouses.[16]

A few economic issues reflected a mild divergence of interest. The burgesses in 1763 expressed concern because some councillors had joined the merchants in objecting to paper money,[17] and four years later when the lower house adopted an "address and scheme" for paper money the upper house refused to agree. The burgesses nevertheless sent the address to the king.[18] On a few occasions the Council protected the rights of property against potential infringement, but this rarely was necessary.[19] The Council first amended an act "for the better regulation and collection of officers' fees" so as to raise at least one fee, and subsequently rejected the entire bill. Possibly, as in Maryland, the prerogative was at issue here.[20]

On several occasions the Council proved itself more humanitarian than the burgesses. It protected the land of the Nottoway and Nansemond Indians,[21] and the dower rights of a widow.[22] When the burgesses passed an act to prevent malicious maiming and wounding, the Council inserted, after "gouging," the words "plucking or putting out an Eye," and after "biting" added "kicking, or stamping upon."[23] The Council also seems to have interceded on behalf of bastard children.[24] It protected the public at large by introducing a bill to prevent the sale of oysters at unseasonable times. This was rejected by the lower house.[25]

The upper house also vetoed a number of bills that probably were popular. Presumably the inhabitants of two counties who applied for new justices of the peace were disappointed by the Council's refusal on the ground that "in few counties there are gentlemen enough properly educated and qualified to meet the trust."[26] "An Act for the encouragement of Settlers on the lands in the upper parts of Augusta County" was also turned down, as was one "to relieve the People from the expence attending the execution of the laws prohibiting the tending of Tobacco seconds."[27] Perhaps the public wanted a bill better regulating the election of vestries, and certainly a majority wished to relocate the capital.[28] In rejecting the latter, the councillors revealed their sectional origins. On the other hand, when the upper house insisted that justices of the peace serve in the militia it may have been closer to public opinion than the lower house.[29] It is impossible to tell whether most Virginians favored such vetoed bills as those that prevented hogs from running at large in Portsmouth and Leeds, or enabled the justices of Amelia County to purchase land for a court house, or one better regulating the collection of county and parish taxes, or one imposing restrictions on vagrants and the care of the poor.[30]

There were a few other disputes of minor importance. One concerned an attempt by the burgesses to obtain their wages "in Money." The Council first rejected this bill in January of 1764. In December the lower house resubmitted the bill, but the Council postponed consideration of it until May of 1765 when it was again vetoed. Not until 1767 did the burgesses succeed.[31] Although the records do not make this clear, the burgesses were probably favoring themselves at the expense of other public creditors. Another controversy occurred when the Council rejected a bill relieving some of Daniel McCarty's land from entail, but did not inform the House. When the burgesses presently requested the Council to "expedite" the bill, they drew an angry response.[32]

In assessing the role of the Council in Virginia one must conclude that it aroused no great hostility on the part of either the burgesses or the public. This was due not to its lack of power but to its restraint in exercising power, and to the fact that there existed no fundamental conflict of interest. Evidently on only two occasions was the Council openly criticized. The first occurred when three members of the Council (Byrd, Blair, and Thornton), acting in their judicial capacities, granted bail to an influential Virginian even though he was clearly guilty of murder. Newspaper attacks followed. The "middle and lower ranks of men," wrote "Dikephilos," were alarmed, for they could not be certain "that persons in power will always act rightly." He continued:

Men in power should be treated with great deference; but this deference should be consistent with British freedom, and not like slaves to a Bashaw. If British subjects know the power of men in high stations, and if men in high stations will exceed their due bounds, has not the meanest subject a right to mention his apprehension and grievance? Has he not a right to endeavour to maintain his privileges?

This was of course a criticism directed not specifically at the Council but against a few councillors—and perhaps against the ruling class generally.[33]

At the very end of the period more serious trouble developed, when in 1775 the Council published an admonitory address referring to the Virginians' "licentious and ungovernable spirit," and intended for circulation with Lord North's conciliatory resolution.[34] The committees of Richmond and Westmoreland counties replied. The Council members, said the latter, "have not acted as they were bound to do from their station in government; which ought to have led them to be mediators between the first magistrate and the people, rather than to join in fixing an unjust and cruel stigma on their fellow subjects.[35]

The conclusion is inescapable that although the power of the Council was, as Governor Fauquier wrote, "very great and extensive,"[36] the burgesses and their constituents did not object to that power as long as it was exercised with restraint. In most cases the burgesses had their way. Only at the very end of the colonial period did a fundamental cleavage appear, and then the conflict was not between the two houses, but between the Council and the people.

New Jersey

New Jersey's upper house resembled that of Maryland in two respects: many of its members were related by intermarriage, and half of the councillors held some other high office, most often a judgeship. But this was not a Council of placemen. As in Virginia, its members did not depend upon their offices, but had large independent incomes. Furthermore, they did not act the part of placemen, for as many became rebels as took the king's side—indeed, those who held offices in addition to their posts as councillors were more apt to be rebels than those who did not. The outstanding characteristic of New Jersey's councillors was their membership in the colony's well-established upper class.

Half of the councillors belonged to the one extended family that was even more influential during the colonial period than the Lloyds of Maryland. Its geographical center was in the town of Perth Amboy, and its members were primarily urban, principally merchants and lawyers. Most of them, however, were also members of the East Jersey Proprietors, to whom the province had originally been granted, and as such were large landowners. The "Perth Amboy group," as it came to be called, was not a cohesive political party. On the contrary, its members were quite diverse in their public behavior. Its significance lies in the dramatic rise to economic and political power of a native elite, whose fortunes were inherited in some instances through several generations, and who formed the basis for an indigenous aristocracy in the upper house.[37]

A West Jersey family contributed three more councillors. Charles Read, a Philadelphia merchant, was the grandfather of Councillor Charles, and his granddaughter (through James Logan of Pennsylvania) married Councillor John Smith, whose brother Samuel was also a councillor. Most of the remaining members of the upper house had similar backgrounds. For example, Daniel Coxe was the fifth of the name, the first Daniel having been chief proprietor of West Jersey, while Francis Hopkinson's father was a member of the Governor's Council in Pennsylvania, and Francis married the daughter of Colonel Joseph Borden, leading citizen of Bordentown. The only councillor without local connections was Frederick Smyth, who was born in England, and owed his appointment as chief justice and councillor to influential friends at home, especially to Lord North. Smyth was therefore the only placeman.[38] Finally, John Ladd, alone among the councillors, succeeded by virtue of his own talents, for his father, a surveyor, was no more than well-to-do.

The foregoing account indicates most of the significant social and economic characteristics of the councillors. Although more than half of them were great landholders, they were not primarily engaged in agriculture, but were merchants (eight, of whom four had retired), or lawyers and judges (nine). They were urban rather than rural. The governors were careful to select an equal number from East and West Jersey, but such a balance did not mean that Perth Amboy was weighted equally with an agricultural hinterland, but only that Perth Amboy, Newark, Morristown, and Elizabeth in the east balanced Burlington, Trenton, and Bordentown in the west. All but one or two of the councillors were wealthy.[39] The councillors' parents were much like their sons. They came from the top social and economic class, and like their sons had accumulated property partly from land but even more from commercial and legal activities. The great majority of the councillors were Anglicans, though among those from West Jersey were two Presbyterians and three or four Quakers. As a group they were well educated and well informed, often with broad intellectual interests. The influence of the East and West Jersey proprietors was strong. Governor Belcher, indeed, had complained of this preponderant interest,[40] but had been unable to counteract it, while subsequent governors made no effort to do so. The councillors therefore could actually pursue their own interests rather than those of the king, though normally their objectives coincided. When the Revolution came, four of them became rebels, five were Loyalists, and two were neutral.

Conflicts with the Assembly were minimized by its almost equally unrepresentative character. The lower house did contain a half-dozen farmers of moderate income, but large landholders had great influence, and merchants and lawyers were even more important. The typical representative was well-to-do, and, like the councillors, usually lived in an urban area. The principal difference between the two bodies lay in the social origins of the representatives. About a third of the Assembly chosen in 1761, for example, descended from the prominent old families (such as Joseph Borden, John Lawrence, Samuel Smith, and the future senators Aaron Leaming and Jacob Spicer of Cape May), but the majority were of ordinary, respectable parentage, their fathers farmers of moderate means. Such men might, on particular issues, contravene the aristocrats in the Council, but neither body really can be termed popular.

Indeed, the period 1763–1776 was marked by very few disputes. One would scarcely have known that a revolution threatened, or that legislatures elsewhere were in turmoil. Most of the bills were originated by the "House of Assembly" or, as the governor referred to it, the "House of Representatives." The Council, which called itself "The House" and termed its presiding officer the "Speaker" when in legislative session, accepted the great majority of bills without qualification. During the session of May–June, 1763, for example, not one amendment was made.[41] Ordinarily such amendments as the upper house did suggest were accepted by the lower. When the Assembly objected the Council usually "receded." Most of the amendments seem to have been minor. The Council rejected only a dozen bills between 1763 and 1775, averaging fewer than one per year, and only a handful of bills caused real disagreement.

Issues that elsewhere caused bitter strife were entirely or nearly absent in New Jersey's legislature even when the colony itself was in turmoil. The rights of both houses were well understood and respected. The Assembly did not question the legislative authority of the Council and did not infringe upon its power. On only one occasion was there a dispute about respective rights: in 1769 the Assembly complained "that upon the delivery of Bills to the Council for their Concurrence the Council received the same without rising, as heretofore has been usual." The Council replied that no disrespect had been intended, and the affair ended.[42]

One prolonged debate began when the treasurer of East Jersey, Stephen Skinner, was robbed of over £6,000 belonging to the colony. Public opinion blamed him for the loss, and demanded that he make restitution, but he was defended by the powerful Perth Amboy group to which he belonged; and when he was forced to resign as treasurer he was elevated to the Council.[43] The Assembly took up the popular cause in a half-hearted way. It could not force Skinner to stand trial, but it tried to provide better security for the future. The provisions of such bills implied Skinner's culpability. The Council rejected these measures, partly because it wished to defend the former treasurer, and also because restrictions upon the office of treasurer involved an attack on the prerogative.[44] At the same time the lower house was trying to secure Skinner's removal and trial, in that order—a sequence that assumed his guilt. The Council, conversely, insisted that he should not be removed, and that suit against him could not be instituted while he held office. The Assembly could do nothing except pass resolutions blaming Skinner for the loss.[45] Not until 1774 was a bill accepted by the Council, after many amendments, that authorized a suit against Skinner; at the same time the Council agreed to a bill obliging the treasurers to provide security.[46]

In defending Skinner, the Council was protecting not only a key member of the Perth Amboy group but a royal official; and it was, of course, a function of the upper house to defend the prerogative generally. This was not a particularly difficult task in New Jersey, where the prerogative was, after 1763, fairly safe. In 1764 the lower house passed a supply bill which provided that not over six hundred men should be raised for military service, and these only if a majority of the eastern colonies as far east as Massachusetts did likewise. The measure did not meet the specifications of the royal instructions, and the Council rejected it, declaring that it was of "so uncertain a nature and so inadequate to the purposes Recommended in his Excellencys Speech as to leave them no Room to hope it can be of any Use." The governor then adjourned the legislature for a few hours. Upon reconvening, the lower house voted to extend the limitation as far as New York only. This satisfied the Council, which recommended that the governor accept the bill.[47] The next year, in bills for the construction of roads and the payment of arrearages to the armed forces, the Assembly made the commissioners accountable to itself, contrary to the governor's instructions. The Council attempted unsuccessfully to alter the measures, and then once again advised the governor to accept them despite his instructions.[48] In 1768 a similar incident occurred. The Council amended a bill appointing commissioners for supplying barracks to provide that the appointments would be made by the governor and Council. The Assembly resolved unanimously that the measure was a money bill and so could not be amended. Once more the Council, "seeing the Absolute necessity of accomodating the Kings troops," surrendered.[49] Finally, in 1769, the Council attempted to attach a suspending clause to a bill for the recovery of small debts, but failed, and recommended that the governor request the king's permission to sign.[50]

In these matters neither house showed any great concern for the details of the prerogative, and the two never were far apart in their views. Several bills provoked arguments, the meanings of which the records do not make clear. In 1772, 1774, and 1775 the Council rejected bills for the regulation of juries.[51] This may have involved an effort to reduce the governor's authority. Another bill would have required justices of the peace and freeholders in two counties to raise some money for a bridge. When the Assembly disagreed with the Council's amendments, the latter unanimously adhered to them, whereupon the Assembly brought in a new and successful bill.[52] An "Act for the Relief of Insolvent Debtors" stimulated at least forty-three Council amendments, of which the Assembly rejected only six, and a conference committee ironed out the differences—the whole process requiring only two days.[53] The records do not reveal any debates over property rights, though on one occasion the Council does seem to have been more vigilant than the Assembly in safeguarding the rights of large proprietors.[54]

The history of the legislature during the prewar years demonstrates that the two houses were in basic agreement on all types of issues. The Council in New Jersey served almost exclusively as a council of revision, for it did not represent an officialdom, nor was it composed of different social or economic interests from those of the Assembly. Although a bare majority of its members remained loyal, it made no real attempt to combat the Revolutionary movement.

NEW YORK

No great extended family dominated New York's Council, nor, despite the fact that it was composed almost entirely of future Tories, were placemen in control. Instead, the councillors belonged to the colony's commercial and seigneurial upper class, who had been appointed because they were known to be prerogative men. They were drawn from what became the Loyalist element of New York's elite, an element that dominated both houses of the legislature before the Revolution, and was deprived of wealth and power after 1776.

The colony had always profited from a flourishing commerce. The bulk of the trade centered in New York City, where it drew on a rich agricultural hinterland. The extensive area between the Hudson River and the Connecticut border was characterized by very large "manors." These were partly speculative in nature, but soon came to be occupied by tenants who produced a sizable agricultural surplus and who paid each landowner rent-rolls amounting to £1,000 or more annually. The close economic connection between these landlords and the city merchants led to intermarriages, so that they ultimately formed a unified social class. They did not, however, confront the newcomer with an impenetrable phalanx, for the immigrant who acquired a fortune could easily enter the elite: wealth opened every door, including that which led to the young heiress. Commerce was an especially promising field for the ambitious, and the portals of even the fairly exclusive Chamber of Commerce were opened to a considerable number of self-made men. The colony had an upper class but not a true aristocracy, unless the manor lords may be considered as such.

The Council was the stronghold of the urban elite. Twelve of the sixteen members[55] who served between 1763 and 1776 were merchants and three others were lawyers. Only one had exclusively agricultural interests, and even he had spent most of his life as an army officer, not as a farmer. The councillors' family backgrounds were also almost entirely urban, for only two or three were farmers' sons. The manor lords were also represented, since two-thirds of the councillors were large landowners, and the great families of the Hudson Valley—the DeLanceys, Van Cortlandts, Philipses, Beekmans, Nicolls, and Van Rensselaers—had relatives in the upper house. Yet the major interest of the councillors was overseas trade. Land was for most of them a by-product of the mercantile success which had enabled them to purchase estates or to marry the daughters of rich country gentlemen.[56] Very likely these broader interests prevented them from becoming parochial, and encouraged an Atlantic-wide view. It is indicative that half of them were born outside of the colony, and all lived in New York City rather than in its agricultural environs. Their connections and viewpoints were imperial rather than colonial.

With one possible exception, all of the councillors were wealthy; indeed, £10,000 was the usual estate. This money was derived primarily from trade or money at interest. Few held profitable offices, either civil or military. Most of them were Anglicans: the two William Smiths, who were Presbyterians, and the two Crugers, who were Dutch Calvinists, were the only exceptions.

Despite the fact that only half of the members were native New Yorkers, the great majority were connected with prominent and wealthy colonial families. Both William Axtell and John Harris Cruger were born in Jamaica, but the Crugers had large tracts of land in northern New York, while Axtell's father, Daniel, a rich merchant, invested in New Jersey real estate. William Axtell moved to the mainland at the age of twenty-six and promptly eloped with a DePeyster girl.[57] Charles Ward Apthorpe's father was a prominent merchant in Boston, where the councillor was born, and he retained a considerable amount of land in Massachusetts and in Maine. Apthorpe also amassed a large fortune in New York City, which he augmented by marrying the sister of James McEvers, an important merchant.[58]

Few of the councillors had had to make their own way in the world. Daniel Horsmanden, the chief justice and the only councillor who might be termed a placeman, was an immigrant and the son of a minister, but the family seems to have been well-to-do lesser English gentry. Daniel went to Cambridge and the Inner Temple, migrating as a lawyer to Virginia, where a collateral ancestor had been a councillor and another relative had married William Byrd I. He soon moved to New York, became associated with the powerful DeLancey faction, and married the sister of Councillor Joseph Reade (whence came most of his money).[59] Roger Morris was another immigrant who made his fortune by a wise marriage. He also came from a substantial English family, and had been able to purchase a commission in the army.[60] Of the other newcomers, the senior William Smith's father was only a tallow chandler, but he had apparently migrated with a considerable fortune, derived in part from his wife, so that the family occupied from the start a high place in a society that had no prejudice against wealth regardless of its source.[61] Hugh Wallace's parents are unknown, but he seems to have been able to enter business at once upon his arrival in 1753; and since one brother was his partner and another was a merchant in Liverpool, he may have had important financial backing.[62] Lastly, Henry White, who arrived from Wales in 1756, apparently also had some helpful connections.[63] Both Wallace and White married exceedingly well: the former won a Van Cortlandt, the latter a Low. Thus, while these two may perhaps be considered fundamentally self-made men, the other councillors began life high up on the economic scale.

No such unity marked the lower house, yet it, too, was far from being a representative body. It contained two elements: the majority remained loyal to England, and resembled the Council in their characteristics; the minority took the rebel side and differed from the councillors in several particulars. The differences resulted, of course, from the elective nature of the Assembly; had the differences predominated, the relations between the Council and the Assembly would have been stormy instead of peaceful.

The lower house chosen in 1769, which proved to be the last of the colonial period, consisted of twenty-eight members. Ten of these lived in the central and northern counties (Dutchess, Ulster, Orange, and Albany), where there were many independent farmers instead of the landlord-tenant society that was characteristic of other areas. In addition, two came from Suffolk on Long Island. Most of these men were well-to-do rather than rich, came from ordinary families, and took the lead in opposing British policies. But the majority of the representatives, chosen from the counties near New York City and the east bank of the Hudson, were wealthy, often were members of the elite families, and were future Loyalists. Therefore, while the lower house was bitterly divided, and while in the Council the Presbyterian party struggled unsuccessfully with the Anglicans, the two branches did not clash, because the same sort of men controlled each. Moreover, the lower house, like the upper, contained more merchants (ten) and lawyers (four) than representatives who depended upon agriculture (twelve), and nearly half were wealthy. Therefore the Council was not called upon to block radical measures or even to repulse attacks upon the prerogative.

As in other royal colonies, the upper house was closely aligned with the executive. Although the governors differed with the Council on various matters, and theoretically the two might have been counterpoised as part of a "balanced" government, in practice the councillors regularly gave the king their full support in return for highly profitable rewards.[64] The British government naturally selected men who could be relied upon and looked for loyalty as a prime qualification for appointment. The Livingstons were excluded during the years following 1763, and only the Smiths, father and son, represented the opposition Presbyterian party in the upper house. William Alexander, the one councillor who became a rebel, retired to New Jersey and ceased to attend meetings after

1765. "A Freeholder" wrote optimistically that the councillors represented the aristocratic element in the constitution and "have a very great Degree of Virtue, when they act with a Spirit of Independency, under a bad administration."[65] But only the Smiths played an independent role. A more realistic appraisal was made by another correspondent who observed that the Council imitated an aristocracy through its legislative and judicial powers, but that it was "in Influence, Privileges and Stability, vastly inferior."[66] The prestige of the Council was also weakened by its small active membership, for there were often fewer present than the quorum of five which was necessary to conduct business.

Such business as the Council transacted consisted chiefly of passing minor amendments to bills originated by the lower house. Many sessions were marked by complete harmony, and during a dozen years the upper house rejected only a dozen bills. The disagreements between the two branches were of three types: matters affecting the prerogative, economic issues, and the rights of the Anglican Church.

The Council seldom had to defend the prerogative. The Assembly was not inclined to attack it, and the Revolutionary movement proceeded primarily outside of, not within, the legislature. Perhaps the prerogative was at issue when the Council refused to allow certain fines to be appropriated for the payment of taxes, but insisted that the money be used for the repair and purchase of arms.[67] More important was the case of a militia bill. The Council made three amendments, of which the Assembly accepted only two. According to William Smith, Jr. (whose motion for a conference was rejected by the upper house), the dispute involved a provision prohibiting the appointment of nonresident officers, which the Council had eliminated on the ground that the governor's power of appointment could not be restricted. Smith argued that from a practical point of view the clause was unnecessary, since there was only one such officer; and the need for a militia was so urgent because of trouble in Vermont that the Assembly would surely give in as soon as it realized that neither the Council nor the governor could accept such a limitation. But neither house would budge and the session ended without a decision.[68] With this rather minor exception, the prerogative was safe from attack by the Assembly.

The Council defended property rights, especially the rights of merchants. When the Assembly passed a bill regulating the sale of food in the public markets of New York City, the aldermen (including the radical leader John Morin Scott) protested to the Council that the measure violated the liberties granted by charter to the city. The Council ceased to hold public hearings, and finally rejected the bill.[69] On another occasion the aldermen obtained a hearing on a bill regulating the sale of firewood.[70] The Council also rejected a bill taxing certain goods sold at public vendue in the city.[71] Creditors may have been pleased when the Council amended a bill preventing suits in the superior court for sums smaller than £100, by reducing the minimum to £50.[72] Property rights apparently were also protected by the rejection of a bill to ascertain the northern limits of Ulster County: at least Smith, who favored the measure, protested that neither private titles nor the interest of the Crown would be injured.[73] These incidents are certainly minor, and indeed there was no reason why the two houses should have differed on economic policies. Thus, when the Council amended a bill that enumerated taxable articles in Orange County so as to exclude money at interest, household furniture, jewels, plate, and clothes, the Assembly agreed without argument.[74]

The last type of dispute concerned religion and politics. During 1769 and 1770 the Council rejected a series of measures that favored the dissenting sects. These bills would have exempted all Protestants from paying compulsory taxes for the support of ministers (aimed at the Anglicans), and enabled non-Anglican churches or congregations to hold property for the support of the Gospel and the use of schools.[75] Cadwallader Colden reported that the bills had been originated by men who had instigated riots (these were the days of the Townsend Act crisis), which he blamed on dissenters in general and above all on those coming from or educated in New England. Colden believed that there might have been more opposition to the bills by the strong Anglican-Loyalist element in the Assembly had the Council's rejection not been certain.[76] However these measures had first been introduced a year before the riots, and probably did reflect the opposing religious views of the two houses. Even this disagreement cannot be called major, and on the whole relations between the Council and Assembly in New York were harmonious.

NEW HAMPSHIRE

New Hampshire's Council contained a curious, indeed a unique, combination of placemen and members of the local elite. Half of the members held high office, and almost all were closely connected with the governor. But whereas the placeman was characteristically not a colonial by birth, in New Hampshire only two of the sixteen pre-Revolutionary councillors were immigrants from overseas. In addition, they received these offices not as rewards or bribes for loyalty (with the above two exceptions) but because they belonged to the small local elite. Controversies between the two houses did not develop out of a debate between placemen and colonials over the authority of the king, but because this little ingroup held power.

This peculiarity of the colony's political history resulted from the fact that during the half-century prior to the Revolution a Wentworth was governor. The Wentworths were wealthy Portsmouth merchants who dominated New Hampshire's economic and political life for three generations.[77] John Wentworth had become lieutenant governor in 1717, his son Benning was appointed governor in 1741, and Benning's nephew John took office in 1766.[78] They profited greatly from their power and filled the Council with their relatives. The upper house therefore consisted essentially of one extended family and its allies and sycophants. The members lived in Portsmouth, engaged in business, acquired wealth, held important offices, and became Loyalists. A few illustrations will characterize the great majority of New Hampshire's councillors.

Theodore Atkinson (1696–1779) was the only son of a councillor from whom he inherited over £1,000. He doubled this by marrying the sister of the future governor, Benning Wentworth. He had meanwhile gone to Harvard and studied law; subsequently he moved from New Castle to Portsmouth, joined the Anglican Church, and rose to power with his brother-in-law, holding at various times the offices of customs collector, naval officer, secretary, and chief justice. His only son, Theodore, who died in 1769, was also a councillor (the widow married Governor John Wentworth). Most of his fortune went to a relative, George King, who took the

name Atkinson, and the estate thus passed from a Loyalist councillor to a rebel senator.[79]

Daniel Rindge belonged to a large family, part of Portsmouth's
upper class, one of whose members married the councillor Mark
H. Wentworth. Daniel's father John was a councillor and a
wealthy merchant. Daniel himself was also a merchant and, like
most members of the family, became a Loyalist. A brother-in-law,
Daniel Rogers, was also a councillor, but Rogers' father was only
an apothecary; and although Rogers added Rindge to his name
(as did his brothers), he became a rebel.[80]

Most of the councillors who were not related to the dominant
group came from the same class.[81] Even Peter Livius, an immigrant, had the same background. He was the son of a rich Portu-
guese merchant, and by marrying the daughter of Colonel John
Mason he became one of the claimants to a huge land grant in New
Hampshire. Presumably for this reason he was made a councillor.
Although he became a Loyalist, he was exceedingly critical of the
Wentworths' economic activities—especially their land speculation, which conflicted with his own interests. In later life he served
as judge of the vice-admiralty court in Quebec.[82] The only other
non-native was the customs collector, James Nevin, who was born
in Scotland and apparently worked his way up in the British Navy.
He was chosen a councillor in 1758 for reasons unknown, and acquired land in over thirty towns. He died in 1769 leaving a moderate estate.[83]

Unless Nevin's father was poor, the Council contained only one
self-made man. We first hear of George Boyd as a houseboy to
Henry Sherburne, who was the father of Councillor John Sherburne (and related to practically everybody). Boyd later became
foreman of a ropewalk and was notorious for his sharp practices.
By 1774, when he left the colony, he was paying a tax twice as
high as anyone in Portsmouth, and was hailed in the press as "the
most lucky Genius of the present Day in the merchantile Way,
though not bred a merchant."[84] All of the other councillors belonged to prominent and wealthy families. Most of them were merchants. Only two were primarily farmers, though many of the
others had large landholdings. All but two lived in Portsmouth.
Nine of the twelve who held office in 1776 remained loyal to the
Crown.

The House of Representatives contained no such powerful elite group, but many members did belong to the same social class as the councillors and a few actually later served on the Council. Representative Peter Gilman, a large landowner from Exeter who married into the Wentworth family, became a councillor in 1771.[85] Similarly, Councillor John Sherburne had represented Portsmouth, as had his wealthy brother Henry.[86] Councillor Thomas W. Waldron, a wealthy landowner, represented Dover until his apointment to the Council in 1772.[87] The town of Sommersworth elected a member of the Wentworth family. About a third of the representatives were wealthy; and nearly two-thirds belonged to New Hampshire's upper class of large landowners, merchants, and lawyers. The rest of the members were farmers, a few of whom also had other interests, but who owned moderate estates even when they were among their towns' more substantial citizens; for the colony was not rich. Most of the representatives became rebels, and many played a prominent part in the Revolution. What made the House an undemocratic body was not so much the above-average wealth and nonfarm occupation of its majority, but its narrow geographical base: practically the entire membership came from a handful of towns near the coast. Until 1770 no town west of the Merrimack Valley was represented. In that year a few new towns were allowed to hold elections, but not enough to make any difference in the composition of the House. The House and Council were therefore similar in many respects. However, the general social and economic level of the representatives was somewhat lower than that of the councillors, and the former were much more influenced by public opinion.

Relations between the two houses were characterized by frequent disagreements and by the representatives' exasperation at the dilatory and obstructive policies of the Council and of the royal government. In New Hampshire the upper house was not empowered to amend bills, but only to propose alterations that might make them acceptable. Had this been done consistently and conscientiously, the effect might have been beneficial, as it often was in other colonies; but as a rule the Council simply rejected any measure that it thought imperfect. Often it did not even inform the lower house that a bill had been disapproved, and the representatives had to inquire whether any action had been taken. Sometimes no action had been taken at all; on other occasions the bill was returned without any explanation for the rejection. On June 8, 1763, for example, the lower house informed the Council that various bills that were essential for the good of the community had been sent up but had not been acted upon by the Council. The representatives requested that these be passed or that the Council communicate its objections so that changes could be made. Nothing happened. In December the representatives again requested information, and this time were presented with a list of nine bills, of which some had been rejected by the Council, others by the governor; but the list did not specify who had done the rejecting or why. The bills were resubmitted the following spring, and again most of them were delayed, so that on June 13, 1764, the lower house was obliged to ask what bills had been passed. Eight days later no reply had been received, and the legislature was adjourned. When it met again in January the request was renewed, but not until May did the Council at last inform the representatives that the bills in question had been rejected.[88]

New Hampshire's Council, intimately connected with the governor by marriage and social class, also acted in concert with him politically. Far from forming an independent branch of government, it was little more than an agent of the executive. When in doubt about a measure, the councillors consulted the governor. In 1765, for example, when the representatives inquired about the disposition of bills regulating interest rates and the value of money, the Council replied that they lay before the governor "as the Council Chused to Confer with him thereon before they concur'd them."[89] On another occasion the Council returned a bill establishing fees accompanied by the objections not of the upper house but of the governor.[90] In another colony such a message would have been returned as unconstitutional.

When the governor and the representatives clashed, the upper house naturally defended the governor. The most important such conflict concerned the governor's salary.[91] This issue had a long background, based on the poverty of the colony and the unwillingness of the lower house to grant permanent funds. For many years prior to 1763 the governor received an annual income derived primarily from an excise. The situation was unsatisfactory from the governor's point of view, partly because he sometimes received no money, and partly because he might be threatened at any time by the withholding of funds. In 1765, for example, the governor sat on two bills desired by the lower house while the latter was discussing his salary. When the representatives discovered that the governor was stalling they sent an angry message, but were kept waiting three more days before the governor gave in. Then, and only then, did they settle down to the business of granting money.[92]

The controversy reached a crisis point in 1767 when the new governor (John Wentworth) attempted to carry out the instructions he had received to obtain permanent funds. The lower house sent up a resolution which the Council returned, objecting first that it granted money for only one year instead of for the duration of the governor's administration, and second that, whereas previously a special fund had been provided, now the governor was simply to be paid from the treasury. Moreover, the councillors said, the grant should be made by an act, not merely by a vote. The representatives pleaded that the colony was too poor to grant permanent funds, but suggested that the passage of the excise bill would be helpful. This measure had been rejected by the Council from 1763 through 1766, and now was again being held up—evidently because of a dispute over who should control the collectors, and other issues concerning infringement of the prerogative. The governor backed up his Council by insisting that the lower house comply with his instructions. The representatives, undaunted, voted a salary of £700 currency for only the duration of the present governor's term, to be drawn out of the excise on spirituous liquor, or other funds if necessary. But if the governor received a salary from home (through the Townsend duties), the act was to be withdrawn, and the excise was to be "farmed" by a committee. The Council could not accept this, and the dispute continued for more than a year, when the upper house surrendered. The salary was thereafter granted annually.[93]

The Council defended the royal prerogative whenever it appeared menaced. One of the more important occasions was the protracted debate, commencing in 1767, over the formation of counties. The disagreement concerned, in part, the number of counties: the representatives wanted four, the councillors two. The primary reason for the Council's intractableness, however, was that the bill established the times and places for holding court sessions, thereby encroaching upon the royal prerogative. In February of 1768 the lower house drew up a bill that evidently yielded on the courts but retained the four counties. The Council rejected it. The debate then returned, in 1769, to the question of courts. The House wanted annual sessions in both Portsmouth and Exeter, whereas the Council preferred holding both in Portsmouth. The representatives pointed out that the end of all government was the good of the governed, and that courts were established for the benefit of the people. Judges depended primarily upon their knowledge of the facts, which were best ascertained by witnesses before juries in the original venue. Besides, they added, traveling to Portsmouth was expensive. These arguments, or the intervention of the governor, were persuasive, for the Council finally retreated after a suspending clause had been appended.[94]

The most far-reaching of all disputes involving the prerogative was that which concerned representation. Some years before 1763 the lower house had attempted to secure the right to control its own membership, but Governor Benning Wentworth had successfully established the principle that towns were given the right to choose representatives by royal authority alone. So complete was his victory, achieved in 1752, that the executive was stronger in New Hampshire than in any other colony, with the possible exception of Georgia. The debate was reopened by the House in 1763 when it passed a bill to allow additional towns to choose representatives. This was rejected either by the Council or by the governor, and re-passed in 1764 with a suspending clause, the absence of which may have been the cause of its rejection previously.[95] In 1768 the legislature learned that the king had refused his consent. So thoroughly had the representatives been cowed, however, that they took no action until 1775. At that point—after the War had started —they refused to admit delegates from three towns that had been authorized by the governor to hold elections, and sent up a brash message insisting upon their exclusive right to determine their own membership. Since the Council was appointed by the Crown, they argued, it was an arbitrary stretch of the prerogative for the governor to issue such writs without the concurrence of the lower house, because both houses would in effect be chosen by the Crown.[96] This challenge came much too late, of course, since the lower house had until then seldom been victorious over the governor or the Council.

Various issues involving economic interests arose during the pre-Revolutionary decade. The representatives passed a bill to regulate the calling of town meetings and the assessment of common or undivided land, but this interfered with the economic interests of the Wentworths and their supporters. The councillors at first procrastinated for a year and then returned the bill, explaining that they "could not see their way clear to pass it as it stood, Neither could they if the Council were not exempted from paying any Tax for their Lands." The lower house refused to alter the measure, which then died.[97]

A dispute over the excise occurred primarily because the House attempted to control the selection of collectors—though a delay of eight months occurred when the Council misplaced the bill. The Council at one point tried to exclude any member of either house from purchasing the post of collector; but the House consistently refused any restriction on its control.[98] The dispute continued until the two chambers compromised by vesting the power of appointment in a joint committee. On another occasion, when the lower house appointed a committee to investigate certain funds, the Council would not concur until the House watered down the resolution to a request that the governor have the proper accounts laid before the House.[99] Attempts by the representatives to regulate the value of money and the amount of interest rates also encountered lengthy delays although the measures finally passed. The Council rejected bills for the relief of debtors, and on several occasions required changes in money bills, fee tables, allowances to members of the legislature, and other financial measures. Various non-economic bills were also rejected or accepted only after changes had been required; but the reasons for such actions can rarely be discovered because the Council seldom deigned to explain its action.

In general the lower house rarely succeeded in overriding the upper house on vital matters. The situation was surely galling to the representatives, who did not conceal their anger when the Council ignored their requests for information or dispatch. But not until the colony was on the threshold of revolution was the Council publicly attacked. Then a bold writer in the *New Hampshire Gazette*[100] cited internal grievances as proof that the people should elect men who would defend liberty, not those who might destroy it. The Council, he observed, could not be among the defenders, for it was essentially a House of Lords: councillors would protect the rights of the prerogative, not the privileges of the people. Perhaps others shared this view, but of course no reform was possible, even of the lower house, as long as the Wentworth group maintained control. Their power was to be broken only by revolution.

The councils that were controlled by a colonial elite differed from those in which placemen were prominent in only a few respects. Both were composed almost entirely of wealthy men. In both, merchants and lawyers—the urban upper class—were very powerful. Both contained a majority of future Loyalists. However, whereas half of the members of the placemen-dominated councils were born outside the colony in which they held power, almost all of the elite councillors were natives. Indeed, the latter often owed their position to a native-born grandfather or even great-grandfather. In every case the colony's most prominent familes were represented; often the councillors were closely related; always they belonged to the highest social and economic rank. When they held offices in addition to that of councillor, as they sometimes did, they did not depend upon those offices for their livelihood. They were financially independent men who supported the governor because they chose to do so—because they were prerogative men, Tories rather than Whigs. Yet, although they were far from typical colonials, they seldom clashed with the elected branch (New Hampshire excepted). This was so partly because the elite was an integral part of colonial society rather than alien to it and therefore shared the colonial view. Equally important was the nature of the lower houses, composed as they were of men of the same economic and social standing as those in the upper houses, and therefore of similar outlook. The elite councils seem on the whole to have been regarded not as foreign bodies imposed upon the colonies against their will, but as a necessary and even valuable, albeit sometimes annoying, component of the local political system.

CHAPTER 3

THE ELECTED

*A*LL OF THE COUNCILS previously discussed were appointed by royal or proprietary authority and served "at pleasure." The three colonies of Massachusetts, Connecticut, and Rhode Island, in contrast, had relatively democratic governments based upon charters. In Massachusetts, the upper house was chosen by the legislature; in the other two it was elected by the voters. Responsible to the people rather than to the king, these councils anticipated the political institutions of the post-Revolutionary states.

MASSACHUSETTS

The government of Massachusetts, after 1691, consisted of a governor, who was chosen by the king; representatives, who were elected by the voters; and councillors, who were selected by the representatives and the outgoing councillors, subject to the governor's veto. In 1774, Parliament virtually revoked the Massachusetts charter in retaliation for the colony's intractableness, and the so-called Mandamus Council of that year was appointed by the governor under royal orders. Until that year Massachusetts was the only colony in which the council was chosen by indirect election. Moreover, it was the only colony in which the councillors were supposed to represent particular geographical areas.

Every year, at the beginning of the May session, the legislature voted for twenty-eight councillors. Eighteen came from "the territory formerly called the Colony of the Massachusetts Bay," four from "new Plymouth" (Plymouth, Bristol, and Barnstable counties), three from Maine, and one from "the Territory lying between the River Sagadahock and Nova Scotia," which for practical purposes also meant Maine. The two remaining councillors were chosen at large. The governor then approved or, if he wished, rejected the nominees. Until 1766 the governor accepted the whole list almost automatically, so that an individual who wished to become a councillor needed only to satisfy the legislators. After that date Governors Bernard and Gage rejected many of those chosen. Until 1774 the vacancies were left empty; no further vote was taken, and the governor could not substitute different men for those he disliked.

The requirement that the councillors be chosen from certain geographical areas did not mean that all parts of the colony were equally represented. The four councillors from the Plymouth area might have been satisfactory had they all actually resided in those southeastern counties, but such was not always the case. In 1765, for example, Peter Oliver, one of the four, did own a fine home and ironworks in Middleboro, but he was primarily a Bostonian, a wealthy merchant, and a member of the city's social elite. Likewise, councillors chosen for Maine, though technically residents of that region, often were in reality land speculators with homes in Boston. Thus Nathaniel Sparhawk of Kittery was born in Bristol, Rhode Island, became an eminent Boston merchant, and moved to Kittery only after he married a daughter of William Pepperell.[1] The councillor chosen in 1765 for the area between the Sagadahock River and Nova Scotia was William Brattle, a Cambridge lawyer and moneylender. Finally, almost all of the men elected to serve from the old Bay Colony and "at large" were easterners, especially in the years preceding 1770. In 1765 the two "at large" members were Benjamin Lincoln (father of the Revolutionary War general) of Hingham, not far from Boston, and Edmund Trowbridge, an eminent Cambridge lawyer and the attorney general. During the whole period from 1763 to 1774, only one-tenth of the councillors came from the interior counties of Worcester, Hampshire, and Berkshire, which occupied two-thirds of the colony; one-eighth came from Maine; three-tenths came from Boston; and the rest—nearly half—lived in eastern towns on or near the coast, such as Cambridge and Medford, which together furnished nearly as many members as all three western counties combined. Therefore, the Council in reality represented towns near the coast, not the rural interior of the colony.

The councillors were even less typical of the average citizen in occupation and social and economic status than in residence. Most of the voters were farmers with modest properties worth a few hundreds of pounds. But only a dozen councillors made farming their primary occupation, though several others were large land-owners. Merchants formed by far the largest element among the councillors, comprising almost half of the membership. Second in number were lawyers. These men often had wide economic inter-ests, especially real property in farms, speculative tracts, or town buildings and lots. Most of the remaining councillors also engaged in nonagricultural occupations—were traders, manufacturers, doctors, or judges.

Moreover, the councillors owned far more property than did the average citizen. In the colony as a whole, judging from probate records, about one-half of one percent of the men were wealthy; 5 percent were well-to-do; 25 percent were of moderate estate; and the rest—over two-thirds—had less property.[2] Yet half of the councillors were wealthy and most of the rest were well-to-do. About one in five had moderate property, but probably none owned less than £500.

The councillors were further distinguished from most citizens by their social position. By 1763 Massachusetts contained an es-tablished upper class which had exercised power and prestige for several generations. Most of these men were merchants, although some were great landowners, manufacturers, or professional men. About two out of five councillors belonged to this elite. Almost all were of old New England stock. The Massachusetts upper house contained more college men than that of any other colony, about 40 percent of the total membership, and many of those without college degrees were well educated.

A final characteristic that separated the councillors from the general populace was the number of outside offices they held. Three-fourths of the councillors held at least one judgeship in addi-tion to appointments as local magistrates. After 1770 the propor-tion was notably reduced; but, even considering the period as a whole, over half of the members held high civil office in addition to posts on the Council, and several were colonels and generals.[3]

The Massachusetts Council thus resembled other northern upper houses in that prominent, well-educated families supplied a considerable part of the total membership, and prosperous merchants from the commercial centers comprised the largest single element. Yet it also differed fundamentally from those previously examined, because as an elective rather than an appointive body it was far more popular than were the royal councils. In the first place, the interior towns were not excluded from the Council, nor did the capital city furnish most of the members, as it did in New York. Moreover, the elite families occupied fewer than half of the seats; the councillors were as likely to be well-to-do as wealthy; and the upper house even contained a small group of men who were little more than substantial farmers or artisans. Probably 20 percent had only moderate properties. Whereas most councillors elsewhere remained loyal to England, half of the Massachusetts councillors became rebels. Finally, the character of the upper house was dramatically changed during the critical years 1766–1770, when the legislature used its appointive power to purge the Council of prerogative men. This transformation, which in the royal councils was impossible, anticipated significantly the changes that became general after 1776.

During the early years the upper house was divided into two elements. A bare majority could be relied upon to support the prerogative on most issues, while the other group was allied with the lower house. These have been called the "conservative" and the "popular" factions, or parties.[4] The governor's allies consisted primarily of wealthy merchants and lawyers of the prominent old upper class. A majority were college graduates and without exception they held high office. The leader was, of course, Thomas Hutchinson, chief justice, judge of probate, lieutenant governor, and ultimately acting governor. Others included Andrew and Peter Oliver, whose father, a wealthy merchant, had also been a councillor and had married the daughter of Governor Belcher. Andrew Oliver married first the daughter of Honorable Thomas Fitch and then Hutchinson's sister-in-law. Belcher's son Andrew belonged to the same group in the Council, as did one of the Leonards of Norton. John Chandler, Timothy Paine, Israel Williams, and Timothy Ruggles—four wealthy westerners—joined them. The only self-made man was Thomas Flucker, whose father was a sea captain and who married first the daughter of Councillor James Bowdoin and second the daughter of General Samuel Waldo, owner of an extensive estate in Maine. Almost all of these men became Loyalists.[5]

The popular party differed from the conservatives in several respects. Most of its members came from small eastern towns rather than from Boston. More than half were merchants or lawyers, but two were farmers, one was a maltster, and another was a surveyor and a doctor. Half came from ordinary, respectable families; their parents generally were of moderate means or perhaps were well-to-do but not wealthy. They were less likely to hold high office, were seldom college men, and several became rebels. James Bowdoin inclined toward the governor's camp until 1768, when he shifted loyalties.[6] William Brattle, a wealthy Cambridge lawyer, started as a supporter of the popular cause, but changed sides and finally became a Loyalist. James Russell, a Charleston merchant, followed a similar course though he never actually became a Tory. James Otis, Sr., also vacillated. These shifts and defections kept the popular party in the Council weak until about 1769.

By 1769 a major change was taking place not only in the political attitude of the Council but in its social and economic composition. Before 1770, 70 percent of the councillors were merchants and lawyers; afterwards that proportion was reduced to 55 percent, while the number of farmers and artisans increased. Wealthy men formed five-eighths of the total before 1770, but less than one-half afterwards. Members of prominent families gave way to those of undistinguished origin. Especially noteworthy was the displacement of high-ranking officials by men without a major office, and of future Loyalists by men who became rebels.

The contrast can be easily dramatized. John Chandler of Worcester was a very wealthy merchant who left property worth £25,505, including a thousand acres. Timothy Paine married Chandler's sister and left £4,381 when he died in 1793.[7] Timothy Ruggles was also a very large landowner and a leading lawyer, while Israel Williams of Hatfield made a fortune in trade, agriculture, and land speculation, and was called the "monarch of Hampshire." These four, all of whom became Loyalists except Paine, a neutral, were replaced by men who were more nearly typical of the west, though none were farmers. Artemas Ward, a Shrewsbury storekeeper whose father was a founder of the town, had only moderate means; John Whitcomb of Bolton was a well-to-do manufacturer (he owned some lime kilns); and Timothy Woodbridge, superintendent of Indian affairs, earned £1 per day teaching Indians.[8]

These changes meant above all that after 1769 the councillors were subordinated to the representatives, because if they assumed too independent a role they would not be re-elected. The governor could, of course, reject men whom he disliked. But this power, had it been fully exercised, would all but have deprived him of a council. Of the old conservative faction only Sparhawk, who defected to the popular side, held office after 1769. Governor Bernard vetoed eleven men in 1769, but those who remained did not support him; Gage had no better luck when he rejected thirteen in 1774. In between, Hutchinson did not even try.

As was true of other royal councils, and despite the peculiar mode of selection, prior to the purge the governor usually could rely on the upper house. Hutchinson himself wrote in 1769: "I do not know that there has been an instance since the Charter until now of the Councils combining against the G[overnor]."[9] John Adams agreed. The councillors had protested against the Revenue Act of 1764 but, according to Bernard, had "played a most steady part,"[10] and when, in 1765, the House had passed a resolution that the courts should open without using stamps, the Council had tabled it.[11] There followed the first attack on conservative members. In 1766, the Council had advised the governor to obey the Quartering Act, and subsequently had defended him against newspaper attacks.[12] As a result, when in 1769 the popular party won control over the lower house, the Council was purged of its prerogative men. Thereafter, the fact that the Council was elected proved to be, as Bernard observed, the "Fatal Ingredient" of the government.[13] From that point on the councillors ceased to act in defense of royal authority and became increasingly rebellious. Hutchinson complained: "I have never been able to obtain their advice or Council to any proposal I have made for discountenancing the ursupation [sic] of the Government by the Town of Boston."[14] They refused to find quarters for the troops;[15] they acted independently of the governor, criticized him, and passed resolutions nearly as strong as those of the representatives. In 1773, the upper house sent a message to the governor defending the colonists against Hutchinson's criticisms, and denied that Parliament had unlimited authority.[16] When the Council joined in calling for Hutchinson's removal, its usefulness, from the governor's point of view, was clearly at an end. The direct consequence of these events was the enactment of that section of the Massachusetts Government Act of 1774 that provided for the Council to be chosen by the governor by a writ of mandamus. This introduced the final chapter in the history of the upper house.

In 1774 Governor Gage invited over twenty men to serve as councillors. When some of these refused he invited others until, all told, thirty-four had been approached. Twenty-five were sworn in during August. Of these, eight soon resigned. A year later Gage added two more men, and was able to meet with nineteen in July. The mandamus councillors were truly the colony's Loyalist elite. Seven of them had served earlier and had been forced to retire. The Olivers now returned, as did the treasurer, Harrison Gray, and the secretary, Thomas Flucker. Paine and Ruggles from the west were invited to rejoin, as was Danforth of Cambridge. To the westerners were added Abijah Willard of Lancaster, a large landowner with a fortune of £7,500, scion of an important family related to the Chandlers,[17] and John Murray of Rutland, a merchant and large landowner who had immigrated as a poor lad from Ireland. A wholly self-made man, he ended by acquiring an extraordinary estate of over £25,000 and marrying a daughter of John Chandler (in that order).[18] Most of the new councillors were rich businessmen from the Boston area, doubtless chosen because suitable Tories were hard to find elsewhere, and because local men could easily attend the sessions. Most of them belonged to the colony's upper class, such as James Boutineau, who was related to the Bowdoins and Faneuils, William Browne, of an eminent Salem family, the two Ervings, and the two Hutchinsons. Naturally they held many important civil and military offices. Two-thirds were Harvard graduates. All except perhaps one were Loyalists. This was a Loyalism not of the Anglicans—only four or five belonged to the Church of England—nor of recent immigrants—only two had been born overseas—but of a native, Congregationalist, cultured, and conservative upper class.

The mandamus councillors had no easy time of it. One writer even informed them that "hardly one in ten of you can boast a descent, from persons above the rank of shopkeepers and mechanics," an accusation which must have irritated men like the Hutchinsons more than most criticisms.[19] They were damned as traitors and beset by angry mobs. Several were obliged to resign, and few could (like Joseph Lee) save their property from confiscation. The councillors collectively lost between £150,000 and £200,000. They lost more than money: they lost their power. While the Mandamus Council was meeting with Gage, another Council very different in origin and composition, was meeting with Hancock. After July of 1775 the latter alone remained.

The transformation of the Council, striking though it was, did not affect relations between the two houses as much as might be supposed. For this there were several reasons. Relations between the colonies and England, rather than local matters, were responsible for the change in personnel; and the position of the two bodies on internal affairs was therefore little affected. More important, the change that occurred between 1765 and 1770 was not a matter of two diametrically opposed forces being reconciled, but of two similar, though not identical, bodies moving in the same direction: the paths that the two houses followed did not begin at polar opposites and meet at a center, but started no great distance apart and slowly converged. The lower house gradually became more radical, and as it did so the upper house was brought into harmony with it. In 1763 the conservatives controlled the Council and had a majority of two to one in the House. Then in 1766 no fewer than forty-two new representatives were chosen, and the first attack upon the Council followed. Even then the lower house was still not a radical body. It initially defeated the Massachusetts Circular Letter of 1768, which vigorously asserted colonial rights, before finally adopting it at the end of the session. Not until 1769 did the popular party win a truly decisive victory, at which point the Council was purged.[20] After that time the two branches followed a similar course. Finally, the Council had never been as independent of the House as were most councils, for the method of selection had always operated to minimize the differences between them and to moderate conflicts. Aside from the conflict over the resistance movement, relations were generally harmonious throughout the period.

The procedure followed by the legislature during its sessions helped to prevent disputes. Petitions and laws were framed by joint committees and then introduced into one or the other house, passed or rejected by it, and sent to the other house for concurrence. Amendments were rarely made, and when disagreements arose they were usually settled by additional joint committees. The houses almost never communicated their reasons for rejection or nonconcurrence; doubtless these reasons were well known through the committee system. Few disputes arose; disagreements ordinarily were limited to petitions on which there were no preliminary consultations.

Therefore, when relations between the houses are examined, leaving external policy aside, the purge of 1769 is seen to have made less difference than might have been expected. The Council at times was just as stubborn after that date as it had been before,[21] with about the same lack of success; for even during the earlier period it seldom emerged victorious in major controversies. The ascendancy of the lower house can easily be demonstrated. When, in 1765, the House advertised in the newspapers that soldiers and their heirs who wanted land should submit their names, the Council protested that it had previously refused to concur in a vote on that subject. The lower house, it conceded, had the power to originate such grants, because they were similar to money bills; but the approval of the Council was essential and ought not be taken for granted. The representatives explained that they had not intended to infringe upon any rights of the Council, but did not reverse their policy.[22]

One of the few instances in which the Council followed an independent course occurred later the same year. While the legislature was not in session, the governor and Council, acting in their executive capacity, withdrew money from the treasury to support a company of soldiers at Castle William. The representatives quickly challenged this action. They insisted that such a procedure was a flagrant infraction of the rights of the lower house, for if the governor and Council could raise one company they could raise ten or a hundred, creating a standing army. The councillors replied placatingly that they had not intended to infringe upon the rights of the House, and might have made a mistake in judgment, for "they pretend not to be infallible," but that when the legislature was not sitting, the governor and Council must have power to act for the good of the people. In this case the people were so agitated that the stamps required by the Stamp Act, which had just arrived, might have been destroyed had they not been protected, and the province would have been forced to pay for them. The representatives retorted that the Council's action was legislative, and therefore incorrect; a more pointed response soon followed with the first stage of the purge.[23] After that event the Council was less apt to follow an independent policy, though it never became subservient. Throughout the period, it was capable of opposing measures desired by the lower house, at times even unanimously.[24]

A major function of the Council in every colony was the defense of the prerogative. This duty was accepted by the Massachusetts upper house, perhaps in part because the governor sat with the Council, perhaps also because so many of the councillors were bound to the government by the offices which they held, and perhaps in many cases by conviction. In 1763, for example, the governor requested that a census be taken. The Council obediently recommended that men be appointed to do so, defining in some detail the procedure to be followed. The House, however, did not intend to give up the power of appointment, and suggested that a joint committee answer the governor. The Council did not concur, but resolved that the governor issue the necessary orders to the selectmen. The House, determined to control the operation, rejected this method; and in the end—after a delay of almost a year—the two houses ignored the governor and agreed that the selectmen should do the job.[25] The outcome was a victory for the lower house. But when the representatives tried in 1765 to set certain fees that were already defined by Parliament, the Council successfully prevented any action.[26] Again, after the purge, when the representatives passed a series of acts that were not drawn in the proper form according to the governor's instructions, these were unanimously rejected by the Council.[27] Still later the Council defended the royal rights in Maine. The governor had called attention to the intrusion of settlers upon ungranted land and the need to preserve royal mast trees. A joint committee submitted a report which defended the settlers, but which did request the governor to prevent further intrusions. The Council accepted the report but the representatives did not. They were willing to issue a proclamation against trespass upon the king's timber, but not upon the land. The Council attempted to add trespass upon the land, but could not do so, and ultimately gave in.[28] The Council thus demonstrated that despite its selection by the representatives it could occasionally be independent of the lower house, and that, to some degree, it was associated with the governor.[29]

One of the most important contests between the two houses was that waged for control over the colonial agent. Throughout the period, the lower house attempted to obtain its own agent, while the Council upheld the principle that the agent should act for the entire colony. In 1763, when Jasper Mauduit was agent, the House of Representatives tried to replace him with his brother Israel. The Council rejected the substitution, and also insisted on changes in the letter that was sent to the agent. For the moment the representatives accepted defeat, but during 1764 they began to correspond with the agent without consulting the Council, and refused to participate in the customary joint committees which had previously been chosen. In 1765, Richard Jackson was selected by both houses, but when he did not act with sufficient vigor during the Stamp Act controversy the House appointed Dennis De Berdt. The Council at first continued to support Jackson, defeating efforts to dismiss him and delaying De Berdt's salary bill. In June of 1767 the salary bill was finally accepted by a vote of nine to six after the representatives had agreed to eliminate a phrase referring to De Berdt as the agent of the lower house rather than the agent for the whole colony. When the governor vetoed the grant the Council joined the representatives in protesting. At the same time the Council condemned the action of the lower house in maintaining a separate agent. Subsequently, when the two houses could not agree upon who should be chosen, the Council appointed William Bollan and tried to prevent the representatives from maintaining De Berdt; but in the end both men were paid and each house consequently had its own agent. The lower house therefore had won its primary objective.[30]

The two houses did not differ fundamentally on economic issues. In general the upper house was slightly more insistent on the prompt payment of taxes and debts, and defended the interests of large property holders. Twice when the House tried to issue treasury notes for the payment of the public debt, the Council refused to concur. Perhaps the Council was unwilling to authorize what amounted to an inflationary measure in the face of British policy; eventually the Council did approve of some such bill in a modified form, the exact nature of which is unknown.[31] The Council may have been reflecting the economic prejudices of its members by twice rejecting excise bills.[32] On several occasions the Council rejected House votes for levying taxes on land owned by nonresidents, a step desired by some newly-established towns.[33] Some attempts on the part of western towns to lighten their tax burden were also vetoed.[34] The Council refused to agree to measures for the relief of prisoners for debt, and for stays of execution for debt.[35] In 1771 and 1772 the representatives attempted to empower justices of the peace to try cases involving debts of less than £10, but were unable to overcome the Council's opposition.[36] On various other occasions the upper house proved less sympathetic to those who owed money or wished to obtain province land cheaply.[37]

Such actions might be thought to show a lack of sympathy for poor people, especially debtors. On the whole this seems to have been true, though the record is not consistent.[38] It was the lower house, rather than the Council, that rejected (unanimously) a bill for the relief of indigent Indians, and was unwilling to burden the towns with additional taxes for the support of jailed criminals. On the other hand the Council rejected a large number of petitions submitted by poor persons seeking relief, which the House approved. One was sent by a man who had encountered many hardships as a pioneer, and then had spent much time and money trying to find a child supposedly captured by the Mohawks. Now, poor and feeble, he asked for land and abatement of taxes. The lower house granted the petition but the Council unanimously rejected it.[39] The Council also refused to appropriate money for the medical care and support of the poor in Boston. Probably the upper house felt that these were local matters.[40] Even more serious to the persons concerned was the upper house's unwillingness to allow the sale of real estate for debt. Thus in 1763 an Indian of Natick, "Planter," requested permission to sell fifteen acres in order to discharge debts "contracted for necessaries" and to enable him to repair his house. This was granted by the House but refused by the Council.[41] Even the sale of land in order that a lad could go to Harvard was considered unjustified.[42] The Council also blocked an attempt by the lower house to amend the law governing such sales.[43]

The two houses also divided on their treatment of minority groups. The representatives once took more favorable action than the upper house toward a Baptist group, and once toward Quakers.[44] In contrast, the Council was much more sympathetic toward the Acadians. This was a special case, for the Council was attempting to carry out the instructions of the British government that the exiles should be well treated, whereas the representatives doubtless reflected a general hostility toward ancient enemies. The trouble began when many Acadians left the towns in which they had been placed and came to Boston, hoping to leave the colony. But they found themselves unable either to leave or to support themselves, while those who remained in the towns were apparently not being properly provided for. The result was a controversy lasting for more than a year, during which the Council tried to obtain sufficient funds and the representatives grudgingly appropriated pittances. Finally, in June of 1766, the lower house resolved that no further money should be spent without a special order by the entire legislature; and when the Council tried to add the phrase, "Cases of absolute necessity excepted," the representatives rejected the amendment.[45] In this matter the Council certainly reflected the more humanitarian attitude of the British government.

Legal and administrative matters also caused disagreement between the two houses. These included petitions for the formation of new towns, or of new districts from old towns, which the Council occasionally rejected,[46] and the organization of new courts or of new meeting places for old courts.[47] The Council also refused to approve a long series of petitions which sought special permission for a tavern license; these were evidently appeals from unfavorable decisions of local justices.[48]

These incidents, and other disagreements, were on the whole minor.[49] The two houses differed, but they never engaged in the prolonged and bitter disputes that plagued many other colonies. Yet they were dissimilar in social, economic, geographical, and cultural backgrounds.[50] The reason for their harmonious relationship was simple: the councillors owed their seats not to the governor but to the representatives. Fully subservient to neither, at the same time they could not be entirely independent. This anomaly was not retained when the Revolution made possible political reforms.

CONNECTICUT

Connecticut and Rhode Island, born within a few years of one another, with Massachusetts their common sire, had histories far more disparate than those of most siblings. Though each founded its government upon a charter with a bicameral legislature chosen by the voters, and though in each the upper house was selected by a colony-wide ballot, the two houses were totally dissimilar. In Rhode Island, the "magistrates" reflected, with reasonable accuracy, the character and views of the entire population; in Connecticut the "assistants" comprised a highly select group quite distinct from the general citizenry. Yet each seemed to correspond to the genius of the colony.

Every September the freemen of Connecticut voted for twenty men who would stand for election in May. No lists of candidates were published for the voters' attention, so that the freemen nominated those whose names were familiar to them—perhaps local leaders first, then men of colony-wide repute—which meant, in practice, the current officeholders, provided they had acquired fame rather than notoriety. The votes were counted in October by the "deputies," as the members of the "Assembly" or "House of Representatives" were called. In the spring the freemen chose twelve out of the twenty, including the governor and deputy governor. In every town the constable called first for votes for the person who had the largest poll in the fall, and so successively through the list. This meant, as one writer observed, that the incumbent councillors were named in order, and thus had an almost insuperable advantage over their rivals, no matter how well qualified. The list therefore tended to become permanent. Moreover, when an assistant died, the vacancy was filled by the governor and the other assistants. Thus the Council became a nearly self-perpetuating oligarchy.[51]

The office was not, however, hereditary. Of the twenty-four councillors who served between 1763 and 1776, only four were descended from and six others related to previous councillors. Such connections certainly helped, but they were not decisive. More important was one's position within the colony's social structure. A majority of the councillors came from Connecticut's prominent old families, which had furnished political, economic, social, and religious leadership for three or four generations. In this respect the upper house resembled some of the royal councils. Such an ancestry was not absolutely essential, however, for nine or ten councillors came from families that were reputable but not outstanding. One qualification seems to have been requisite: Connecticut birth.

By what process did these men come to be politically distinguished? In the overwhelming majority of cases, it was through the legal profession, usually preceded by an education at Yale. Attendance at Yale was more common among sons of the wealthy than among those of slender means, but it was not limited to the former. Shubael Conant's father, a third-generation American, was a surveyor and farmer of apparently moderate income, but Shubael went to Yale, became a lawyer, judge, and councillor, and left a personal estate of £1,657.[52] Colonel Robert Walker's father, Deacon Robert, left an "extensive farm," but was not a wealthy man; nor did Robert Jr. have any advantageous family connection, but he, too, went to Yale, became a lawyer, the king's attorney, and then assistant.[53] A college degree was not, in those days, essential to a legal practice, and several of the assistants made their way without it. Andrew Burr did so, but then he came from a long line of wealthy landowners, judges, and assistants.[54] The lawyers William Pitkin and his son lacked college degrees, as did Hezekiah Huntington, but these, too, were born to the purple; while William Griswold, who attended college but did not graduate, inherited thousands of acres and a secure place in society.[55] Other assistants demonstrated that the law could lead to success even when one had neither college degree nor influential relatives. Roger Sherman, a typical self-made man, was born on a farm, started as a cobbler, and achieved success through surveying, storekeeping, and the law.[56] Benjamin Hall, whose father was a farmer, may have benefited from the fact that his mother was the only daughter of the Reverend Charles Chauncey. He became a judge and an assistant without legal training.[57] Joseph Spencer's father seems also to have been a farmer; at any rate, Joseph had no particular advantages, but studied law and became a judge some years before he rose to political power.[58] What Zebulon West's father did is uncertain, but he was probably a farmer. Zebulon acquired a respectable landed estate of over seven hundred acres and held the office of judge of probate, but he was never more than a large farmer of moderate income. He left a small property to his oldest son.[59]

The typical assistant after 1763, then, was a fourth-generation Connecticut-born son of a prominent family. The parents of the assistants often were large landholders; others were ministers, lawyers, or merchants. They were usually at least well-to-do.[60] After graduating from college,[61] the future assistant entered the law or perhaps a business (fifteen were lawyers, four were merchants). He held local offices, served as a deputy in the Assembly, and became a justice of the peace. If he had not attained a judgeship before elevation to the upper house, he did so then—to this there is not a single exception. He was elected to the upper house before he reached fifty years of age. There he might expect to remain until he died or retired, for it would take a real cataclysm, such as a revolution, to displace him.[62] Almost all of the assistants were Congregationalists. Half of them held high military rank. Obviously they were trusted leaders. They demonstrated their economic competence by acquiring much property when they had not inherited large estates, though the Connecticut economic elite did not, as a class, compare in wealth with the upper classes of most colonies, and it was probably not primarily wealth that determined their high position.

Colonel John Chester's lengthy obituary in some ways characterizes the whole group of men who dominated Connecticut's political life. Referring to his "train of honorable Ancestors," the eulogist noted that he was "liberally educated at Cambridge," and, he continued, "his inclination and Genius, equally with his affluent Circumstances in life," made him, while in office, "unbias'd either by popular Applause or Disapprobation, to act contrary to his Sentiments."[63]

Affluent the assistants were, unbiased they could be only up to a point: Chester chose the unpopular side in the Stamp Act controversy and lost his job. The guarantee of tenure was thus not absolute, for an aroused electorate did displace men who forgot, or did not care, that they were popularly chosen. Connecticut's upper house, though perhaps an oligarchy, was continuously exposed to the democratic elements in the government.

Annual elections undoubtedly made the assistants reluctant to risk public disapprobation by too vigorous opposition to the deputies. Moreover, two major sources of disagreement elsewhere were absent from Connecticut: no royal or proprietary prerogative needed to be protected, nor was it necessary to defend the particular interest of an appointed governor. Relations between the two houses were therefore generally harmonious.

The first important controversy involving the upper house after 1763 generated repercussions which were felt for a decade. For the first time the assistants became the object of criticism and the people's high regard for them declined. The issue concerned external policy, specifically the Stamp Act. When the Act was received, a great majority of the deputies were opposed to its enforcement. Strong resolutions condemning the Act were passed by the Assembly, where only five men opposed them. Among these five was Thomas Fitch, Jr., the governor's son.[64] The councillors agreed to the resolutions, and when Governor Fitch attempted to enforce the unpopular law he found a majority of the upper house against him. Only four assistants took an oath to support the Act. Like Fitch, these men were from the southwestern part of the colony. Their stand was more courageous than popular, and in the next election all five were defeated and none was ever chosen again. They were replaced by candidates whose record on the Stamp Act was satisfactory. The change had the incidental effect of doubling the number of businessmen and decreasing the proportion of lawyers; but otherwise the social and economic characteristics of the upper house were unchanged.

During the next few years continual efforts were made to reelect Fitch and his supporters. Their candidacy was pressed not because of their position on the Stamp Act, however, but on the basis of several quite different arguments. After the disastrous (to the Fitch group), election of 1766, articles were inserted in the principal newspapers calling for a geographical reapportionment. It was argued that the more populous and wealthy towns west of the

Connecticut River were now underrepresented in the upper house and on the bench (for selection as an assistant led at once to a judgeship). Many important trading centers, it was claimed, were not represented by an assistant. The articles urged western voters to vote for only half-a-dozen candidates, particularly those who had been defeated, and to resist all attempts at intimidation. By this tactic the re-election of Fitch and his supporters would be assured.[65] This argument was countered by the reminder that the Fitch group had "virtually deserted the colony in time of their greatest danger." Fitch and his supporters might be able and honest, but they had been greatly mistaken, and there was no evidence that they had altered their views. To re-elect such men might suggest that the people had changed their minds about the Stamp Act.[66] An effort was made to demonstrate that the new distribution of assistantships was fairer than the old (though in fact there was little difference). Other observers noted that in Connecticut one town was much like another, whatever the location. Factional strife should be avoided, they said, and people should unite to choose the best men no matter where they resided.[67]

Meanwhile, Fitch's admirers sought to obtain his election as chief justice in order to increase his influence. Indeed, at first he was chosen by the lower house but was rejected by the upper. In the end, although many representatives felt that he was now "well fixed in the principles of liberty," others were still dubious, and when a poll was taken, most of the deputies were unwilling to vote openly against public opinion.[68] The fact that Fitch had more support in the lower house than in the country as a whole led some of his supporters to suggest a constitutional change by which councillors would be chosen by the Assembly instead of by the voters. The major proponent of this strategem was Benjamin Gale, one of the few deputies who had voted against the anti-Stamp Act resolutions. Gale urged that the charter be interpreted so as to permit the change; he also argued that the councillors should be deprived of their veto power and of their influence over the appointment of officials. In this way, conflicts might be avoided. Other critics felt that the freemen had the right to vote for anyone, not just the twenty nominees.[69] Gale himself, and probably others who agreed with him, were reacting to various factors: Gale identified the New Lights, whom he despised, with the easterners, and he blamed both for the success of the Susquehanna Company's Pennsylvania project, now being supported by the reformed Council but opposed by the lower house. The eastern land speculative interest was accused of responsibility for Fitch's defeat, the Stamp Act affair being only "a plausible Handle to raise a popular Outcry against him and some others."[70] The upper house was thus enmeshed in the complex political issues of the period. After the purge of 1765, however, it came to reflect primarily the views of the dominant "radical" eastern group—the pro-Susquehanna, anti-Stamp Act element.

From that date until independence the two houses were seldom opposed to one another, although the assistants did tend to be slightly more conservative. Resolutions against the Intolerable Acts passed the Assembly in May of 1774, but the upper house tabled them until October, when they were approved. The following spring the Assembly insisted upon, and obtained, a stronger protest to Lord Dartmouth than the councillors desired.[71] In economic matters, the upper house blocked a reduction of taxes passed by the deputies in 1764. Again, in 1765, the assistants tried to establish a tax rate of twopence on the pound, but the deputies insisted upon a penny only. Twice more, in 1769, the upper house attempted to increase taxes and was rebuffed.[72] The presence of many merchants in the upper house may have led to disagreements. "A Memorialist" complained that no successful economic reform could be instituted because the traders would not agree to it; the legislature, he urged, should contain at least one-half farmers.[73] Yet no evidence has survived that indicates serious disagreement between the two houses as long as Connecticut remained a colony. The Council could not represent separate views even though it was composed of business and professional men rather than farmers, because annual elections obliged it to heed public opinion. When some of its members showed signs of independence on a vital issue, they were promptly purged, and the assistants never again ventured seriously to challenge either the people or their deputies.

Rhode Island

Rhode Island's upper house consisted, before the Revolution, of "assistants" or "magistrates"[74] chosen annually by the voters, the twelve receiving the largest number of votes (including the governor and the deputy governor) being elected. The system differed from that in Connecticut in that no preliminary fall election was held. Nominations were therefore not made officially. However in practice two "factions" presented slates to the people. These were the Ward group, based in the south, and the Hopkins party, headquartered in Providence. Both had followers throughout the colony, but the Ward faction was strongest in Newport and other towns roughly south of Coventry, Warwick, and Warren, whereas the Hopkins faction won a majority in the north. There seem to have been few differences between the two groups other than personal and geographical, though the Hopkins party was more conservative economically and proved to be slightly less enthusiastic about the Revolution. Both embraced merchants and farmers, rich men and men of small means, men from leading families and those of humble origin. The Ward party contained more Quakers and Baptists, but Hopkins himself was a Quaker. The leading authority states that by tradition each of the five counties sent two magistrates,[75] but by the Revolutionary era factional disputes had put an end to this equality. In 1767, for example, Providence and Newport each sent three, thus furnishing half of the membership. The 1770 upper house included five from these towns and two others from commercial centers on Narragansett Bay. The whole mainland area from the two Greenwiches south sent but two. However, by comparison with most other councils, Rhode Island's magistrates were sectionally well distributed.

Regardless of which faction was successful, the upper house was radically different from councils elsewhere. Rhode Island was, as Judge Horsmanden, the New York councillor, asserted, a "downright democracy."[76] If the wealthy Rhode Islanders had united, or if the merchants had combined to carry the election, the upper house might conceivably have resembled the royal councils; but insofar as Rhode Island contained an aristocracy, it was divided by the Ward-Hopkins conflict. Men of wealth were chosen, but they were greatly outnumbered by men who were well-to-do, and in fact nearly half of the assistants had only moderate property. More merchants were elected than their numbers warranted, but since Rhode Island depended upon trade, their economic importance probably justified extra seats. The remarkable feature was that more farmers than merchants were elected. One-fourth of the magistrates belonged to Rhode Island's prominent old families, but half were of humble origin. Whereas in the royal colonies most councillors were Anglicans, in New England only a small minority belonged to the Church of England, while in Rhode Island's upper house there were an exceptional number of Quakers and Baptists.

The fathers of the magistrates, even more than the magistrates themselves, were representative Rhode Islanders. Only four fathers were merchants, two were doctors, two were ministers, and four were artisans. By far the largest number were farmers who held moderate properties or were at most well-to-do. The parents were generally above average in wealth and the percentage who were urban was larger than for the general population; but by comparison with fathers of councillors elsewhere they were reasonably typical of colonial society. Thus, the magistrates sprang from the people.

Three examples will suffice to characterize the men who sat in Rhode Island's upper house. John Gardner of Newport was chosen deputy governor in 1756 and served until his death. His father, Joseph, was a cooper. John became a prominent merchant, a judge, and, during the 1740's, treasurer and commissary general. He was a Baptist and a member of the prestigious Redwood Library.[77] John Almy of Portsmouth was a fifth-generation Rhode Islander. His aunt married William Ellery and their son, William Ellery, Jr., was a signer of the Declaration of Independence. Almy was also related to the Rays, Wards, and Lippitts—all prominent families. His father left a personal estate of £2,375 sterling, and bequeathed to the magistrate land in Portsmouth, Tiverton, Little Compton, and Newport.[78] Jonathan Randall was one of the nineteen farmers who served during the period. He lived in Cranston, and owned two slaves in 1774. His father, William, of the third generation, owned 175 acres and a mill, and left a modest personal estate of £180. Jonathan was the fifth son and did not rise above his father's economic status, although he served many years in the legislature.[79] It was the presence in Rhode Island's upper house of men such as Randall that made it unique during the colonial period.

The two houses seem to have been similar, perhaps even identical, in their composition, and therefore fundamental disagreements are not to be expected. The attitude of the magistrates tended to reflect the political desires of the party in power, and since both the Ward and Hopkins factions were vying for votes, they depended upon public opinion. Both houses derived their authority from the same source, and therefore did not struggle for supremacy; the functions of each had been clearly established by generations of usage. Almost all measures originated with the lower house, though the upper could and did take the initiative on occasion. Many matters were referred to joint committees, whose reports were then acted upon, ordinarily by the lower house. The upper house usually concurred with the acts and resolves. Its refusal to concur ended the matter. Sometimes amendments were made and sent down for approval. Seldom was there prolonged debate. In 1762 the lower house attempted to reduce the authority of the magistrates in conducting elections, but the magistrates protested successfully and there was no further argument over the relative power of the two bodies.

The existence of factions in the legislature occasionally resulted in disputes. In 1765 a petition by Stephen Hopkins and others encountered trouble from the Ward-dominated upper house, and the following year a petition from another Hopkins supporter was rejected; two years later the victorious Hopkins group denied a petition from Thomas Hazard of the Ward faction.[80] On the other hand the Hopkinses protected Elisha Brown even though he was a Ward man, possibly because he was an uncle of John and Moses Brown of the Hopkins party.[81]

The upper house adopted a cautious policy toward relations with England. This attitude obviously was not due to any prejudice in favor of the prerogative, nor did the policy go so far as to oppose resistance to British measures. The caution—and it was no more than that—was evidenced especially by the Hopkins group, and perhaps helps to account for its defeat in 1765, just as the Fitches were ousted in Connecticut. In 1763 the lower house requested the governor (Hopkins) not to administer the oath of office to newly appointed customs officials in Newport and Providence. The magistrates, however, proposed that if the surveyor general, John Temple, took the oath, then the other officials might also do so. The lower house refused to make any concession and a stalemate resulted.[82] The next year a memorial to the Board of

Trade protesting British policy was amended so as to be sent only if some other northern colonies agreed with it.[83] A few years later the Council, once more controlled by the Hopkins group, rejected a vote of the lower house concerning the losses sustained by Augustus Johnston during the Stamp Act riots. Johnston, a member of the Hopkins faction, had suffered considerably for his unpopular stand at that time. The magistrates pointed out that full evaluation of the damage had not been made nor had Johnston received compensation, and therefore the resolution was unsatisfactory.[84]

Similarly, in the spring of 1774, the upper house, still with a Hopkins majority, refused to recommend a general contribution for Boston and instead only expressed a "tender Commiseration for the Poor," promising to help them in the future "as their Necessities may require and the Abilities of the Colony afford."[85] This may have been a strategic move, since the colony was still trying to obtain reimbursement from England for expenses incurred in the French war. Yet many of the Hopkinses were lukewarm toward the resistance movement. Stephen Hopkins himself favored the Galloway Plan whereas Ward opposed it. In April of 1775 Governor Wanton, Deputy Governor Sessions, Thomas Wickes, and Simeon Potter, all Hopkins men, dissented from a vote to raise 1,500 men, and Peleg Barker absented himself.[86] In the next election Barker was displaced by John Collins, the future governor; Wickes was defeated by James Arnold, Jr.; Wanton was re-elected but refused to serve and became a Loyalist; Sessions and John Congdon, also a Hopkins man, lost their positions. By the end of another year there had occurred an almost total transformation in the membership of the upper house. Samuel Dyre, another Hopkins magistrate, became a Loyalist. However, it is fair to say that a majority of the magistrates of both factions were rebels, and nearly all of the measures taken in opposition to the British acts were approved by both houses.

On matters pertaining to taxes, interest rates, and finances generally, the upper house usually took what was presumably the popular position of lower taxes and interest rates, more money in circulation, and lower fees. The Ward faction was more disposed than the Hopkins group to adopt such stands, but both depended upon public support: annual elections, a wide suffrage, and stiff competition for office required that the politicians at least pretend to be democratically inclined. Thus, in 1766 the upper house rejected a tax bill on the ground that the people could not pay so large a tax, and suggested that a smaller amount be collected payable in lawful money or in old Tenor at a depreciated rate. The treasury, said the magistrates, could borrow additional sums.[87] On several occasions the upper house preferred to issue legal tender notes at a low interest rate, thus putting more money into circulation, rather than to levy taxes.[88] The magistrates also tried to limit interest rates.[89] Nearly all of these contests took place while the Wards controlled the upper house. The Hopkinses were much less favorably disposed toward such policies: in 1762 they tried to increase taxes, and in 1775 the magistrates raised the interest rate on money borrowed by the colony.[90] The Wards at other times opposed making real estate liable to attachment for debt, whereas the Hopkinses ultimately favored such a measure;[91] and the Wards opposed a bill requiring the destruction of barberry bushes because it would necessitate expenditures so great as to ruin many people (instead, those who wanted to destroy the bushes could do so at their own cost), whereas the Hopkinses accepted it.[92] The Wards doubtless gained approval when they opposed higher fees for lawyers,[93] though the Hopkinses competed for public favor by adopting a popular stand on the collection of taxes,[94] and rejected a supplementary allowance for certain judges.[95]

Such actions by the Rhode Island upper house are astonishing when one considers the usual activities of councils, and testify to the uniqueness of the colony's government. Indeed, one seldom recognizes any relationship between the magistrates and councillors elsewhere. Councillors in all colonies would have applauded the magistrates when they amended a bill designed to tax Rhode Islanders' money and trading stock anywhere in the world, so as to exclude investments in the public funds of Great Britain and exempt goods taxed elsewhere; but few councillors would have approved the magistrates' rejection of a bill providing for the taxation of unimproved land,[96] nor would they have insisted on lower salaries for tax assessors.[97]

There was rarely disagreement between the two legislative branches on what may be called humanitarian measures. On one occasion the upper house substituted a jail term for whipping; on the other hand it amended a bill expelling certain prisoners from the colony so as to have them whipped if they returned.[98] On another occasion, when the lower house voted that persons in jail having the liberty of the house and yard should receive no support, the magistrates did not concur; but they balanced this humanitarian gesture by rejecting an import duty on slaves.[99] In a dispute over the Newport work house the upper house, in a humanitarian spirit, tried to protect the children of poor people, and objected to a clause that discriminated against Indians, insisting that they should not be harshly treated nor in any way be discriminated against.[100]

There were many other occasions when the two houses disagreed, but the disagreements were almost always minor.[101] Even the disputes discussed above were not really significant. Evidence that relations were almost uniformly amicable, that differences were unimportant, is found not only in the journals, but also in the almost complete absence of any serious altercation in newspapers or in private correspondence. Indeed, there is only one disagreement mentioned in any Rhode Island newspaper. The real issue in politics was not prerogative *vs.* legislative supremacy, creditor *vs.* debtor, merchant *vs.* farmer, governor *vs.* Assembly, but which faction should control the government. The function of the upper house in Rhode Island seems to have been to reflect the views of the party in power, and to reject, amend, or accept bills as the magistrates saw fit, without any consistent application of economic or social biases. In this capacity—essentially that of a revisory body, a check against the lower house—the Council anticipated the role of the senates after the Revolution.

The elected councils of the three New England colonies resembled the royal and proprietary councils in certain respects. Merchants and lawyers were exceedingly numerous, comprising in fact half of the membership; and when those with other nonagricultural occupations, such as judges, doctors, and manufacturers, are added, the urban element accounted for at least three-fifths. Most of the councillors owned large estates. Scions of prominent old families were present in about the same proportion as elsewhere, and their educational attainments were exceptional.

On the other hand, the differences were striking. Farmers and artisans appear in significant numbers; most of the members were well-to-do rather than wealthy, and about one in eight owned moderate property. Most of the elected councillors were not sons of the established upper class but men whose parents were respectable, ordinary citizens. Half were descended from farmers, artisans, and the like—from the great middle class of small property owners. If an excessive proportion came from the larger towns, rural areas did have their representatives; even in Massachusetts, much more in Connecticut and Rhode Island, the councillors came from all over the colony. Finally, the great majority became rebels.

The attitude of all three of the elected councils toward the Revolution changed from conservative to radical; and the membership of the Massachusetts upper house was drastically altered. The transition was completed at the time of the Stamp Act crisis in both Connecticut and Rhode Island. In Massachusetts the change began at the same time but was not completed for several years, partly because public opinion moved more slowly, and partly because the executive branch opposed it. In the end all three bodies, which—for the times—had always been democratic, became even more so.

Because in Massachusetts the upper house was chosen by the lower, and in the other colonies both houses were elected by the voters, the two branches of the legislature adopted similar rather than conflicting policies. Disputes did exist, but as a rule they were easily disposed of by the committee system. The principal function of these councils was not to block, but to review, amend, and improve the bills and resolves sent up by the lower house. They were a little more inclined to favor the prerogative, the status quo, the upper class, and property rights—that is, to represent the aristocratic principle; but this bias was not obstructive. In their functions as well as in their composition the elected councils anticipated the changes that the Revolution was destined to make in all of the newly independent states.

Pre-Revolutionary Councils: A Summary

HE COLONIAL COUNCILS, viewed as a whole, were composed of the provincial aristocracy, which defended both the royal prerogative and the interests of the local elite. They resembled the King's Council in England in that they were chosen by the royal authority, held office "at pleasure," and had both executive and judicial functions. They resembled the House of Lords in that they acted as an upper house of the legislature; but whereas the Lords sat by hereditary right and were therefore independent of both the Commons and the king, the councillors depended upon the king for their appointment and in theory always supported the governor.

The ideal councillor, from the point of view of the prerogative, was perhaps the placeman, because his loyalty was assured. But the royal government was forced to win colonial support, and to do so meant appeasing important colonials. The governors could not perform their duties and earn promotions without local allies, so the king appointed men of prominence, or members of powerful families, whose loyalty brought rewards of offices or other favors. The governors sought out the provincial equivalent of a nobility and attempted to make of the council a sort of subservient House of Lords. The effort was only partly successful, and the council either became ineffectual (from the governors' point of view), as in Virginia, or it ultimately had to be composed of placemen, as in the Carolinas. Gradually the councils modified their role and became upper houses of a type unknown in England and unintended by the king. The elected magistrates and assistants led the way, but the process was perceptible everywhere.

Other than the increase in the number of placemen at the close of the colonial period, the composition of most of the councils remained about the same throughout the years 1763–1775. Despite the majority of farmers in the population, there were relatively few farmers in the upper houses. Probably not more than a third of the members derived their principal income from the land, and few indeed actually farmed. Most of the latter were large landholders, especially southern planters, who often had other economic interests. The agricultural point of view may also have been expressed by the many business and professional men who invested in land: all together, over two-fifths of the councillors were great landowners. Primarily, however, they were merchants and lawyers, plus a few doctors, officials, and manufacturers. They were thus predominantly urban rather than rural; even many of the great landholders lived in such towns as Savannah, Charleston, New York, or Boston. They were biased in favor of their own sections and interests, and were not sympathetic to the needs of ordinary farmers and westerners. Moreover, their residence placed them in the richest cultural milieu of colonial America, and in continuous, almost intimate contact with Europe. More than half lived in major ports or cultural centers and most of the rest could be reached by ocean-going vessels. The councillors were citizens of the Atlantic world, often cultured gentlemen, educated far above the average, and many doubtless regarded themselves as more European than provincial. Certainly they could appreciate the problems of empire and could sympathize with the governor.

They were distinguished from the majority of colonials in other ways as well. Their wealth hardly needs re-emphasis. Even when those from Connecticut and Rhode Island are included, about five-eighths of the councillors had property worth £5,000—a figure equivalent to perhaps a quarter of a million dollars in 1965. Most of the others owned property worth at least £2,000. About half were born to wealthy and prominent parents, belonging by birth to such aristocracy as the colonies had produced. Others came from the same class in the Old World. Of the remaining councillors, most were members of what is known today as the comfortable middle class—substantial, respectable farmers, artisans, and professional men. Probably one in eight was of humble birth, a self-made man, often one who had married into the local elite. The overwhelming majority, except in New England, were Anglicans.

The role of the council evolved from its theoretical position as part of the royal authority and its real position as part of the colonial power structure. Obviously the councils defended the prerogative. The actual substance of that function varied widely. Where placemen were powerful, the prerogative was vigorously and even aggressively defended. In other colonies, either the prerogative was seldom endangered, as in New York and New Jersey, or the upper house was half-hearted in its defense. The councils also defended their own existence and powers as well as the rights of their members. Had the councils' activities ended there, few colonials would have approved of their existence, and probably the unicameral systems of Pennsylvania and Delaware would have been greatly admired and much imitated. But the councils had other functions. They defended the economic and political interests of colonial businessmen; moreover they protected creditors and large property owners in general. They also represented the social and to some extent the cultural interests of the colonial upper class. The degree of activity in these fields depended, of course, upon the position adopted by the lower house, which frequently reflected the same views. But almost everywhere the councils embodied the aristocratic principle in government. In this capacity they won the support of the colonial elite.

Perhaps even that powerful aid might not have been enough to assure the council's survival in an anti-monarchical, anti-aristocratic postwar climate. But there were other functions that did. The council in most colonies was an extremely active legislative body, in many cases originating bills, passing resolutions, considering and acting upon petitions. In others, it served primarily in a revisory capacity, reviewing and improving legislation. Since the councillors were men of better education, wider experience, and, as a rule, greater intelligence than the representatives, they proved to be exceedingly valuable. The histories of both Connecticut and Rhode Island proved that conflicts between the two branches were not at all inevitable; the histories of all of the colonies suggested that the councils, properly remodeled, might be converted into highly useful instruments of government. The opportunity for reformation came in 1776.

Part Two

Post-Revolutionary Senates
1776–1788

$\mathcal{T}$HE SINGLE most important political change wrought by the American Revolution was independence from king and Parliament, which offered the new states the possibility of reforming their own governments. Seizing the opportunity, they hastened to complete the subordination of the executive to the legislative branch and to modify the power and the functions of the upper house. Accompanying these constitutional changes was a *de facto* shift of power in every state. Its most dramatic evidence was the democratization of the upper houses. The degree of change varied, of course. In those states where prior to independence councillors had been elected, much had already been accomplished in the years between 1765 and 1770. The composition and the powers of the other upper houses were now altered also, often radically. Even those senates that were intended to be aristocratic were indelibly marked by the vigorous democratic movement.

CHAPTER 4

The Aristocracy

*T*HE ABSENCE in America of a hereditary nobility complicated the task of those who wished to establish senates controlled by an upper class. Three techniques were available by which some local aristocracy might be granted power. A system of indirect election would presumably ensure the selection of an elite. Long terms of office might guarantee the senators' independence of public opinion. Finally, property qualifications, if sufficiently high, might restrict membership to the rich. However, only two senates—South Carolina's and Maryland's—contained a majority of wealthy members and only in one other—Virginia's—did half of the members belong to the pre-Revolutionary elite. Among all of the eleven senates, Maryland's alone was truly aristocratic.

MARYLAND

The conservative planter class, which had led Maryland into war and independence, had no intention of relinquishing its political power. The state constitution of 1776 was drawn up by nine of Maryland's wealthiest and most prominent leaders, who zealously endeavored to preserve upper-class rule: indeed, the new government was too aristocratic even for some of the senators.[1] The Senate consisted of fifteen men, six of whom resided on the Eastern Shore. It was designed to serve as a counterweight to the democratic elements in the lower house. Stability and independence were expected to ensue from five-year terms. An upper-class majority was obtained in three ways. Every senator had to own £1,000 worth of real and personal property. This requirement was not so restrictive as it seems, however, for the figure was in current money, equal to £600 sterling, with the result that even many small planters were eligible.

Probably more important was the method of election: the unique device of an electoral college. Two electors were chosen by each county. The rural, conservative Eastern Shore, which had supported independence reluctantly, was given a voice almost equal to the rest of the state. The electors resembled the members of the House of Delegates, in which many of them served, but they included more merchants and lawyers (one-fourth of the total), had more property (they were required to have property worth £500 [£300 sterling], about that of a prosperous farmer or artisan), and more often belonged to the prewar elite. They chose men who were like themselves, but who were even more markedly representative of the upper class, especially of the business elite.

Finally, the upper-class orientation was reinforced by the constitutional provision that the Senate itself fill all vacancies. The method was significant because there were numerous resignations. Therefore, over one-third of the senators who served between 1776 and 1788 were first chosen by the other senators. Furthermore, if a senator wished to remain in office he could usually do so, for the electors preferred to vote for incumbents. Thomas Stone and Charles Carroll of Carrollton served three terms, and several others were chosen twice. In short, death or refusal to serve were almost the only reasons for replacement, and the Senate became a nearly self-perpetuating body.

The Senate resembled the pre-Revolutionary Council in many respects. Both were dominated by men of wealth. Although the majority of the members were not primarily engaged in agriculture, in both houses large planters formed an influential minority; and, since many of the other men invested extensively in real estate, large landholders were a majority. In both bodies, one member in five was a merchant and one in three was a lawyer. Both contained a proportion of college-trained men that was quite unusual at the time. Both were composed largely of Anglicans. Many members of both the Senate and the Council had served first in the lower house. Two senators previously had sat in the Council, while a number of senators were related to councillors. The extensive Lloyd family, which had comprised a minority rebel group in the Council, contributed nine members to the Senate.

On the other hand there were several striking differences between the Council and the Senate. The absence of placemen in the latter was of major significance. All but one of the councillors had held offices granted by the governor, and of course owed their Council appointments to him. Few senators were officeholders, and they were in no way dependent upon the executive. The economic and social characteristics of the upper house also had changed, at least in degree. Only two of the councillors lacked extensive wealth, but about four out of ten senators were well-to-do rather than wealthy. The great majority of councillors belonged to the colony's elite, whereas half of the senators were born into the lesser planter class; the old aristocracy, though still very strong, had become a minority. In fact, the Senate resembled the pre-Revolutionary House of Delegates more than it did the Council, and several senators had been delegates. The Senate, however, had many more merchants and lawyers, considerably more men of wealth, and more representatives of prominent old families, than the prewar House of Delegates.

Robert Goldsborough was a typical senator. His father, Charles, was the son of a chief justice and wealthy landowner. Charles became a lawyer, commissary general, and a member of the Council. He married Elizabeth Ennalls, of a prominent family.[2] Though not related to the Lloyds, he was a protégé of Colonel Edward Lloyd, and was a political moderate. Robert studied law in London and inherited a large fortune. He served as attorney general for a few years, and sat briefly in the lower house, where he was a moderate like his father; but he declined an appointment to the Council and soon afterward became one of the most prominent Revolutionary leaders.[3]

John Henry of Dorchester (1750–1798) was descended from a Presbyterian minister and graduated from the College of New Jersey. He thus represented a religious element new to the upper house. His father, Colonel John, founded the family fortune by marrying an heiress, the daughter of Colonel John Rider (grandson of a councillor). John Jr. studied law in London, and, after 1777, served continuously either in the Senate or in Congress, eventually becoming one of Maryland's first United States senators, and finally governor. In 1783 he owned 3,504 acres valued at £4,294, as well as 56 slaves and 125 head of cattle.[4]

Goldsborough and Henry were two of the twelve lawyers who comprised a third of the Senate's membership. Thomas Contee (1729–1811) was one of a half-dozen merchants. His great-uncle John was an immigrant, who served on the Council, and who died in 1708 without heirs. John's nephew, Alexander Contee, a younger son, was born in England. He took over his uncle's property, became a large landowner and a prosperous merchant, and married the daughter of Colonel Thomas Brooke. Thomas Contee, a second son of Alexander, inherited the large Brooke estate in Charles County, and carried on the mercantile business in Georgetown, Nottingham, and Port Tobacco, acting as consignee for Contee relatives in London. He served in the House of Delegates from 1769 until the Revolution.[5]

Persons with purely agricultural interests, though in the minority, still accounted for a third of the Senate's membership. Samuel Wilson is a good example of the prosperous, though not wealthy, planter. His grandfather was a Presbyterian minister. His father, born in Ireland, immigrated before 1700 and left a large landed estate to Samuel and an older son. Samuel also was a Presbyterian. He represented Somerset in the House of Delegates for many years, and was a leader of the court party, to which most delegates from the Eastern Shore belonged. He became a rebel, however, served on the Council of Safety, and helped supply the American (and perhaps the British) Army. In 1783 he held 1,426.5 acres in Somerset and also owned 2,250 acres and 24 slaves in Accomac County, Virginia.[6] It is worth noting that none of these men was new to the colony, nor had any risen from humble circumstances; indeed, only four senators were born outside of Maryland, and only one started from scratch.[7]

The Senate frequently took roll-call votes, about three-fifths of which reveal a fairly consistent alignment. The majority group, the apparent successor of the court party, adopted conservative economic policies, defended the aristocratic principle in government, and often opposed the wishes of the lower house. The members came almost exclusively from prominent old families of great wealth. Nearly all were very large landowners (though a few had other interests as well), and almost all were Episcopalians. Most of the Eastern Shore men belonged to this group, which was also supported by the Annapolis and Anne Arundel County senators. The most important leader was Charles Carroll of Carrollton. Other leaders were his cousin, also named Charles Carroll (a manufacturer and large landowner), Daniel of St. Thomas Jenifer, Matthew Tilghman, and Brice T. B. Worthington. Their opponents sometimes took the more popular side. They represented western Maryland, usually the Baltimore area or the Potomac Valley. Although a few were primarily large landowners, the rest pursued nonagricultural careers. Several were Episcopalians but at least as many were Presbyterians. Their fathers, as a rule, were men of lesser standing than were the sires of the conservative group; several of these senators were new to the state and a few were self-made men. Some of the leaders of this group, such as Richard Barnes and George Plater, belonged to the same social and economic class as their opponents, but Thomas Stone's father had been no more than a substantial farmer,[8] and Samuel Hughes was an Irish immigrant who became an iron manufacturer in the western part of the state.[9] It is curious and probably significant that, as prewar delegates, these men had voted together in opposition to Worthington and several others who were now on the conservative side in the Senate. The members of this minority group, though obviously eminent citizens, had perhaps a wider acquaintance with and evidently a greater sympathy for the majority of Marylanders. But this sympathy was a matter of degree, for on many significant issues the Senate stood united against the House of Delegates.

Had the composition of the House of Delegates after 1776 remained unchanged, conflicts between the two houses might have been few and minor. But the Revolution had also transformed the lower house, so that the differences between the two bodies were actually greater after the event than before it. The change did not include a geographical shift of power, for Maryland's rather small frontier area gained only slightly; nor was there a substantial increase in the number of delegates. Rather, there occurred a significant downward transfer of power in which the typical delegate, instead of being a well-to-do or wealthy planter, became a successful farmer, or at most a prosperous but not affluent planter.

The fathers of the delegates were obscure men, and when they appear in the records at all, it is as ordinary farmers.

While the contrast between these men and their predecessors in the 1765 House of Delegates is sharp, that between them and the senators is even more striking. About 60 percent of the senators, but at most one-fourth of the delegates, were wealthy; at the other end of the scale the Senate contained only one man who may have had only a moderate amount of property, whereas over a third of the delegates were men of modest means. There were a few merchants, lawyers, and doctors in the House of Delegates, most of whom were men of property, but they comprised only a fourth of the members, whereas such men accounted for over half of the senators. About the same proportion of large landholders—slightly more than one-third—sat in each body. In the Senate, the balance of power rested with the businessmen, many of whom, of course, had landed estates as well; whereas the House of Delegates was controlled by the agricultural interests. No ordinary farmers sat in the Senate, but perhaps a third of the delegates were farmers rather than planters—a large enough group so that, with some support from the planters, they could achieve a majority.[10]

The aristocratic quality of the Senate, though it may have reflected the true nature of Maryland's social structure, as a contemporary believed,[11] resulted not in a harmonious, balanced government but in discord. Several newspaper articles had from the beginning demanded a democratic form of government that would contain either no upper house at all, or a popularly elected Senate.[12] What the majority of the people preferred is impossible to say—they were not asked—but the type of upper house created certainly resulted in acrimonious disputes between the two branches of the legislature.

The lack of harmony was evident even in procedural matters. At the first session in 1777 the senators suggested that the method of conducting business should be the same as in colonial times: a large number of formal messages instead of the more intimate joint sessions.[13] The delegates preferred to confer at once when any disagreement arose, thereby avoiding a long series of amendments, written explanations, and further amendments, but the senators insisted that the formalities be maintained. The use of joint committees was, they declared, "not altogether regular" and "produc-

tive rather of delay than despatch."[14] Evidently the upper house
was attempting to safeguard its full power and independent existence: it was a small body (eight of its fifteen members constituting a quorum) and might easily have been overwhelmed by the
more numerous delegates.[15]

The Senate was especially careful to uphold its authority with
respect to money bills. It had good reason. The constitution provided that all such measures should originate in the lower house,
and that the Senate might reject but not amend them. The restriction, of course, reflected pre-Revolutionary experiences. Money
bills were defined in the constitution as those levying taxes for the
general support of the government. That meant, according to the
Senate, that local bills, and bills in which money was incidental,
were excluded: the Senate could amend any measures other than
those in which the general revenue was the main subject.[16] The delegates interpreted the constitution differently, for they were anxious to prevent amendments wherever possible. Often they incorporated into a money bill subjects that were related to the main
measure but were not essential to it. In this way legislation dis-
tasteful to the upper house could be introduced without giving the
Senate a chance to make amendments, and the Senate might then
be obliged to swallow the pill because the measure as a whole was
necessary. Although the delegates were prohibited by the constitution from using such a procedure, this provision was open to various interpretations, and the lower house adopted that which gave
it maximum power. The Senate naturally—and on the whole correctly—took a firm stand.

Examples of disputes over money bills are numerous. During
the first session, even before the delegates had a chance to claim
that a bill for quartering soldiers was a money bill, the senators
returned it with the demand that it be separated into two different
measures.[17] In 1779 the Senate reluctantly accepted a tax bill containing provisions that it disliked.[18] The upper house was especially irate when, in 1780, a legal tender clause was inserted in a
money bill. The practice of "tacking on" such disparate matters,
wrote the senators, deprived them of their constitutional right to
prepare amendments, and was indeed precisely what the constitution had intended to prevent by a careful definition of money
bills.[19] They rejected the measure, but advised the delegates that if

separate bills were submitted the tax bill would be accepted. On this occasion the two houses failed to agree and no tax law at all was enacted during that session.[20]

In 1785 the senators rejected a bill levying import and export duties, and submitted a long list of alterations which, they promised, would make the measure acceptable. The delegates expressed great concern. The Senate had no right to suggest changes in a money bill, and the bill was urgently needed. Once more the Senate yielded and passed the bill.[21] On still another occasion a Senate bill for the regulation of indigents was rejected by the delegates on the ground that it was a money bill.[22]

A more prolonged and significant dispute involving the relative power of the two bodies occurred in 1787, after the Senate had rejected several popular measures to relieve debtors, including the introduction of paper money.[23] During the Revolution the state issued various forms of paper money. The Senate could not prevent this, but it could and did limit the legal tender quality of the money.[24] After the War the senators steadfastly rejected new issues.[25] Such money, they insisted, would surely depreciate, and Maryland should solve its financial problems by additional taxes rather than by borrowing.[26] The delegates thereupon insisted on an adjournment, hoping that public opinion would force the Senate to change its position. During the recess, both sides appealed to the public through petitions and published speeches. In the long newspaper debate the Senate was alternately attacked as an aristocratic body representing only rich men, especially merchants, moneylenders, and lawyers;[27] and vigorously defended as consisting of great and able statesmen.[28] The paper money group, led by Samuel Chase, one of the state's most prominent leaders, insisted that the bills were essential and were desired by a majority of the people, and that the Senate should obey the wishes of the majority. "Power in the rulers or governors of the people is like the reflected light of the moon, and is only borrowed, delegated and limited by the grant of the people," Chase declared. The Senate, he conceded, should be independent of the lower house, but "from the nature of a government by *representation*, the *deputies* must be subject to the will of their principals. . . ."[29] The senators, his supporters asserted, were oppressing the people, who therefore had a right to demand redress. Granted that the people might become "oppressive and tyrannical," still, history proved that disorder and convulsion came more often from the "insolence of rulers."[30]

On the other side, some senators and newspaper commentators denied that the people had any right to interfere with the upper house. When the people retained legislative power, warned the Senate's defenders, the government was a "strict democracy"; when they chose legislators, it was a "government, by representation." The latter form was preferable because the mass of citizens could not reason as well as could those of superior talent.[31] The Senate, declared "an Elk-Ridger," was intended to be the "aristocratical" part of the government, the function of which was "to be a check on the democratical, as being subject too much to their constituents, which might create anarchy and confusion."[32] Most members of the upper house, however, were unwilling publicly to deny all responsibility to the people. The Senate's official statement was written by Thomas Stone, a moderate. It argued only that the delegates were attempting to force the senators to accept a bill that they had unanimously rejected. If this attempt succeeded, the Senate could no longer arrive at judgments independently, and the totality of legislative power would be held by the lower house. No longer would Maryland have two separate branches as provided by the constitution.[33] In the end, the Senate successfully repelled these attacks. Thus, on the eve of the Federal Convention, the principle that legislators might be independent of public opinion was upheld in Maryland.

Most of the major disputes between the two houses were over economic issues. The Senate consistently defended the property rights of the wealthier Marylanders, especially of creditors, and tried to hasten the collection of debts. The option to delay payment, the senators said, was one reason for the improvidence of debtors. Such delays were costly and unjust to the creditor, who then refused to loan money, which in turn was a reason for the lack of credit and the scarcity of cash. The delegates were unimpressed and rejected a bill that the Senate had sent down.[34] The crisis of 1787 was brought on in part because the Senate rejected bills for the relief of debtors, particularly a stay law and a "valuation bill," which provided for evaluation of a debtor's property by appraisal instead of by auction—the latter method usually enabling the creditor to profit enormously.[35] When the legislature reconvened, the delegates scored a clear verbal victory by entrusting to the Senate the job of relieving debtors. The senators were not enthusiastic. Protecting debtors, "without interfering with the contracts of individuals," they said, was a matter of "considerable difficulty." The lower house thought it impossible, but suggested that in time of great distress such interference with contracts was justified. In the end, the Senate did grant some concessions, but on major issues it stood steadfastly on the creditors' side.[36]

The Senate's position on these economic questions and on various other issues seems to have run counter to the wishes of most Marylanders. For example, when the delegates attempted to amend a recruiting bill so that poor as well as rich men could benefit by the hiring of substitutes, the senators rejected the amendment.[37] Again, when the lower house tried to reduce expenses and postpone tax collections during the postwar depression, the Senate urged prompt collection of taxes and rigorous prosecution of delinquent collectors.[38]

Loyalists usually found the Senate more sympathetic than the lower house. During the legislature's first session, the senators adopted several amendments to a punitive measure sent up by the delegates. These eliminated a clause punishing people who enticed disaffected colonials to return to Great Britain, who discouraged people from supporting independence, who depreciated the currency, and who maliciously published false news. The Senate also struck out a loyalty oath. The senators' stand concerning the Loyalists was due to, or at least justified by, their conviction that freedom of speech should be preserved. No government, they asserted, should delve into the secret thoughts of its subjects. Oaths would not prevent revolutions. "Tests of this nature, it is true, have been imposed by our ancestors, but we wish to imitate their wise not impolitic institutions."[39] "We are unwilling," the senators declared, "to tarnish the lustre of our glorious cause by any measure which may have the appearance of unnecessary and vindictive severity."[40] The Senate lamented that the delegates' "acquaintance with the laws, opinion and customs of barbarians, as well as civilized nations, has not enabled you to point out a remedy adequate to this evil, without introducing a greater mischief." The delegates tartly replied that it was unfortunate that the senators, "who are much better acquainted with the laws, opinions and customs, not only of the civilized nations of Europe, but of barbarians and savages," were unable to discover an adequate remedy for an offense admitted to be highly criminal.[41] Newspapers published several angry denunciations, one of which suggested that both houses ought to be chosen annually by the people.[42] The upper house compromised, but continued to intercede on behalf of Tories and neutrals.[43] Curiously, however, the Senate in 1785 opposed granting the right to vote and to hold office to those who had refused to take the oath of allegiance, insisting that indulgence and persuasion had been tried in vain, and that such nonjurors were potentially dangerous to the state. The delegates found themselves presenting the same arguments once employed by the Senate. In the end the Senate backed down.[44]

The Senate delayed for nearly a year a bill to confiscate Loyalist property. Such a step, said the upper house, was unjust, impolitic, and unnecessary, and deprived of their property people who were not really enemies of the state. The delegates insisted that the need for money was desperate, and charged that some senators were personally concerned (which at least two of them were). But the Senate was defended by newspaper articles in which it was argued that if money was available for the purchase of such property money was equally available for taxes or for loans to the state. The senators were "gentlemen of family, fortune, knowledge, experience, and abilities." The delegates were not impressed by such eulogies and their persistence, together with the pressing need for money, finally forced the upper house to accept the bill. However, despite the delegates' objections, it exempted certain types of property, notably debts.[45]

The senators were more conscientious defenders of personal liberty than were the delegates. The upper house rejected an *ex post facto* law, passed a bill enabling clergy of the Anglican Church to preach after taking an oath (this was vetoed by the delegates),[46] eliminated a fine for Quakers who preached without taking an oath,[47] substituted imprisonment for whipping,[48] permitted slaves to earn money by working on holidays,[49] and just missed, by a tie vote, allowing theatrical performances to be held during the War.[50] On the other hand, the Senate twice rejected bills incorporating churches of non-Anglican denominations,[51] and once insisted upon taxing a college's property.[52]

The justice of the Senate's position on economic matters and on treatment of the Loyalists is a matter of opinion, but the upper house indisputably was valuable as a council of review. Thus in 1777 it rejected a bill to indemnify those who had suffered from the British Army. The senators argued that in the future some people might destroy their own property in the hope that a similar bill would be passed. Moreover, the extent of damage was hard to determine, so that the wiser course was to postpone any such law until a later date, when equal justice could be done to all sufferers.[53] The Senate generally exercised greater fiscal responsibility.[54] Many changes it recommended in tax bills seem proper, such as reducing the duty on salt—an article used by the poor as well as by the rich—and eliminating export duties.[55] The Senate was instrumental in establishing a court of chancery to handle many of the cases that had been taking up much of the legislature's time.[56] A very large number of bills originated by the lower house were extensively revised by the Senate, and these amendments were accepted with little debate by the delegates.[57] The Senate often kept the delegates at work finishing essential business when the latter tried to adjourn prematurely,[58] asserting on one occasion that it was "willing to adjourn when the necessary public business is dispatched."[59] It should be added, however, that the sessions were prolonged unnecessarily by the small size of the Senate, which made it difficult for the members to accomplish their tasks, and by absenteeism, which often prevented a quorum. The delegates tried on several occasions to make attendance compulsory, but these bills were either rejected outright or passed only after the senators had excepted themselves.[60]

The Senate also refused to allow the delegates an increase in their per diem allowance, which led to an angry exchange of insults.[61] The delegates seized the opportunity to point out that men of "wisdom, probity, and zeal for the general welfare" might be excluded from the legislature, whereas those "of opulent fortunes," not distinguished for these virtues, would establish an aristocracy, oppress the people, and subvert the government. The senators suggested that if any legislator was impoverished he might be given a larger allowance, but observed that financial independence was the best security for integrity. The delegates replied angrily that the Senate ought to avoid "unbecoming sarcasms and irritating sneers," and insisted that men of small estates should not be obliged to reduce them in the public service.[62] The delegates continued to press for a raise. The following spring the upper house consented to an increase, but only for that particular session. (Charles Carroll of Carrollton dissented even from that.) On another occasion when the Senate rejected the delegates' attempt to obtain seventeen shillings and sixpence instead of fourteen shillings per day, the latter promptly sent up a bill reducing in the same proportion the salaries of all officials and the fees of officers and lawyers. The senators immediately rejected this, and observed that while they were sorry to give offense, they thought fourteen shillings was enough, since in Virginia and Pennsylvania the legislators received only twelve shillings and sixpence. However, the delegates did obtain a permanent increase during the next session.[63]

The Senate similarly favored lower payments to certain other government officials. Twice the fees allowed justices of the peace were reduced, and once the upper house attempted a more general reduction.[64] But in the case of judges, economic considerations were counteracted by political philosophy. The senators wanted judges' salaries to be higher, and granted permanently rather than annually, in order to render judges independent. The delegates refused to accept these recommendations, whereupon the Senate retreated, warning that it would not do so again.[65] In this case, the senators ultimately were successful. In 1786 judicial salaries were raised from £500 to £1,000 and were made permanent, and in the following year a bill repealing the act was rejected unanimously by the Senate.[66]

Finally, the Senate was more attentive than the House of Delegates to the needs of Congress. On one occasion it appropriated more money;[67] on another, it upheld the precedence of a treaty over a state law.[68] In 1786 the Senate refused to ballot for commissioners to meet with representatives from other states for the purpose of considering a uniform system of commerce. That was the function of Congress, it said, and such a meeting might delay the collection of money owed to Congress. "Innovations in government," the conservative senators declared, "when not absolutely necessary, are dangerous, particularly to republics, generally too fond of novelties, and subject to change."[69] When Congress itself issued a call for a convention the next year the Senate was more eager than the delegates to send representatives.[70] Almost all of the senators became Federalists.

Thus the Maryland Senate, the most aristocratic of all such bodies, consistently adopted a conservative position on economic and political issues. Although it demonstrated its usefulness and was superior in certain respects to the lower house, it often opposed the desires of most Marylanders. As a result, the legislature was plunged into conflicts more bitter and protracted than any that occurred elsewhere in the new nation.

South Carolina

With the onset of the Revolutionary War, the merchant-planter upper class of South Carolina found its power threatened by the Charleston artisans, by the small farmers, and more seriously by the inhabitants of the interior districts. The eastern elite moved promptly to solidify its control through constitutions which discriminated against the west and the small property owners. Yet its dominance was not so absolute as that of Maryland's upper class, and even the Senate, by design an aristocratic body, felt the effect of the democratic impulse.

The constitution of 1776 established a "Legislative Council" which was chosen by the "General Assembly" consisting principally, though not exclusively, of easterners. The upper house was therefore deprived of its independence and subordinated to the lower. Naturally, the councillors who were selected came almost entirely from the coastal parishes, and nearly all were wealthy members of the colonial upper class. Practically all were great landowners. Half were also engaged in commerce or the law. Yet there were a few exceptions which proved that the effects of independence were already evident. LeRoy Hammond, from western district ninety-six, had become well known before 1776, but, far from being a member of the colony's elite, he was born in Virginia, presumably was a farmer's son, and had made his own way up by trading in Augusta and in the Carolina back country.[71] Also chosen was Joseph Kershaw of Camden, who immigrated from England about 1750, started as a clerk in Charleston, moved west, and by 1776 had made a fortune by numerous undertakings, including farming, milling, trading, brewing, and distilling.[72] Men such as these could have met almost any property qualification and perhaps did not materially differ in their economic outlook from the men of Charleston and the rice country; but in other respects they were a new breed.

The lack of a property requirement in the 1776 constitution was corrected two years later when the governmental structure was again modified. This time an independent Senate was created, chosen by the voters rather than by the lower house (which was renamed the House of Representatives). Each senator was supposed to have a freehold worth at least £2,000 currency, which in South Carolina would be about the same as sterling. The provision was not enforced, however, and indeed there were certainly more than a dozen senators, perhaps twice as many, who had less than the required property. Each parish or district chose one senator for a two-year term. He did not have to be a resident, though if he were not, the property requirement was higher. In practice the senators almost invariably were residents. The one-per-district system discriminated against the west, which, though it contained about three-fourths of the voters, had relatively few political units compared to the east. Each Senate consisted of thirty members, of whom about half lived near the coast and several others in the contiguous districts. Still, at least a dozen were westerners, whereas before the Revolution there had been no western representatives in the upper house and only a few in the lower. Perhaps one could not have expected the eastern planters to make a greater concession, especially since the west's loyalty to the new nation was doubtful.

This geographic diffusion of power was paralleled by other changes in the senates elected between 1777 and 1788. The largest single economic interest was agriculture. Over half of the senators who served during this period were exclusively farmers, most of whom had large estates. The planters therefore had greatly increased their influence in the upper house. However, the Senate's composition was far from a true reflection of the occupational distribution of the state. One out of every five senators was a merchant, and one out of every ten was a lawyer. Three were large manufacturers, two were artisans, and two were doctors. Many of these, of course, were also large landowners; the purely urban element was quite small—about one-fifth—but it was still more than was warranted in a society so largely rural. A majority of the senators were wealthy, and over four out of five were at least well-to-do, as required by the constitution; yet it seems that about one-sixth had only moderate property. Most of these were western farmers, who, of course, introduced a new element into the upper house.

The prominent old South Carolina families who before the War had dominated the Council and had comprised half of the Assembly, were unable to maintain control even of the Senate. They held only a little over one-third of the seats. Another third were men born in the colony but not of prominent parents; the final third were men new to the colony, of humble origin. The proportion of new men was much larger than in the colonial legislature and was due primarily to the greater representation granted to the west. About a third of the senators grew up on great plantations, and a few others were children of prosperous merchants or lawyers, but many came from families of the middle rank or even lower. Several of their fathers were artisans or shopkeepers, and at least a dozen fathers were farmers. Most of those whose origins are unknown (a sizable number) undoubtedly came from ordinary families.

One type of senator is represented by General Stephen Bull and General John Barnwell. Bull was the grandson of William (1683–1755), nephew of Governor William Jr. (1710–1791), and son of Stephen (1707–1750). His father was a wealthy planter and the general owned 233 slaves in 1790.[73] Barnwell was not quite as rich, but he belonged to the same class. His grandfather, John, who immigrated in 1701, was a member of the Council. The daughters of the first John's oldest son, Nathaniel, married Colonel Thomas Middleton, the wealthy son of Councillor Henry Middleton, General Stephen Bull, and William Elliott, father of a councillor. Senator John had 83 slaves in 1790.[74]

A more typical senator was Thomas Ferguson of St. Paul's. His father, James, seems to have been a small planter who married the daughter of a large landowner. Thomas distinguished himself by marrying practically everyone in sight (in sequence) including a Rutledge and a Wragg. In 1768 he had 672 acres and apparently was well-to-do rather than wealthy.[75]

Still another type of senator was Richard Richardson. He was born in Virginia about 1704 and fought in various Indian wars, becoming a colonel by 1757. A decade later he owned 3,680 acres in the west and shortly thereafter sat in the Legislative Council. His son Richard (1741–1818) also served in the Indian wars, became a captain under General Sumter and a colonel with Marion, both of whom were senators. He, too, served in the upper house.[76] Most of the senators resembled one or another of these men, yet there were other sorts too: John and Richard Hampton, for instance, whose father was a flax breaker, and who became small planters and Revolutionary officers like their more famous and prosperous brother Wade; or Philotheos Chiffelle, son of a minister, a Charleston merchant who left a personal estate of only £376 when he died.[77]

The Senate, containing so many westerners and well-to-do but not wealthy men, was not a truly aristocratic body. Neither was the lower house genuinely democratic. Although westerners were somewhat more numerous there than in the Senate, the eastern parishes were greatly overrepresented and, in combination with the transitional districts a little farther inland, sent a large majority of the delegates. More men of modest means sat in the lower house, but about one-third were wealthy and another third well-to-do. The lower house contained nearly the same proportion of men representing non-farm interests. Therefore, the two bodies were not diametrically opposite, but resembled each other in many ways. The House, however, had been affected far more by revolutionary social change: a larger proportion of its members were small property owners, new men from humble homes.[78]

The two branches of the legislature were similar enough usually to agree on fundamentals, yet different enough occasionally to divide on specific issues. Because both houses contained several factions, groups, or parties with divergent interests, disputes seem to have erupted when a particular point of view temporarily triumphed in one house but not in the other. The division within the Senate, as revealed by a number of roll-call votes taken during 1787–1788, was not entirely along class lines, for although one group consisted principally of wealthy men, the other group also contained several men of wealth. The distinction was basically sectional. One faction included westerners in the proportion of three to one, the other easterners in about the same ratio.[79] The westerners naturally were almost all new men, of varying degrees of wealth, engaged in diverse occupations and, incidentally, were almost always of high military rank; the easterners were apt to come from old and often prominent Carolina families, were generally wealthy, and usually were large planters. All of the easterners became Federalists, whereas the westerners were more apt to be Antifederalists. Since the same groups existed in the House, obviously the contest was not simply that between an aristocratic Senate and a democratic House. However, it is true that the more aristocratic, eastern party was stronger in the upper house, whereas the representatives were somewhat more democratically inclined.

Relations between the two houses were not legally defined until the constitution of 1778 vested in the House the power to originate money bills, and deprived the Senate of the right to amend them. In other respects the two were equal, and in practice the upper house obtained equality with regard to money bills as well. When the first tax was introduced in the fall of 1778, the Senate presented a schedule of amendments. The first objection made by the lower house to this procedure, curiously, was to the Senate's failure to read the bill twice. Actually, the Senate seems to have given the bill a second reading, and therefore returned it. The representatives protested again, but turned their attention to the more serious issue: that it was "repugnant to the spirit of the Constitution and the Practise of this House to give a Reading to any Schedule of Amendments from your House on a Tax bill."[80] The Senate replied that it was "parliamentary just and Reasonable," and in accordance with the spirit of the constitution, for the Senate after the second reading to propose amendments which were needed, and which, if incorporated, might prevent a rejection. Moreover, the senators appealed to precedent: they pointed out that during colonial times the Commons had considered schedules of amendments to tax bills sent by the Council. In this they were correct, though the lower house had challenged the practice at the end of the colonial era. The representatives, impressed by these arguments, then did consider the suggested amendments, and accepted most of them; but they also passed a resolution that restated their position and cautioned that only the "Very Critical Situation of Public Affairs" had obliged the House to be silent: no precedent had been established.[81] Nevertheless, the Senate in later years frequently suggested changes in tax bills, and these proposals were considered by the House in the same way as were any other amendments, without further protest.

In other respects the two houses, after some initial sparring, quickly recognized each other's rights. The exchange of messages between them was, as in colonial times, quite formal. Even before independence the Legislative Council insisted upon being addressed as "Honourable" instead of "Mr. Speaker and Gentlemen."[82] Most potential disputes were adjusted on an informal basis by numerous conference committees. The Senate in South Carolina was no mere revisory body. It initiated all sorts of measures, examined with great care those presented by the representatives, and sometimes substituted entirely new bills. Often both bodies had committees working on the same subjects. The Senate received a large number of petitions, passed resolutions concerning them, and sent these down for concurrence. The action taken by one house was usually accepted by the other.

The Senate was much more resistant to demands for constitutional change. The first recorded instance involved a court of chancery, which was not authorized by the constitution. When the House tried to ballot for a master in chancery, the Senate replied that it could not; this position was upheld by a conference committee.[83] Later in the year the House passed a bill to "regulate" a court. The Senate felt that this violated the constitution because no alteration could be made without ninety days' notice or the consent of a majority of both branches. The House pleaded that the bill was necessary to protect widows and orphans; that the Senate was not supposed to know how many representatives were present; that a review of the constitution had been announced during the previous session; and that the change was legal because the constitution stated that its provisions were valid only "untill otherwise altered by the Legislature." It was "an universal Rule in the constitution of a Law so to expound it, as to give efficacy if possible to every part of it"; therefore if that clause were to be given force, change was legal.[84] This broad interpretation was rejected by the Senate, but the House warned that constitutional reform would be considered at the next session.

In the spring of 1784 the Senate demanded and obtained a series of amendments to a new bill, on the ground that the powers granted to the court were too much like those under a monarchy, and should be delimited so as to accord with the constitution. One interesting change was the substitution of the phrase "during good behaviour" for the "during pleasure" that had been customary under the royal government. The two houses then agreed.[85]

Much more serious was the issue of a general constitutional revision. Precisely what the reformers had in mind is uncertain. The House wanted to make the constitution "more consistent with pure republican principles and the equal rights of Mankind."[86] A bill of rights was to be added. An illuminating pamphlet entitled *Conciliatory Hints* defended democracy as the best form of government and called, in general terms, for the purging of aristocratic elements in the constitution; but the author was not specific, except that he defended a bicameral legislature.[87] The demand for change came principally from the west, beginning with petitions from the district "between the Broad and Catawba" and the "Spartan" district.[88] Votes taken in the lower house indicated a chiefly sectional alignment,[89] though in the Senate reform was pressed by Joseph Atkinson, a self-made man who was a merchant from St. Thomas and Denis on the coast. Probably the westerners wanted more seats in both houses; perhaps they would have abolished the Senate entirely. In the debates over the 1776 constitution the Council had been retained by the narrow margin of forty to thirty,[90] and according to David Ramsay, in 1784 many people were opposed to the upper house.[91] The Senate seems to have feared such a fate, for in 1785 the representatives, calling for a convention, added reassuringly: "and it is hereby recommended in the strongest terms, that the Delegates be not empowered to vote for the abolition of either branch of the Legislature." However, the Senate, which had unanimously rejected the proposal in 1784, once again refused its assent, this time by a vote of sixteen to five. Atkinson tried in vain to reverse the decision later in the session. Further attempts were made in 1786 and again in 1787. The Senate, after first insisting that delegates to a convention be denied power to abolish either branch, finally blocked any change at all, arguing that the constitution had no defects.[92]

Men of the uplands were also displeased when in February of 1786 the Senate rejected the removal of the capital from Charleston. The alignment on this question was largely sectional, for although a high location was climatically favorable, Charleston was in every other respect more comfortable, as well as more civilized, and more convenient for the eastern legislators. On the other hand, westerners disliked the long trip and the higher prices in Charleston, and there was probably a rural, perhaps even a class, bias as well. The Senate did not hold out long, and in March the bill was approved after the designation of the shift as "permanent" had been eliminated.[93]

On other issues the Senate's course was erratic. In most states the lower house often sought an early adjournment even when business remained unfinished. But in South Carolina the Senate almost always favored an earlier end to the session. Finally, in 1788, it reversed its position, righteously insisting that it would adjourn only "when the business now pending before the Legislature shall be finished."[94] The two houses agreed on relations with Congress. They also usually concurred on officials' salaries; in the exceptional instances the Senate's stand was not consistent.[95] A curious dispute arose over the legislators' per diem. The lower house tried to allow $2.00 per day to any member lodging in a tavern or boarding house. This policy favored those who did not have houses in the city or friends there with whom they could stay, and who were not wealthy enough comfortably to pay their own expenses. The Senate probably showed its upper-class bias by objecting to the plan, and by trying instead to grant the sum to anyone applying for it, rich or poor.[96]

The treatment of Loyalists, so important and controversial a question in most states, seems not to have aroused any major dispute between the two houses. The gaps in legislative records during the war years may deprive us of the evidence of such a contest; but the usual postwar debate did not develop. Perhaps this was owing to the large number of Revolutionary Army officers in the upper house. As late as March of 1787 they still comprised a majority, and they probably did not sympathize with the Loyalists as the upper-class senators in other states often did. The Senate was, it is true, somewhat more lenient in its treatment of former enemies. British merchants were given more favorable consideration, as were certain Loyalists who wished to return to the state, and the Senate was more willing to restore property that had been confiscated. But on most such petitions and on most issues relating to Tories the two houses agreed.[97]

Economic disputes, which in many states were the most serious and acrimonious of all, rarely occurred in South Carolina. Since a majority in each house came from the eastern, large planter class, the demands of the western section and of smaller property owners in general, insofar as these differed from the interests of the state's dominant minority, were defeated in the lower house, and never reached the upper. Moreover, even the large planters had fallen so far into debt that they favored laws that elsewhere were indignantly rejected by the upper class. The two houses did not always agree, but the disagreements were comparatively minor.

The attitude of the Senate toward taxation seems most often to have reflected the wishes of the strong nonagricultural element, rather than a desire to raise, lower, collect, or postpone taxes. But any generalization is hard to substantiate. During the 1779 session the Senate levied some additional duties, including those on town lots, farm animals, and stock in trade. But a few years later the upper house reduced the tax on slaves. In 1784, it lowered the rate on four items and raised it on two. It accepted an important bill establishing graduated taxes on different types of land. The Senate amended the 1785 tax bill to eliminate the tax on trade, professions, stock, and money (though the last was later restored). The tax bill of 1786 passed without amendment. In the following year the Senate eliminated a special import tax on slaves but added one on wine. The House protested but finally acquiesced. None of these disputes resulted in a long controversy or a public debate, and on the whole the record testifies to fundamental harmony.[98]

The Senate often showed a mild pro-creditor bias. A stay law that had been passed in 1782 was eliminated the next year from a bill for continuing acts in force.[99] When a special session was called in October of 1785 to aid debtors, the Senate was reluctant to act other than to permit the suspension of executions for debt until the next session. Commissioners were to be appointed to decide before a suit was initiated whether the debt was unpaid because of "unforseen accidents," in which case the delay might be granted, "but in all cases to hold the Debtor to give other personal Security or a Mortgage to the Creditor for the amount of his Debts."[100] In 1787 the Senate tried to amend a new bill so as to protect the creditor, particularly by forcing the debtor to pay the creditor's expenses incurred while trying to obtain the necessary security; it retreated, however, when the House took a firm stand.[101] The next year the Senate refused to extend the time for paying debts under an installment bill.[102] These policies are reminiscent of Maryland's Senate. But creditors could not rely upon the upper house. In 1785, the representatives, responding to pressure by debtors, passed a reform bill; the Senate voted down an amendment that would have weakened the bill and then passed it unchanged.[103] Two years later a majority of senators rejected several amendments to an installment bill that were intended to protect creditors.[104] Though certainly more sympathetic toward the creditor, the upper house did not prevent the passage of these important pro-debtor laws.

The Senate also gave ground on the paper money issue. After vetoing a paper money bill in 1784, it accepted one the next year.[105] The change of heart was not out of sympathy with the small debtor farmers, however, for the law was designed to aid the large property holders. A borrower could obtain up to £200, but he had to furnish security worth three times as much in land or two times as much in silver, and pay 7 percent interest. Anyone who borrowed was obliged to pay his private debts, and could not take advantage of the valuation law. The measure ought to have been entitled "an act to assist well-to-do members of the legislature and their friends," for almost the entire sum of £100,000 was lent out to them. A list of those who received loans in 1786 included twenty-six senators and at least thirty-nine members of the House![106]

The passage of the paper money and pro-debtor laws in 1785 was thus due partly to the selfish economic interest of the senators. However, it also reflected the pressure of public opinion, for in the election of the winter 1784–1785, over half of the senators, including almost every westerner, were defeated, and replaced, undoubtedly, by men who favored these bills. On other economic issues a similar sensitivity to the wishes of the voters was manifested.[107]

On the whole the Senate of South Carolina, supposedly an aristocratic body, accepted with little dispute the decisions of the lower house. This general harmony was the product less of design than of circumstance: the lower house was not a truly democratic body, but included a majority of well-to-do easterners; and the Senate was not strictly aristocratic, but contained a strong leaven of democracy.

VIRGINIA

Virginia was the only other state in which the prominent old families still controlled the Senate. However, this control was more precarious than in Maryland and South Carolina. The Virginians did not recreate their aristocratic Council, which had contained only members of the first families. Instead, they constructed an entirely new chamber.

The delegates to the constitutional convention of 1776 seem to have had no clear idea of what should be done with their Council. They apparently agreed that a senate should exist; but who should select it and how often, from what constituencies and with what qualifications—these questions were probably debated at length by the designers of Virginia's new government. In the absence of a Madison to preserve the debates, it is impossible to know precisely what arguments were used. Two articles in the *Virginia Gazette* indicate a few of them. "Democritus" proposed a lower house which would be elected annually by the freeholders, with a rotation by which delegates could serve only for a given number of terms. However, he warned, "even under these restrictions, an overgrown popularity may be dangerous to the safety of the state, or an arbitrary representative body may find means of imposing partial temporary laws on the people." He therefore advocated a second house, with a veto power, consisting of a "small number of the ablest men in the nation." Elections by the people at large would, he thought, be inconvenient, and choice by the lower house absurd, because independence would give way to subservience. Therefore, he proposed that the people in each county elect a committee, who in turn would select twelve members. Presumably, although he did not say so, the elections would be annual. On the other hand, the author of "A Government Scheme" favored an upper house of twenty-four, chosen by the representatives, who would serve for seven years.[108] Carter Braxton preferred life terms; Thomas Jefferson advocated either nine years or life; and

George Mason suggested indirect election, very high property qualifications, and four-year terms.[109]

The outcome was evidently a compromise: twenty-four senators chosen by the voters, one-fourth elected annually, their independence presumably secured by four-year terms. Since the idea of senators-at-large had not taken hold, and since there were more than twenty-four counties in the state, Virginia was divided into twenty-four areas consisting of at least two counties each. The system favored the east—Gloucester and Middlesex, for example, were weighted equally with much more populous Loudoun and Fauquier—but on the other hand even the westernmost counties were assured of representation. The Shenandoah Valley chose one senator and shared one with what is now West Virginia, which also had another; and the southwestern part of Virginia, including the Kentucky region, also elected a senator. Tidewater counties controlled only about half of the seats—a notable change from pre-Revolutionary days. No provision was made for rotation, and, in fact, John Jones of Brunswick and Robert Rutherford of Frederick served every term between 1776 and 1788, while Archibald Cary of Chesterfield, William Ellzey of Loudoun, Henry Lee of Prince William, Burwell Bassett of New Kent, Edward Stevens of Culpeper, and John P. DuVal of Harrison served almost as long. Senators had to be resident freeholders of their districts, but there was no other property qualification.

The membership of the Senate differed from that of the prewar Council in almost every respect. It was a more representative body in that men from the Piedmont and western regions were included. Like the Council, it contained a high proportion of merchants and lawyers (about one-third), and was dominated by great landholders; but it also included several doctors and a few farmers. The councillors, with one or possibly two exceptions, had been wealthy, but about one-third of the senators were no more than well-to-do and at least a half-dozen had only moderate means. The typical councillor owned ten thousand acres and probably two hundred slaves; the senator owned two thousand acres and forty slaves— hardly a small property, but only one-fifth as much as his pre-Revolutionary counterpart. All but one of the councillors came from prominent old familes. These men controlled the Senate too, but only by a bare majority, for many men from respectable but ordinary backgrounds were now included, and a dozen or more were entirely self-made. The parents of the post-Revolutionary senators were usually neither poor nor obscure, but they did represent more diversified backgrounds than those of the councillors' fathers. With one exception, all of the latter had been wealthy landowners, and frequently merchants as well. Although a majority of the senators had been born into large landholding families, there were also a half-dozen farmers' sons, several sons of professional men, and some two dozen senators of unknown origin, almost all of whom were doubtless children of farmers. In these respects the Senate was more representative, or at least less unrepresentative, than the Council.

There were other differences as well. All or nearly all of the councillors had been Anglicans; now, although Church of England men predominated, others, particularly Presbyterians, appeared. All of the councillors were well educated, half of them having studied in England, whereas only one in nine senators had been trained abroad, and one in five had attended an American college. A few others had excellent private educations, but far more had little or no schooling. In short, probably 60 percent of the senators came from the same social, economic, and cultural environment as the councillors. The remaining 40 percent rose from the lower ranks, seizing the chance that the Revolution gave them.

As much as the upper house had been affected by events, it was certainly not a democratic body. Though when compared with the Council, it seems almost representative, when compared with the postwar House of Delegates, its aristocratic quality becomes obvious. This was true because the lower house also had undergone a considerable change, the delegates of the 1780's standing in much the same relationship to the burgesses of the 1760's as the Senate to the Council. The prewar House of Burgesses was almost identical to the Senate: an aristocratic body with certain democratic features. The proportions of wealthy men (about half), of large landowners (70 percent), and of members of the prominent old families (about half) were the same, and the parallel could be greatly extended. Indeed, a very large number of senators had been burgesses. Had the personnel of the lower house remained unchanged, senators and delegates would have represented the same interests in society. But the gradual process of democratization, which affected a part of the Senate, was greatly extended in the lower house, so that the latter became, if not perhaps completely democratic, much more representative than before.

The differences between the two branches can be briefly stated. Compared with the House of Delegates, the Senate contained proportionately twice as many men with nonfarm occupations, and only a third as many farmers. Half of the senators and one-fourth of the delegates were wealthy, while the delegates included a much larger number of small property owners. The senators held about twice as much land and twice as many slaves (the medians being 2,000 acres and 40 slaves compared with 1,100 acres and 20 slaves). Socially, more than half of the senators belonged to prominent old families, whereas only one-fourth of the delegates did. In short, the Senate was controlled by the large planter-businessman class, the delegates by lesser planters who came from respectable but not eminent backgrounds. Thus, the two houses represented different elements in Virginia's society. At the same time, these distinctions ought not to be exaggerated, for representatives of all of the various social, economic, and geographical groups that made up the voting populations sat in both houses; only the proportion varied.

A few illustrations will characterize Virginia's senators. Burwell Bassett of New Kent was the son of William, a wealthy planter and a councillor. Bassett was one of the richest Virginians of his time, owning 6,124 acres in New Kent and Hanover, 156 slaves, and 294 head of cattle. He married Anna Maria Dandridge, of an old Virginia family, sat in the House of Burgesses before the Revolution, and was a senator continuously after November, 1777. Bassett represents the colonial elite which provided leadership both before and after the Revolution.[110]

David Mason of Sussex was a fifth-generation Virginian. His grandfather, John, left a personal estate valued at £830, including 13 slaves and 1,338 acres—a typical holding of a lesser planter, perhaps not quite well-to-do (depending on the value of the land), but more than moderate. David rose a full step up the economic ladder, for he owned 2,830 acres in Sussex and Lunenburg and 38 slaves. He served in the House of Burgesses from 1758 on, was a justice of the peace, a colonel, and, in 1776, a senator. Mason typifies the well-to-do planters of old but not prominent families who dominated the lower house and were well represented in the upper.[111]

Finally, Paul Loyall sat for Princess Anne County in 1779–1780 and from 1785 on. There is no trace of a Loyall family prior to Paul himself; probably he was an immigrant. From 1745 to 1752 he was a ship's captain. By 1763 he had settled down as a merchant and had become the mayor of Norfolk. He married the daughter of Colonel George Newton, of an old Virginia family, and formed Loyall, Newton, & Co. Their firm claimed to have lost £2,821 by the destruction of Norfolk and Loyall himself was reported to have lost £1,932.[112] He also acquired other property—370 acres and 26 slaves in Norfolk County and City. In 1776 he had seven slaves but no land in Princess Anne. Loyall represents that interesting minority (about one-fifth) of senators who had no apparent roots in Virginia. It is noteworthy that virtually all of these newcomers made their reputation and fortunes not in farming but in commerce or a profession.[113]

The differences between the two houses, especially the aristocratic quality of the upper, suggests that controversies as intense as those in Maryland might be expected. Surprisingly, they were virtually absent. Perhaps the power structure within the lower house placed authority in the hands of the upper class there as well as in the Senate. However, the primary cause seems to lie in a unique feature of the state's constitution: the Senate was entirely a revisory body. All bills and resolutions originated in the House of Delegates. The Senate could only amend or reject them, and money bills could not even be amended. As a result of this limited role, the power and influence of the Senate were much reduced. Several Virginians protested that the upper house lacked prestige and was unable to hold out against the more popular body. The fault was usually attributed to the short term of office, direct popular election, or lack of high property qualifications; but comparison with other states where the senate did have power equal to that of the lower house indicates that the cause is probably to be found in the feature peculiar to Virginia.[114] Legislative leadership had to be assumed by the lower house, which therefore attracted more men of ability. One critic even asserted that the Senate was "contemptible in point of Capacity."[115] Clearly the failure to grant equality to the upper house meant that it could neither effectively represent the aristocratic principle nor provide a true check upon the delegates.

The upper house was further weakened because it did not present a solid front. The number of roll-call votes that have been preserved is not sufficient to permit detailed analysis of the internal divisions, which perhaps were not as sharp as those in some other states. However, the senators seem to have voted in accordance with their sectional origins, the men from the Northern Neck and the eastern (Tidewater) counties allied against those from the rest of the state.[116] Such lack of unity, as in South Carolina, further prevented the Senate from effectively opposing the lower house.

The Senate approved without change most of the bills that were submitted to it. When amendments were recommended they were often minor and were accepted promptly by the lower house. If the delegates resisted, the senators usually acquiesced. Few prolonged disagreements occurred. The senators seldom rejected acts or resolutions. Some contests did develop, but unfortunately it is seldom possible to discover whether the Senate consistently adhered to certain principles, because amendments were not printed in the Senate journals, and were rarely printed in those of the House. The Senate was not obliged to give reasons for amendments, and when an exchange of views did take place the medium was a conference, the minutes of which were not recorded.

The Senate did not engage in any extensive defense of its prerogatives, because it had none. It did insist on receiving all letters and papers pertaining to legislative business,[117] and it did make a number of amendments. The Senate successfully repulsed efforts by the delegates to expand the definition of money bills. During the first year under the new constitution the Senate occasionally revised resolutions appropriating money. Then, in December of 1777, the House of Delegates objected to one such amendment, arguing that the resolution was essentially a money bill. The delegates conceded that they had previously acquiesced in such changes, but argued that both the constitution and English precedent demonstrated that the practice was wrong, so the error should be corrected before it became inveterate. The Senate replied that the procedure had been established from the first by the very men who had drafted the constitution and who knew the meaning of its words, while English precedent was of no use, for in Virginia both houses represented the people. The delegates continued the battle verbally but in practice came to accept such amendments.[118] Subsequently, the delegates submitted a bill that included a legal tender provision and a clause punishing counterfeiters. The Senate passed the measure, but under protest, because of the immediate need for it, and when the delegates submitted a similar bill during the next session the upper house rejected it. At the same time the Senate sent one of its rare messages, explaining that the subjects of these bills were extraneous to the power over money bills. The delegates replied that their monetary control was meaningless unless the money was guarded against counterfeiters and had "its common attributes to give it currency." However, the lower house then proceeded to pass two separate bills, which were accepted.[119] The control over money bills became an issue again when the Senate amended a bill for the payment of taxes in kind, and the delegates asserted that the whole bill had to be either approved or rejected. The result was a temporary stalemate, but the Senate later passed a similar law.[120]

In other economic matters, the Senate sometimes reduced sums appropriated by the delegates but at other times increased them. The upper house was more inclined to press for the prompt collection of taxes, yet in 1787 it took the other side.[121] The controversial law of 1785 that postponed collection of half of the taxes was approved without objection. The Senate protected persons who owed money to British creditors,[122] and on another occasion favored debtors within the state.[123] According to one observer, the Senate was influenced by land speculators.[124] Actually, it does not seem to have represented any particular economic or political interest.

The senators rarely disagreed with the delegates on political matters. They tried unsuccessfully to prohibit members of Congress from serving in the legislature.[125] The Senate usually favored increasing the authority of the governor,[126] though on one occasion it restricted his power.[127] Twice it rejected a bill establishing a new county,[128] but such bills were usually approved. The Senate did occasionally defend the rights of Loyalists: a resolution threatening reprisals against British subjects if the invading army did not stop its "barbarities and unwarrantable depredations" was defeated, as was a bill confiscating British property.[129]

Similarly, the Senate adopted no consistent policy on social or cultural issues. Perhaps the presence of many large slave-owners accounts for an effort to obtain monthly patrols of slaves' and servants' quarters by the militia, whenever trouble was suspected, and a provision that no Negro or mulatto could be enlisted into the army unless he produced a certificate that he was a freeman.[130] The changes made in an important bill guaranteeing religious freedom seem to have been minor; Madison called them "frivolous indeed."[131] In general, the Senate was active and useful as a revisory body, and Archibald Stuart was too harsh when he wrote that the senators "have not sufficient confidence in themselves to Oppose the voice of the Delegates upon any Occasion."[132] The Senate did, in fact, occasionally defeat the delegates. But it certainly was not an equal in power or influence, and it clearly did not represent the aristocratic principle of government by an elite. As Jefferson remarked, Virginia had not obtained, from its bicameral legislature, the benefits that such a separation of powers was supposed to confer.[133] The Senate was an aristocracy in its composition but a mediocrity in its functions.

The senates of Maryland, South Carolina, and Virginia were the most aristocratic of all upper houses of the post-Revolutionary years. Yet they demonstrated that the colonial elite had failed to preserve its power intact. The aristocratic principle was retained in Maryland, where high property qualifications, indirect election, and long terms of office created a body which was much admired by conservatives and which did succeed in preventing the passage of popular legislation. Yet even in Maryland the Senate contained an element unknown to the prewar Council: men who came from the lesser planter class and who were no more than well-to-do. Moreover, the Senate was divided internally by a group of men who sided with the lower house. South Carolina's Senate was elected directly and for a shorter term, so that only the higher property qualification secured for it a measure of independence and partial adherence to the aristocratic principle. Yet here, too, the original objective was imperfectly attained, for about one-third of the senators were *nouveaux riches* and another third also came from families outside of the old elite.

Perhaps it can be argued that in a fluid society, where status depended more upon property and achievement than upon birth, an aristocracy did not exist, or, if it did, it consisted of large property holders of diverse origins. But South Carolina, like Maryland and Virginia, did in fact contain a large number of families that had been wealthy for several generations. There were more than enough Bulls, Draytons, Elliotts, Guerrards, Hugers, Middletons, Smiths, and their like to have supplied the Senate with colonial-style aristocrats. Instead, such men occupied scarcely more than a third of the seats. Moreover, two out of five senators were not wealthy. In Virginia, the displacement of the former elite was carried even farther, and the Senate there was almost useless as an arm of the aristocracy because it failed effectively to check the lower house.

Another highly significant development further distinguished these upper houses from their predecessors. In all three, two different factions or parties appeared. In each, a minority group took the more popular course of supporting the lower house. The characteristics of the two opposing elements were the same in all three states, and indicate the form that political alignments were to assume throughout the country. Before a detailed description is undertaken, however, the evidence afforded by other senates needs to be considered, for the tendencies which the three aristocratic bodies only suggest become unmistakable in the more democratic legislatures.

CHAPTER 5

DEMOCRACY: THE FACTIONS

*T*HE THREE SENATES that have been discussed so far all contained a majority of wealthy or near-wealthy men, who at least partially carried forward the aristocratic tradition into the post-Revolutionary world. No other states had senates of that nature. Rather, the proportion of rich men ranged from two-fifths down to only one-sixth. Thus, even in states where the senate was intended to be an aristocratic body, it became instead, like the lower house, the scene of political conflicts which gradually assumed a predictable, consistent character. Members regularly voting together in opposition to other members formed alliances or alignments, which ultimately evolved into parties. Moreover, the senators were obliged to appeal to the voters for support, and gradually they ceased to represent an aristocracy or even an upper class. They represented the people.

This process occurred to some extent everywhere, but it was most obvious in New York, New Jersey, Delaware, and North Carolina. All of these states created senates that were entirely unlike the prewar councils in both composition and functions.

NEW YORK

The wealthy upper class of southern New York, which had controlled both houses of the legislature during the colonial period, was shattered by the Revolution. Although many of its members furnished leaders for the new government, collectively they now played inferior roles. Power was seized by men who were new to the political scene, or who had previously held only lesser offices, and who derived their strength primarily from the support of up-state farmers. Their leader, George Clinton, was governor continuously after 1776.

The constitution of 1777 was drawn up by those moderates, or moderate conservatives, who had survived the crisis, but they were forced to make fundamental concessions to the democratic element. They had at first proposed that senators be chosen by an electoral college as in Maryland, but the final draft provided for popular election. The requirement that voters own a £100 freehold was not truly restrictive, for it gave the ballot to most farmers; senators themselves needed to possess merely a freehold. Had the Senate genuinely been "designed to represent the wealthiest citizens," as one historian believed,[1] the qualifications would surely have been increased.

The constituencies from which senators were to be chosen combined in a curious way the geographical and the at-large principles. The state was divided into four districts which were assigned a number of senators roughly proportionate to the population. Within any particular district, senators were chosen at large. The southern district, including Suffolk, Kings, and Queens counties, all on Long Island, New York City, Richmond (Staten Island) and Westchester counties, chose nine; the middle district, composed of Orange, Dutchess, and Ulster counties, elected six, as did the western district, consisting of Albany, Columbia, and Montgomery counties. Finally, the eastern district, formed by Washington and Charlotte (Vermont) counties, sent three men. The twenty-four senators each served for four years. Every year, as in Virginia, one "class" of six senators rotated. Therefore, the upper house had an element of continuity while at the same time the principle of frequent elections was recognized.

The two branches had the same powers, and the constitution provided that a conference be held whenever a disagreement arose. The usual function of the upper house as a revisory body was diluted by the existence of a Council of Revision, which had a limited veto. Another special council made appointments.

The Revolution transformed both the Assembly and the Senate. Before the War the Council, as has been seen, was composed entirely of wealthy merchants, lawyers, and large landholders living in New York City, who were descended, with few exceptions, from fathers of identical status. The Assembly had been a little more representative, since upstate counties did send about a third of the members, perhaps a fourth of whom were farmers. Nevertheless, the class of wealthy or near-wealthy merchants, lawyers, and large landholders had a decided majority. With some exceptions, this group was opposed to the Revolutionary movement, and most of them became Loyalists or neutrals.[2]

After 1776, the influence of this old elite was sharply reduced. The new constitution transferred power to the areas in which yeoman farmers were dominant; for the counties west of the Hudson and north of Westchester now chose a majority of both houses. As a result of these developments, the balance of power shifted northward from New York City and downward both socially and economically. After 1776, not over 40 percent of the senators and only one-sixth of the representatives were wealthy. Three out of four councillors had been merchants, but now only one in four senators and one in seven assemblymen were in commerce. Farmers, almost excluded from the colonial legislature, now comprised one-third of the senators and actually outnumbered men of the upper class in the Assembly. The family background of the legislators was radically different from the prewar era. Descendants of prominent old families were powerful in the upper house; but even here they held only between a fourth and a third of the seats, while in the lower house they were a nearly ineffectual minority. The members were characteristically well-to-do rather than wealthy, and came from respectable rather than prominent families.

James Duane is an excellent example of a senator who was descended from the wealthy, established upper class. His father started from scratch as an Irish orphan and became a naval purser, but once in New York he married Eve Benson, daughter of a wealthy merchant, moneylender, and large landowner. The elder Duane then became a prosperous merchant and bought thousands of acres. James received a good education, and solidified his social and financial position by marrying the daughter of manor lord Robert Livingston, Jr. He became a lawyer, a large land speculator, and a political conservative. Lewis Morris, another member of New York's elite, was a senator almost continuously. Eldest son of the second manor lord, he was educated at Yale and married into the Walton family, thereby acquiring as relatives Beekmans, Crugers, and DeLanceys. He was rather more favorably disposed toward the Revolution than was Duane, but otherwise was no less conservative. These men, with other senators of the same ilk, such as Philip Schuyler and Abraham Ten Broeck, formed the core of the anti-Clinton faction.

More typical senators were Ezra L'Hommedieu and Henry Oothoudt. L'Hommedieu's grandfather immigrated from France and by 1690 was a trader and a miller in Southold, Long Island. Benjamin, his eldest son, married into an old Sandwich family and presumably took over the family business. He died when Ezra was just of age. Ezra went to Yale, studied law, and married the sister of William Floyd, also a senator and a member of a wealthy Long Island family (another Floyd sister married the brother of Senator Jesse Woodhull). L'Hommedieu became a trusted public servant, and was continually chosen to public office. He owned £1,000 worth of land on Long Island. Like Morris and Duane, he became a Federalist.[3] Henry Oothoudt's father had acquired large tracts of western land, but Henry never made anything from them and seems to have been nothing more than a substantial farmer; in 1790 he owned fourteen slaves. He was well educated but did not attend college. Oothoudt was a stanch Clintonian, representing the rural constituency of Ulster County.[4]

Still a third type of senator, while not previously unknown to New York politics, only now became important. This was the newcomer, usually a farmer, often of small means. Alexander Webster, for example, immigrated from Scotland about 1772 with his father. The family evidently brought some money with them, for they built a good house. Webster became prominent at once, rose to the rank of colonel, and served as a judge. A loyal Clintonian, he represented Washington County, an area of small farms, for many years.[5]

The most interesting of the newcomers was Ephraim Paine. He was the son of a Canterbury, Connecticut, blacksmith and farmer. Paine was at first apprenticed to a farmer, but made money on a West Indies voyage, served as chief manager to a wealthy widow, studied with a doctor, practiced medicine, and preached. Robert R. Livingston remarked that he had "run thro' the whole circle of sciences practizing Law & phisick six days in the week and preaching on the seventh.'"⁶ According to one account he was a New Light Congregationalist. In 1784, an effort was made to expel him from the Senate because he had preached to a Baptist congregation in New York City (ministers could not hold office), but the Senate voted that he was not a minister. Certainly he was a farmer, and a good one, for he won a prize for the greatest quantity of hemp seed produced from one acre. He publicly expressed sympathy for the Vermonters and enmity for merchants and contractors, wore homespun both in public and at home, and was an avowed believer in democracy and the right of revolution. In politics he was an ardent Clintonian, representing Dutchess County for several years.⁷

Allied politically with Paine and Webster was William B. Whiting. Like Paine, he was born in Connecticut, presumably into a family of farmers. His brother tried pioneering in what was then western New York, but gave it up and sold out to William. Whiting at once became a leader, held local offices, built mills, and became a colonel and a justice of the peace. The political views of his constituents are suggested by the fact that they unanimously rejected the New York constitution on the ground that every inhabitant ought to be able to vote and hold office.⁸

Insistence here on the division between the scions of prominent old families and the newcomers is justified not merely by an examination of the senators' backgrounds but by the realities of New York politics. The Senate, like the state generally, was divided into two major parties, the allies and the adversaries of Governor Clinton. The Clintonians derived their strength primarily from the upstate farmers. Scores of votes in both houses, revealing a consistency unusual for legislatures of that period, show the Clinton group supporting pro-debtor laws, opposing a strong central government, and advocating bills favorable to its rural constituencies. In the lower house the popular party was almost always successful, but in the Senate, which contained a far larger proportion of the wealthy elite, the two sides were quite evenly matched.

The nature of this division can be expressed in various ways. With few exceptions, the senators from New York City and other counties of the southern district were anti-Clintonian, while those from the more northern counties usually supported the governor

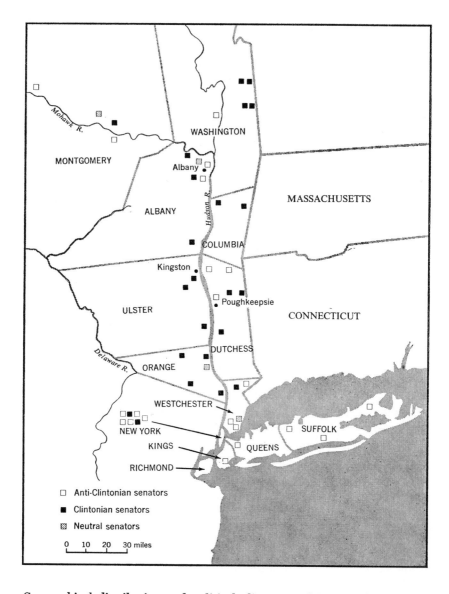

Geographical distribution and political alignment of New York senators, 1780–1788. (Map by the University of Wisconsin Cartographic Laboratory.)

(see map on facing page). Episcopalians usually took the conservative side, while Congregationalists and Presbyterians tended to vote against it. Men of wealth opposed Clinton by a three-to-one margin; those of moderate property supported the governor by the same margin. This class alignment was associated with an occupational division. With very few exceptions, the merchants, lawyers, and large landowners voted against the farmers. Merchants were particularly opposed to Clintonian policies. These economic differences were far more significant than were those based upon education, for although the Clintonians included fewer college men, they were equally energetic in support of educational activities; economic differences were more important, too, than civil or military offices held, for although the anti-Clintonians were slightly more numerous in Congress and in the rank of general, they included fewer judges and colonels.

A final distinction between the two groups was statistically the most significant and not the least interesting: their contrasting social backgrounds. The descendants of old, established, respectable, but "middle-class" families were found in equal numbers on both sides. However, the members of the pre-Revolutionary upper class were overwhelmingly opposed to the Clintonians[9] while the new men who came from outside the state, or were born of humble New York families, almost invariably supported the governor.[10] The economic situation of the fathers emphasizes the point. If a man was wealthy, his senator son was nearly always an anti-Clintonian; if poor or of unknown property (therefore probably poor), his offspring was a Clintonian two times out of three. Farmers begot Clintonians with even greater frequency, but merchants and large landowners seldom did so.

These internal divisions have been emphasized because they are essential to an appreciation of the Senate's role in New York. The two branches of the legislature were not fundamentally different. The upper house did contain more men of means and of distinguished families than the Assembly, which was the stronghold of farmers who owned much less property. These contrasts led to disagreements, some of which were important. But basically the two branches represented the same geographical areas and contained the same social and economic elements. As a result, the legislative history of the state after 1776 was distinguished by conflicts not primarily between a democratic Assembly and an aristocratic Senate, but (as it were) between the democratic and the aristocratic elements for control of each house. The party led by Governor Clinton competed with the opposing party for power in the legislature as a whole.[11]

Most of the conflicts between the two houses developed when the anti-Clintonian party obtained a temporary majority in the Senate, where they were stronger than in the Assembly. Occasionally, too, the Clintonians in the upper house blocked measures passed by their opponents in the lower. In addition, the two houses sometimes disagreed over issues that did not involve party disputes, but derived from the social and economic differences between the two bodies as well as from the traditional struggle for supremacy between them.

The contest over their relative powers was settled without difficulty. The Senate jealously defended its constitutional rights, and, after a few trials of strength, each house respected the other's dignity and authority. The only such dispute of any consequence concerned the ubiquitous question of money bills. When the Senate passed a resolution authorizing the governor to offer rewards for the arrest of several criminals, the money for which was to be provided by the legislature, the Assembly rejected it and substituted an identical one of its own. The Senate asserted that the Assembly was claiming an exclusive right to originate all "Money Matters." The issue was settled, for the moment, when the Assembly composed a resolution with different wording; but a week later the lower house insisted upon its sole right, arguing that the colonial assemblies has possessed such a power and that the state constitution granted the same privileges to its successor (which was not the case).[12] The following spring the Assembly tried to prevent the Senate from amending money bills, but the Senate did so anyway and the Assembly was forced by practical considerations to give in, while still rejecting the principle.[13] These contests were won by the upper house, but the Senate failed in an attempt to increase its influence over the appointment of officials.[14]

The lower house provoked the final skirmish over the two houses' respective authority when it decided to transmit messages to the Senate by one person instead of two. Colonel Hugh Hughes, a representative from New York City, claimed to have initiated the move, ostensibly because it was "ridiculous" to send two men, but probably because he and his friends regarded the upper house as controlled, at the time, by an "Aristocratic junto," whose pretensions and powers needed to be curtailed. In any event, the senators' feelings were hurt, and they sent an angry message to the Assembly, which replied in kind; but the lower house was unwilling to press the point and reverted to the previous practice. Hughes took the opportunity to inveigh against the danger of delegating power, and the matter was then dropped.[15]

Other minor disputes require only brief mention. The senators united in opposing the Assembly's persistent efforts to adjourn before all of the legislative business was accomplished.[16] They also frequently disagreed with the Assembly's selection of a meeting place, the vote being almost entirely sectional, depending upon what locality could momentarily win the approval of each house. Thus one year the Senate preferred Kingston to Albany, but the next year it voted for Albany instead of Kingston; at other times the upper house supported Goshen and Schenectady, but never New York City.[17]

More important was the Senate's effort to protect the rights of Loyalists and their friends. At various times it accorded them equal treatment with respect to Vermont claims, allowed former councillor John Watt's sons to purchase his forfeited estate (this was a straight party vote), defended some friends of the former treasurer, Abraham Lott, and rejected a bill to confiscate Tory property.[18] The debate over the confiscation of Loyalist estates continued for several years, the Senate occasionally trying to slow down the process.[19] The anti-Clintonians were primarily responsible for this leniency, though they often obtained some support from sympathetic members of the other side.

The conservative inclinations of the Senate were also shown with respect to economic issues. In rare instances the Clintonians controlled the Senate, and their foes the Assembly. Then the upper house might reflect the pro-debtor, pro-farmer policies of the governor and his followers.[20] As a rule, however, the Senate tended to favor higher taxes and higher salaries.[21] Factional considerations sometimes overrode all others, as when Abraham Yates tried to deprive Chancellor Robert Livingston of any salary at all.[22] The conservative group was responsible for a series of attempts to modify the paper money act of 1786 by striking out a legal tender provision, reducing the sum to be issued, limiting the duration of the issue, and protecting creditors.[23]

The influence of party alignments is evident on many other economic and political issues. The Clintonians' opponents in the Senate succeeded in preventing the use of various certificates for purchasing public land, and tried to legalize certain land titles that had been granted by the king.[24] They may have been responsible for limiting the governor's power over military stores but both factions agreed in lowering the amount of money that he could borrow for frontier defense. (The Senate may here simply have been guarding against excessive power in the executive branch.[25]) Other disagreements between the two houses followed no distinct pattern, though several illustrate the factional division.[26]

The same lack of consistency applied to questions concerning federal-state relations. In 1780 the Senate supported the ascendancy of Congress over the state, but four years later it refused to send additional delegates to Congress—a move favored by advocates of a strong central government.[27] During 1787 the Clintonians in the Senate insisted upon sending three delegates instead of five to the Federal Convention, with the vote following party lines; they also attempted to place strict limitations on the powers of the delegates, but failed when two Clintonians changed sides. The Assembly later tried again to add two delegates but the Senate once more refused. The following spring the balance of power had changed, and the Senate agreed, by a narrow margin, to convene a ratifying convention.[28]

If factional and sectional aspects are eliminated, the residual characteristics of the Senate indicate an attitude that might be termed conservative or even aristocratic. Even Hamilton for a moment in 1777 feared that the upper house might "degenerate into a body purely aristocratical,"[29] as Hugh Hughes thought it had already done. The Senate did indeed contain more men of property than the Assembly. But this aspect is relatively unimportant. Insofar as there was a contest between aristocracy and democracy in New York, it is to be found not in a struggle for supremacy between the two legislative bodies, but in a political conflict between two factions, or parties—a conflict that encompassed both houses as part of a broader battleground. The role of the Senate, whether

New Yorkers recognized it or not, was henceforth to be determined not by theoretical considerations of checks and balances, but by the cold political reality of intraparty strife.

New Jersey

Just as the Revolution caused a geographic, social, and economic shift in the locus of power in New York, so in New Jersey the aristocratic Council was reformed into a much more representative body. The Perth Amboy group which, with its equivalent in the Burlington area, had once controlled the legislature, now lost its dominance to other factions and even to individuals in various parts of the state. The new constitution provided that each county select one member, which meant that several counties sent their own delegates for the first time. However, the Legislative Council was not intended to be a democratic body, for £1,000 worth of property was required for membership. To be sure, this was local money, equivalent to £600 sterling, little enough to admit substantial farmers and artisans, but nevertheless about 80 percent of the men were eliminated. Actually the restriction was never challenged, and probably did not prevent the occasional election of men with less property.

By comparison with the former Council, the new chamber was remarkably democratic. The merchants, lawyers, and large landowners were now balanced by men of the middle ranks—less well-to-do professional men, artisans, and farmers. Fewer than half of the members were wealthy and a fourth were men of moderate property. Anglicans were scarcely more numerous than Baptists, but Presbyterians, who gained the most from the Revolution, furnished as many senators as all of the other denominations combined.

Of particular interest is the change that occurred in the social origins of the new body. Apparently only three of the senators' fathers were merchants, one was a shopkeeper, and two were lawyers. Perhaps a dozen were large landowners. Fewer than one-third belonged to the colony's prominent old families. The great majority of the parents were farmers, men of small estate, some so obscure that nothing is known about them at all. At least one senator out of every five is known to have started without property.

Thus, New Jersey's upper house, like senates elsewhere, reflected the great changes brought about by the Revolution, and contained men who knew the wants of most Jerseyites.

Illustrative of the senators whose origins were humble is Colonel Ephraim Martin. He was born somewhere in central New Jersey of unknown parentage; presumably his father was a farmer like most men of that region. The future senator was an early settler in Sussex County, a farmer, and by 1774 a coroner. The Revolution made him prominent. He served on local committees and became a colonel on active duty. In 1779 he moved to Somerset County where he kept an inn and which he represented in the legislature almost continuously. He also served as deacon of the Baptist Church. His personal estate was inventoried at only $463.45, but since he owned a half-dozen lots, 3 houses, and 240 acres, he evidently had more than the average amount of property.[30] Jonathan Jenkins (d. 1779) represents the yeoman farmer element. His father probably was Nathaniel Jenkins, who left a personal estate of £21 and some coastal land in Cape May County. Jonathan himself was a miller and a substantial farmer with 319 acres in 1774.[31] Similarly, Elijah Clark was born to a respectable landholder of Gloucester County, who left personal property worth £208. Elijah moved to the town of Gloucester, served in the Provincial Congress and as county clerk, was commissioned lieutenant colonel, and became a prosperous storekeeper, miller, and farmer.[32] Silas Condict's father acquired several hundred acres near Morristown. Silas (who served in the Continental Congress) added to the property, leaving $17,676 at his death. Both Clark and Condict were Presbyterians.[33]

Striking as is the presence of such men with little more than average income, they did not entirely dominate the upper house. Perhaps a third of its members were wealthy, and the prominent old families were strong enough so that they could occasionally carry the day. The fairly high property qualification was probably designed to assure that the Senate would contain large numbers of "the most learned and rich."[34] John Stevens, of the prewar Council, was re-elected a number of times, as were Samuel Ogden, son of Councillor David Ogden, Robert Morris, bastard son of Councillor Robert H. Morris, and Joseph Smith, son of Councillor Samuel Smith. Senator Robert Lettice Hooper's father and great-grandfather both had been councillors. General Philemon Dickinson, brother of John Dickinson, belonged to one of the wealthiest families in the middle colonies. Many others were men of only slightly less repute.

But these men were exceptional. The typical legislative councillor was well-to-do rather than wealthy, a farmer of substantial means or a professional man, the son of a farmer, a Presbyterian and a man with no college education, who rose to prominence during the Revolutionary War by taking an active part, often as an officer, frequently as a member of the Provincial Congress. Such men did not belong to the state's social or economic elite, yet they now became prominent political leaders.[35]

Had the lower house remained as it was before the War, the Legislative Council would actually have been a slightly more democratic body than the "General Assembly"; but instead both branches had been reformed in the same direction. The lower house was, indeed, an extraordinary body for the times—perhaps for most times. Of the thirty-nine members in 1785, nearly half were farmers of moderate property. There seem to have been only four or five men of wealth. Their fathers were almost invariably obscure men, usually farmers of small estate. Only six came from prominent families.[36]

The marked social and economic differences between the two houses suggest that if the members voted according to their economic interests, conflicts would develop whenever the Council was controlled by the wealthier, nonfarm element. Such was, in fact, the case. Just as in New York, the legislature of New Jersey divided, at least part of the time, into two parties; and whenever one dominated the Assembly and another the Council, disputes occurred. Also as in New York, the basis for that division was both geographical and economic.

Statistically, the most significant distinction was geographic. The smaller of the two groups, and that which differed most from the Assembly, consisted principally of south New Jersey (historically, West Jersey) men, including those from Monmouth County. Most of the Bergen representatives voted on the same side, but those from the extreme southwestern corner (Salem and Cumberland) were divided. The rest of the counties sent men who ordinarily opposed the southern party. Essex, Morris, Sussex, Somerset, and Middlesex, in particular, were pitted against Monmouth, Burlington, Cape May, and Gloucester.

This regional difference was perhaps less important than certain other aspects of the division. Although business and professional men were found on both sides in almost equal numbers, farmers (other than large landowners) were generally associated with the northern group. An even more decisive economic distinction was based on possession of property. Most of the wealthy councillors voted with the south, while all but one of those known to be of moderate property were aligned with the north. The parents of the members of the latter faction were almost invariably farmers with small incomes, but half of the southern delegates had inherited considerable means; in other words, the progeny of the eight wealthy fathers uniformly aligned on one side, whereas fifteen out of nineteen fathers of moderate means furnished sons to the other. Councillors from prominent families were opposed, with few exceptions, to those of humble origin. A curious and perhaps an important fact is that the northern group consisted largely of Presbyterians, whereas the other was composed of equal numbers of Presbyterians, Baptists, Quakers, and Episcopalians.

How did these two sides differ politically? The full explanation is complex and lies far beyond the scope of the present discussion. The relevant point here is that in general the southern group represented the hard money, creditor influence, and that conflicts between the two branches of the legislature often occurred because the northern party, which supported the Assembly, sometimes lost control of the Council. In short, the situation in New Jersey was strikingly similar to that in New York.[37]

The Legislative Council of New Jersey had powers equal to those of the Assembly, including the right to originate, amend, and reject bills, except that it could not draft or alter money bills, but only accept or reject them. Moreover, such bills, as well as certain other legislation, required the approval of a majority of the total membership of each house, which meant seven councillors, regardless of the number present. Seldom were more than ten or eleven members in attendance, so that a small minority might block important measures. Obviously either of the two political groups could insist upon the recognition of its views. It was this provision, rather than the high property qualification, that gave to the Council such aristocratic quality as it possessed; for the southern party, though fewer in number, could block the passage of laws desired by the Assembly.

The upper house defended its peculiar powers with as much tenacity as the prewar councils had protected their prerogatives. The first dispute of importance began when the Council objected to an Assembly resolution authorizing payment to the treasurer of £125, because its assent had not been obtained. The lower house replied that it had promised the money in consideration of the treasurer's accepting the office. The Council indignantly answered that no money could be spent without its assent, which had not even been asked. The councillors observed that they were careful not to infringe upon the rights of the Assembly, and had to defend their own. The Council was just as representative of the people, and, as an independent and equal branch of the legislature, was equally obligated to ensure that all appropriations were proper. The lower house responded apologetically that the measure was justified because the Council had lacked a quorum and the Assembly had been forced to make the best bargain it could. The Council apparently was placated, perhaps influenced by the same considerations later expressed by "An Elector," who wrote that both houses were "creatures of the people," and "all disputes about privilege and prerogative are mere *loga machies*," so that they should not waste time "determining with mathematical exactness, the peculiar rights of each house."[38]

The only other such debate also concerned the power of the purse. In December of 1780, the Council suggested that the constitutional article that prohibited the alteration of money bills might be so interpreted "as greatly to embarrass publick Business," to avoid which a conference was suggested. The lower house rejected this proposal, whereupon the Council proceeded to amend a bill raising troops. The Assembly promptly returned the bill with the message that the amendment was unconstitutional. The Council then cited sixteen precedents and ended by unanimously vetoing the measure. Thereafter the lower house acknowledged reality and evidently refrained from mixing money bills with other legislation.[39]

The two bodies constantly held "free conferences"—informal joint sessions in which most potential disputes were discussed and the necessary compromises arranged. These effected a real harmony between the houses which was seldom interrupted, except for periods when they were controlled by different parties. In those cases one group could and did use its superiority in a particular house to prevent action. Ordinarily disagreements occurred when the minority group of south New Jersey exercised a veto power in the Council.

Most of these disputes involved economic issues. Several tax bills, or bills appropriating money, were rejected for unknown reasons. The Council sometimes protected the interest of creditors.[40] A stay law was rejected, as were two bills for the relief of insolvent debtors.[41] The Council twice defeated measures to extend the authority of justices of the peace over cases involving small sums.[42] The paper money forces encountered strong opposition which first intentionally misconstrued the clear meaning of petitions advocating legal tender notes, then twice rejected a paper money bill, and finally accepted it after amendments had been made.[43] On the other hand, the Council contained enough farmers of moderate property so that it did occasionally protect the debtor.[44] The Council was somewhat more inclined than the Assembly to support Congress, although a resolution that "every separate and detached State interest ought to be postponed to the publick Good" passed by only a single vote.[45] On other occasions it protected the property of a Loyalist,[46] and attempted to prosecute delinquent tax collectors.[47] There were, of course, many minor disputes: for example, the Council was less inclined than the Assembly to support Vermont's independence,[48] and on one occasion insisted upon remaining in session when the lower house wished to adjourn.[49]

On the whole, however, the two houses avoided potential controversies with remarkable success. In the October, 1786, session, for example, more than three weeks passed without so much as a minor disagreement, and ultimately the Council rejected only three bills and amended just one. Not all sessions were so peaceful; but clearly the Council did not represent a competing political force. The aristocratic element, though present, was seldom able to act effectively. As a result, the upper house occasionally protected particular interests, but usually it merely modified bills submitted by the slightly more popular lower house. It thus served primarily as a council of revision rather than as a true check upon the workings of democracy.

DELAWARE

During the colonial period Delaware, like Pennsylvania, had no upper house, but unlike its neighbor it created one after independence. The constitution established a House of Assembly and a Council. The latter consisted of nine members, three from each county, chosen for a three-year term, one-third rotating every year. Delaware therefore had the smallest upper house of all the states, and, since many men served for more than one term, only thirty-two councillors held office between 1776 and 1788.[50]

Whereas New Jersey made some effort, through property qualifications, to refine the membership of its Senate, Delaware abandoned any selective principle other than the usual freehold requirement. The absence of special qualifications did not prevent the voters from choosing many of the state's most outstanding and wealthiest citizens, including Richard Bassett, Richard Cantwell (the chief justice), General and later Chief Justice Thomas Collins, John Dickinson, George Read, Caesar Rodney, and President (governor) Nicholas Van Dyke. Apparently no merchant was ever elected—Delaware was not noted for trade—but seven or eight lawyers sat in the upper house, as did a dozen men of large landed estates. At the same time the voters selected an equal number of farmers, and most of the councillors came from ordinary families.

The incomes of the councillors were above the average. According to the 1783 assessment lists, the median annual value of Delaware residents' property was £8.[51] The figure is certainly much too low. Probably the true income was double or triple that given, not including food and other articles that the people provided for themselves. Be that as it may, the data at least permit some comparisons. All of the councillors exceeded the median. About 5 percent of the people (exclusive of slaves) were assessed for £50, which probably meant that they were well-to-do, with property worth at least £2,000. Nearly half of the councillors owned more than this amount. On the other hand seven of them received incomes estimated at less than £25. In brief, about one-third of the members were wealthy, almost as many had modest properties, and the rest were men of substance but not of large estates. The Council was certainly not an aristocratic body.

Thus the new Council contained a wide range of individuals. Richard Cantwell of New Castle County (d. 1787) represents the upper-class element. His father, "Gentleman" Richard, left eight hundred acres and other property. The younger Richard seems to have added to the estate, for he was assessed for £130 annually. A colonel, he was elected to the first Council, re-elected in 1779, and then retired to become chief justice.[52] From the same class came Vincent Loockerman of Kent, whose large landed estate near Dover produced more than twice as much income as did Cantwell's. His great-grandfather, a Dutch merchant who immigrated in 1633, had been (according to one source) the richest man in North America.[53] A more nearly typical councillor was John Baning of Kent, the son of an immigrant, who served almost continually in the upper house and frequently as county treasurer. Baning's property was assessed for £70 annually.[54] George Craighead of New Castle derived a substantial income from his law practice. The son of an immigrant minister who left a four-hundred-acre farm, Craighead had enough money to equip his own regiment, which he then led into battle.[55]

On the other hand most of the Sussex County men had small, rather unprofitable farms. William Conwell was assessed for only £8. He seems to have been the younger son of a farmer.[56] John Polk was one of four Polks who were chosen, all of whom appear to have been farmers' sons, and only one of whom rose above his father's position. Finally, James Tilton of Kent, parents unknown, had so small an income despite an M.D. from the College of Philadelphia that he was assessed for only £6 annually.[57]

Like many of the upper houses, Delaware's Council did not present a united front to the other legislative branch. Its diversified composition was reflected in internal divisions similar to those of New York and New Jersey. The number of roll-call votes taken is not sufficient to permit a detailed analysis, but the votes do indicate the general nature of partisan politics. One party or faction included most of the wealthy members and the few descendants of old families. They came from the more northern counties (New

Castle and Kent) and were led, probably, by General and Chief
Justice Thomas Collins, and Richard Bassett and George Read,
both wealthy lawyers and large landowners. Doubtless, President
John Dickinson was on the same side, though there are no voting
records to prove it. The other group, usually in the majority, was
strongest in Sussex. It consisted primarily of farmers, mostly men
of moderate means and humble origins. Leaders included the Polks,
Conwell, and Tilton. President Nicholas Van Dyke, a wealthy lawyer and large landowner, was associated with them, and so was the
well-to-do lawyer, George Craighead; but Silas Snow of Kent and
Henry Neill of Sussex were probably more typical of this group:
nothing is known about them at all.[58] The latter faction commonly
sided with the lower house when disputes occurred, and may be
considered as belonging to the more popular or "radical" party.

Since Delaware's legislators had no experience with the bicameral system, one might have expected debates over procedure, and
conflicts in which both houses jockeyed for position. No such controversy occurred, however, and the respective rights of the two
branches were quickly established. The Assembly at first tried to
establish a permanent system of joint committees which would consider what legislation was needed (a practice common elsewhere),
but the Council preferred to remain entirely independent. Such a
procedure would be "irregular and productive of confusion," it
thought; instead, all business should originate in one house and
then be referred to the other.[59] Probably the Council feared that its
smaller membership would make it inferior in such preliminary
conferences.[60] Nevertheless, *ad hoc* joint committees were in fact
often used, sometimes even replacing more formal means of com-
munication. The Council carefully protected its right to appoint
members to these committees. And, indeed, other than the Assembly's right to originate all money bills, which it jealously
defended,[61] the two bodies were equal, and the Assembly did not
try to encroach upon the Council's prerogatives.

The principal function of the upper house was that of a conscientious revisory body. Most of the bills originated in the Assembly, and the Council then made amendments which were, as a rule,
clearly justified. It was careful to see that bills were properly
drafted and that they conformed to the constitution.[62] Over eighty
amendments were made to one measure.[63] The Council in other

ways showed itself to be the more responsible chamber: for example, it twice insisted that the legislature finish all of its business when the Assembly tried to adjourn.[64]

The upper house also was a more zealous protector of personal liberties. Freedom of speech inevitably suffered during the War but the Council preserved it as far as possible. The definition of treason was narrowed so as to preclude the "misconstruction of words or expressions used in common conversation"; the councillors hoped to protect "the freedom of speech and privelege of freemen" against "a race of informers, the pest of society, and . . . the engines of tyrants in every State. It is to be hoped," they continued, "that the just cause in which all America is embarked is not to be injured by the speeches of rash, foolish, or wicked individuals."[65] They also sought to reduce prison terms for men of doubtful loyalty because "it is frequently found, by experience, that ignominious and disgraceful punishment hardens more offenders than they reclaim."[66] The upper house protected conscientious objectors, maintaining their right to hire proxies, while the Assembly was insisting that everyone who received protection from the laws of the state ought to help defend it.[67] The Council also preserved the right of every accused man to a proper trial.[68]

The councillors also vigorously encouraged education. When the lower house omitted schoolmasters from a list of those exempt from military service, the Council issued a ringing defense of the importance of teachers. There were so few masters that they should be encouraged in every possible way:

We consider the very few engaged in that service so necessary for the education of the youth of the State that every encouragement should be given to them to pursue that business with the strictest attention. Every parent who reflects upon or regards the welfare of his offspring, every guardian of the rights of a free people, must wish to encourage and promote learning; and such has been the fatal effects of the times on schools and seminaries of learning in this State that we think it worthy the attention of the Legislature to afford at least the proper exemption to the teachers in them.[69]

The Council seems also to have taken the higher ground with respect to enlistments. According to the militia bill as sent up by the Assembly, exemptions could be purchased. The upper house objected that no one who could buy a recruit would enlist, and that since only those "in easy circumstances" had enough money, the poor people would be injured. Success in the War depended upon support among all "ranks," so that measures discouraging to the majority ought to be avoided.[70] The Council was probably correct, too, in trying to strengthen the executive branch,[71] and to increase the allowances of delegates to Congress[72] and the incomes of other officials.[73]

On economic issues the upper house reflected its upper-class composition. However, since during most of these years both houses were controlled by the same sort of men, few disagreements occurred. Not until January of 1783 did any conflict develop. At that time the Council attempted to increase the anticipated tax revenue from £26,250 to £39,000. Its position was probably taken because of the momentary dominance of the conservative party. At the same time, the upper house undertook to make collections more efficient, arguing that more money was needed for the restoration of credit, and that centralization of authority in the state government would lead to an increased revenue. In this the councillors were certainly correct.[74] They succeeded in taxing not only real but personal property, again by a strict party vote.[75] Subsequently, when the lower house imposed excises on spirituous liquors and riding carriages—taxes that affected the well-to-do rather than the poor—the Council added taxes on various offices as well. Since these were held by many assemblymen, the lower house refused to accept the amendment.[76]

During the depression years of the mid-1780's, the debtor element tried in Delaware, as it did elsewhere, to obtain relief through favorable laws, and, as elsewhere, the Council was reluctant to pass them. In 1786 the upper house rejected a paper money bill and defended its action with a characteristic statement: before the Revolutionary War, the councillors asserted, paper money had maintained its value, but later events proved that nothing short of a bank at which paper could be exchanged for hard money would prevent depreciation. Moreover, the paper could not be used by Congress, nor would it circulate out of the state. As a result, the property rights of industrious and worthy citizens would suffer. They were sure that debtors did not deserve this relief: debts were due to "men's living beyond their income, or speculating indiscreetly upon their neighbors' property, and but very rarely from inevitable misfortune." The solution was to limit borrowing, not to encourage it.[77] A few months later the Council rejected a stay law and the following year refused to grant an extension of time for the collection of back taxes.[78]

No doubt these actions were unpopular, but there is no evidence of any great outcry against the Council, nor were the offending councillors unseated. Indeed, by the end of the decade the Council contained a conservative majority. Despite these disagreements, the two houses seldom differed fundamentally and on the whole did not represent sharply conflicting elements in society.

NORTH CAROLINA

The Revolution, which brought great changes to all of the southern states, affected North Carolina perhaps most of all. The consequences for her upper house were dramatic: whereas during the dozen years prior to independence eighteen men had served, in the same period of time after 1776 over 250 senators were elected. Furthermore, most prewar councillors were men of some reputation, but the senators, with few exceptions, were obscure then and are generally unidentifiable now. The old upper class was still present, but it was submerged, and its plaintive cries for help echo feebly through the letters of such men as Samuel Johnston and James Iredell. In many of the new states the principle was adopted that the Senate should be a small body of the best (or the wealthiest) men. Constituencies tended to be large, property qualifications sometimes high, terms long. In North Carolina, the Senate was scarcely less popular than the Commons. Each of the state's numerous counties was entitled to elect a member; property qualifications were sufficiently low (three hundred acres) that farmers of substantial means could serve; and elections were held annually. Counties did not invariably choose a senator, or find one who would attend, but the membership always numbered at least forty and exceeded fifty after 1783. Tenure seldom was long. During these twelve years most of the counties sent five or more different men, and one county chose nine. A few senators were almost permanent fixtures, such as James Coor of Craven who served every year except one; but the average senator retired after three terms. In short, the Senate, like the lower house, was directly responsive to public opinion.

North Carolina was almost entirely agricultural, and the upper house, which before the Revolution had contained only a few planters, now had an overwhelming majority of men who derived their principal income from the land. Nearly 90 percent of the senators were either planters or farmers, in about equal proportions. The merchants and professional men who were chosen had little power to affect legislation unless many landholders took their side. Before the War most of the councillors were Anglicans and came from the coastal counties; now the Senate was diversified both in religious make-up and in geographical distribution.

Since slaves were included in the census of 1790, some generalizations can be hazarded concerning the economic status of the senators. If the ownership of twenty slaves defined one as well-to-do in North Carolina, and if the possession of fifty made one wealthy, then the membership of North Carolina's upper house can be analyzed as follows: among the senators whose property in slaves is known (nearly 90 percent), 18 percent were wealthy—by far the lowest proportion of any state outside of New England—48 percent were well-to-do, and 34 percent were of moderate means or even poor. The last percentage was by far the highest in any southern or middle state. Other sources, such as they are, confirm these estimates. The senators had considerably more property than the average citizen, and probably more than the assemblymen; but by comparison with members of other legislative bodies they were almost poor. Certainly the aristocratic element was small.

The family background of the senators also testifies to the transformation. In a large number of cases nothing is known about their fathers. This is true partly because there exist few genealogies of North Carolina families, and partly because essential sources such as marriage, birth, and death records, wills, and tax lists have largely disappeared. Above all, the state was characterized by high mobility, both horizontal and vertical. A large proportion of its citizens were immigrants, or had moved from Tidewater to Piedmont; many had started poor and had then acquired a settled property. The nearly one-fourth of the senators who are of unknown parentage probably came to North Carolina from another colony or from Europe; certainly their fathers were men of little consequence. One out of four senators was surely or probably new to the state. Not more than one in twelve was desended from a prominent old family, and the remainder—the largest single group—were born in the colony of respectable but ordinary parents. Apparently the fathers represented nearly a cross-section of colonial society.

The Senate's membership divides roughly into the following groups: one out of five was a large landowner with perhaps some other occupation as well, a wealthy son of a prominent and wealthy or well-to-do planter, and possessed of considerable knowledge of the outside world. One-fourth were well-to-do lesser planters, sons of established farmers, locally born, with little experience beyond that of their state, except that which might have been gained during the War. One-fourth were farmers of moderate property, who either started from scratch as immigrants or rose from humble local beginnings. Finally, about the rest, of whom practically nothing is known, it can be surmised that they were not rich, not prominent, not of eminent families, not merchants or professional men, and not famous soldiers or politicians. They are remarkable only for their anonymity.

Typical of the first group were the Jones brothers, Allen and Willie. Their great-grandfather had immigrated to Virginia, and their father was a lawyer and large landowner in North Carolina. Both were educated in Europe (in which respect they were unusual), and married well. They took the side of the government against the Regulators, were ardent rebels, and members of the Continental Congress. Both were tolerant in religion and supported education. Allen was a general (indeed over half of these men were colonels and generals), a conservative, and a Federalist, while Willie became a leader of the popular party and an Antifederalist. Both had varied business interests but were primarily planters. In common with the great majority of this group, both lived in Tidewater counties. Thomas Person represents an interesting deviation from this type. Born probably in Virginia, he became a surveyor for Lord Granville and acquired a huge estate. However, he was a Regulator, a radical revolutionist, a philanthropist, and a leader of the democratic element.

The four members of the Bryan family in the Senate typify the well-to-do planters of respectable yeoman descent. The father of two Bryans was a cut above that rank, for he was worth £49,344 local money—perhaps £5,000 sterling—when he died. One son, Arthur (b. 1749), a justice of the peace, owned 1,505 acres in 1784 and 10 slaves in 1786. His brother Hardy (b. 1753) owned 962 acres and 14 slaves. He, too, was a justice but held no other office. Their uncle Needham (1726–1784), a colonel, sat in the lower house before the War and in the Senate after it. He was a wealthy planter, and a grandson of the immigrant. A different line led to Nathan, son of another Hardy (a successful farmer who died in 1760), who held 2,110 acres and 16 slaves in 1779.[79]

Another type of senator was Frederick Harget, who represented Jones County continuously beginning in 1784. His background is unknown, for no one of that name is recorded in the extensive list of North Carolina wills. In 1779 he was a prosperous farmer with 530 acres, 6 slaves, 6 horses, and 19 cattle. By the end of the 1780's he had added a tract in Tennessee and acquired ten more slaves, thereby rising from the status of the moderately wealthy to that of the well-to-do farmer. Nothing else is known of him. Finally, there is John Birdsong of Chatham. No one of that name left a will. He is not found on surviving tax lists or census records. He emerges from obscurity for one year and then returns again. That such a man could be chosen to the Senate—and Birdsong was far from unique—proves that democracy had indeed come to North Carolina.

Since the Senate was nearly as representative a body as the lower house, disagreements between them were seldom serious. In fact, the Senate, far from opposing the Commons with united force, was divided internally. Sometimes a slight majority of the Senate sided with the Commons, sometimes not, the balance often changing with a new election. Therefore, as in so many of the states already discussed, an analysis of the Senate's role in North Carolina requires not simply a review of the differences between the houses, but a description of the internal divisions within the Senate itself.

The Senate contained two groups of nearly equal strength, consisting in each case of about thirty men. About ten others occupied neutral positions, while the rest cast too few votes for any certain estimate of their affiliation. In most respects the two groups were comparable to the parties that have previously been described. Geography was the most obvious distinction. One group consisted almost entirely of representatives from the northeast, the dividing line running from Warren County, on the Virginia border, roughly 125 miles from the sea, diagonally southeast through Nash, Dobbs (now Greene and Lenoir), and including Onslow on the coast. Senators from the southeast occasionally lent support; those from the next tier of counties to the west—Wake, Johnston, Wayne, and Sampson—were divided. The rest of the state sent men who almost always voted on the other side on critical issues. The consistency of voting increased as time went on, becoming most evident in 1787.

There were other, less significant, differences. The two sides were much the same in wealth and occupation: both were composed of farmers, of both substantial and modest means. The northeastern group consisted primarily of old North Carolina families, a few of which were prominent. Western senators were usually born outside of the state and were of humble social origin. Practically all of those known to be Presbyterians lived in the west and voted on that side, whereas the northeasterners included a variety of religious groups. In other respects the rather spotty biographical data reveal no difference between the two, though it may be significant that most of the northeasterners became Federalists while the westerners were opposed to the Constitution. In general the former supported "conservative" and the latter "popular" policies.

Although the composition of North Carolina's upper house was more democratic than that of most other senates, it was just as jealous of its prerogatives. The first legislature under the 1776 constitution at once became involved in a dispute over procedure, in which the Senate insisted upon its right to participate in nominations and elections, and to determine the allowances to its own clerk.[80] Although contests between the houses were never so serious as to create deep animosities, the Senate continued to maintain its authority. On one occasion it resolved that there should be no informal conversation between members of the two bodies while they were in session, because such intercourse might lessen their "independent unbiased freedom of Debate."[81] The Senate was in fact equal to the Commons in every respect except numbers. It could originate money bills and any other laws, and it amended and rejected an important quantity of legislation. In doing so it frequently differed with the Commons. These differences, however, were not owing to any fundamental and consistent divergence, but, as has been noted, to the balance of power at that particular moment.

The senators had no firm convictions about expenditures. During 1778 the upper house was more anxious than the lower to increase the travel allowance and daily pay of the legislators, with westerners taking the lead.[82] But the following year the House of Commons raised the amount, and in 1781 it doubled the allowance.[83] The Senate upon several occasions increased the salaries of various officials, yet delegates to the Continental Congress owed their raise to the Commons.[84] The Senate was a little more willing to allow a larger profit to men supplying the army and building roads, but on one occasion it reduced the "ration."[85] The position taken clearly depended upon considerations of the moment rather than upon any consistent philosophy.

The Senate similarly varied its position on revenue. Ordinarily the two bodies agreed. In 1784, the Senate favored higher taxes on land and polls, and during the following year it pressed for collection; but in 1787 it defeated an attempt by the Commons to raise land taxes west of the Appalachians.[86] The Senate rather than the Commons tried to classify land according to its value—a measure usually supported by the smaller farmers; and the upper house also came to the defense of tenants.[87] The cession of western lands to Congress was first approved by both houses, but the Senate subsequently objected.[88]

Land speculators found support in the Senate when, in 1777, titles purchased from the Indians were legally recognized on the ground that "valuable considerations" had been given, and that "the scheme of agrarian law is altogether chimerical in an enlightened age and a commercial country." This position, which was taken by the northeastern group, elicited energetic criticism from Thomas Person, who attacked monopolies and argued that "the property of the soil in a free State is one of the essential rights of the collective body of the people."[89] Other vested economic interests were also protected when the Senate rejected bills limiting the inheritance of estates by foreigners and prohibiting the export of corn.[90] On the other hand, creditors were angered when the Senate favored making paper money legal tender, refused to limit the amount of money issued, supported an emission of paper, and on several other occasions took the soft money side against the Commons.[91] The Senate favored lower lawyers' fees, and its position on economic matters, though erratic, generally aroused the anger of conservatives.[92] They were especially irate over the senators' failure adequately to protect Loyalists and Loyalist property. In its first session, the Commons resolved to set free prisoners who would become good subjects of the state, but the Senate rejected the suggestion. Two years later a series of memorials in behalf of absentees, which the Commons had referred to a joint committee, was not even considered by the upper house.[93] The Senate refused to allow a Wilmington merchant accused of Loyalism to return to the state, rejected his petition for the restoration of his property, and insisted upon retaining the basic confiscation law.[94] James Iredell wrote his wife that the "cursed Senate" would not "suffer any plan of moderation."[95] In later years the Senate became more lenient, blocking further punitive measures; yet upon occasion it voted against Loyalists and was opposed to enforcing the British treaty.[96]

In humanitarian matters there was almost no difference between the two houses—in fact, the Commons acquitted itself quite well. The Senate tried to protect the Moravians by allowing them simply to take an "affirmation" renouncing fidelity to the king, rather than requiring them to swear loyalty to the state.[97] But the upper house proposed that the Quakers be taxed seven-fold instead of four-fold,[98] rejected a bill for the encouragement of ministers,[99] and refused to approve a bill that would have permitted Quakers who were conscientious objectors to slavery to free their slaves.[100]

No consistent pattern can be distinguished in the Senate's other differences with the Commons. The upper house rejected a half-dozen bills providing for the establishment of new counties, but it also approved many others.[101] The senators were reluctant to grant power to the governor,[102] delayed for several years the establishment of a court of chancery,[103] and were skeptical of the merit of justices of the peace, apparently because most members of the Commons were justices.[104] Senators elsewhere often favored longer sessions than did the lower house, but in North Carolina the Commons was just as apt to delay adjournment.[105] All of these issues found the senators divided among themselves in the same manner as were the members of the Commons, and disagreements between the two houses developed not because of any fixed opposition based upon fundamental differences, but only when a temporary majority in one was opposed to a temporary majority in the other. Disputes are therefore to be understood in terms of political alignments rather than as a contest between branches of the legislature.

The architects of the New York constitution intended to make the Senate an aristocratic institution. Probably the property qualification in New Jersey and the three-year term in Delaware were designed for a similar purpose. But the framers were disappointed. These three upper houses did sometimes protect property rights and the rights of the local elite, but they were often subject to popular control, while the Senate of North Carolina was a frankly democratic body from the start. Moreover, a development occurred that seems to have been unforeseen and was generally deprecated. The senates became the scenes of what were then called "factional" combats. With the benefit of hindsight, it is apparent that the factions were nascent political parties. They were based (or so the evidence indicates) primarily on social and economic considerations, although there was a clear tendency for Presbyterians to oppose Anglicans. One of these embryonic parties may be called "popular," "radical," or "democratic." Its members were likely to be "new" men—either immigrants from Europe or from another colony, or men of humble social origins. They sided with the lower house and advocated paper money, stay laws, anti-Loyalist legislation, and tax policies and other laws favorable to farmers, and took "antifederal" positions. They drew their support from rural areas and from the small property holders. The opposing side consisted of townspeople, of men from the older parts of the states, of individuals born into prominent families, of merchants, lawyers, and large landowners—in short, of the economic and social upper class. The senate was supposed to have been their stronghold, and they did have more influence there than in the lower house. But the senates were ceasing to be a haven for the elite and were developing quite different roles.

The functions that the new senates were now performing can be ascertained from the accounts that have already been given. But they can be perceived even more clearly in those states where the issues are less clouded by questions of aristocracy and party strife. The New England states furnish such examples.

CHAPTER 6

Democracy: New England

$\mathscr{T}$HE New England legislatures of the post-Revolutionary era were more democratic in their composition than any of those previously discussed, except that of North Carolina. The assistants of Connecticut and Rhode Island continued to be popularly elected. New Hampshire's royal Council became an elective body, while the Massachusetts upper house, though designed to represent property rather than numbers, nevertheless contained chiefly men of the middle ranks. The New England senates were distinguished also, but less happily, by their failure to take and record roll-call votes. Internal divisions, so prominent in other states, therefore cannot be traced in detail, although they did occur. However, other characteristics emerge with greater clarity.

MASSACHUSETTS

The coming of independence in 1776 did not immediately affect the upper house in Massachusetts. The first impact of the Revolution had been felt earlier, as in Rhode Island and Connecticut, principally in the 1769 purge. In 1773–1774 a further shift of personnel took place. As the Revolutionary movement accelerated under increasingly radical control, Loyalists or neutrals who had retained their posts now retired: Brattle, Danforth, John Erving, Sr., George Leonard, Jr., and Isaac Royall all departed. Other members, such as John Hancock and Artemas Ward, undertook new duties. The men who replaced them were, of course, enthusiastic rebels, some of whom were now becoming very prominent: Samuel Holten, Jr., Moses Gill, Samuel and John Adams, Benjamin Austin, and Francis Dana all served during 1775 and 1776.

For several years after 1776, the upper house continued to be elected by the lower under the old charter. As before, most of the councillors were chosen from the former Bay Colony. The turnover was more rapid than during colonial times, because councillors were often elected to other offices and resigned their seats (though plural office-holding was still common.[1] The social and economic transformation of the Council, a process that had begun about 1765, continued, though it was now more gradual. In particular, the influence of Boston was further reduced, and that of the western counties correspondingly increased. Fewer merchants were chosen, and many more farmers and artisans. Between 1770 and 1774, 44 percent of the councillors were wealthy; during the years 1775 to 1779, only 17 percent. The proportion of college men, of officeholders, and of men belonging to prominent families did not vary, though the fathers possessed somewhat less property.

The final significant change in membership occurred as a result of the constitution of 1780, which, though in many respects conservative, further democratized the upper house, now called the Senate. The rejected constitution of 1778 had provided for a Senate of twenty-eight persons, each of whom had property valued at £400. Of these, ten were to be chosen from the three northeastern counties of the old Bay Colony, six from what had been Plymouth, four from Maine, and eight from the west. This assured the west of increased representation even though the basis for the reapportionment was the tax paid rather than the population. The method of election proposed was similar to that in Connecticut: a preliminary vote every November would yield a list of candidates double the necessary number, from which the voters would then choose in the spring. Vacancies would be filled by the House of Representatives from the list of nominees.

Objections to the proposed Senate came both from those who thought it was too aristocratic and from those who, like Theophilus Parsons, felt that it was too democratic. The former apparently were more numerous, for the constitution of 1780 lowered the property requirement to £300 in real estate and allowed, as an alternative, £600 in personal property.[2] The latter requirement is a curious one. Most merchants and professional men could qualify under the real estate provision. The men who needed the alternative were, above all, the artisans and small shopkeepers; but the £600 figure excluded perhaps 90 percent of them. In general, the personal property requirement could be met by only 5 percent of the men and the real property qualification by about 40 percent. The new Senate was larger, with forty members, but Maine still had only four and the west eleven, so that the continued dominance of the eastern counties was assured. The outlying areas were, however, better represented than in colonial times. Had numbers rather than taxes been the basis, the three western counties would have had thirteen seats instead of eleven, Suffolk's share being correspondingly reduced.

The new constitution provided for a single election in which each county chose its senators. Voters were required to have a freehold estate worth £3 annually, or £60 all told, which meant, according to the 1771 assessment lists, that about 40 percent of the men were disfranchised by the first provision, but only about 25 percent by the alternative (excluding indentured servants and slaves). A majority vote was needed to elect a senator, and the lower house would ballot to fill any undecided seats. At first about three-fourths of the senators received the necessary majority, but in later years, as the number of candidates proliferated and the contests grew more heated, the outcome of more electoral battles was resolved in the House. The House felt no obligation to name the candidate with the highest number of votes, but chose from the first two or three on the list, depending upon the balance of political power. The people tended to re-elect the incumbent—thirteen men each served at least nine years—but there was a considerable turnover in the elections of 1785 and again in 1787. The excessive strength of Suffolk County, the property qualification, and the influence of the lower house in filling vacancies all were intended to create an aristocratic body.

The Senate after 1780 did indeed contain an undue proportion of well-to-do townsmen of good family; yet it could not be called aristocratic, and proceeded still further along the course that the purge of 1769 had anticipated. Merchants now made up one-fourth of the membership. One-eighth were lawyers, and the rest were evenly divided between farmers and those with nonfarm occupations such as doctors, judges, and artisans. Farmers therefore were in the minority; but since others from agricultural areas often, perhaps usually, supported them, they formed a larger proportion than at any time previously. One-fifth of the senators were wealthy, one-third were well-to-do, and most of the rest had a moderate amount of property; a few were poor and could scarcely have qualified if challenged. The influence of property had therefore been further reduced.

The constitution forbade plural office-holding; senators and representatives were specifically required to resign if they accepted most high offices, though the prohibition did not apply to the lesser judicial posts. As a result fewer senators held such offices than before. The number of college graduates declined, though the proportion of such men—30 percent—was still high for the period. The prominent old families suffered a further attrition of power, their members now comprising one-fifth of the Senate—about half the proportion of colonial times. One out of five was a self-made man. The great majority came from respectable middle-class families. The fathers less often were merchants, lawyers, or large landholders (19 percent as contrasted with 36.5 percent before 1775 and 27.5 percent between 1775 and 1780). Instead they were usually farmers or artisans. In social origin the senators did not differ greatly from the majority of the state's voters. However, they were considerably above the average in wealth, even more so in education and political experience, and most of them were engaged in nonagricultural pursuits.

The Senate had roots in the colonial past, and families or even individuals illustrate a continuity between the Council and its successor. James Bowdoin, William Sever, and Walter Spooner were among those who sat in both bodies. Two Cushings served before and four after 1776. Benjamin Lincoln was a councillor from 1753 to 1769, and his son of the same name sat briefly the next decade. Senator John Pitts, who was chosen from 1778 to 1783, succeeded his father, Councillor James Pitts; while the town of Stockbridge in Berkshire county furnished, first, Timothy Woodbridge to the Council and, then, his nephew Jaheel to the Senate.[3] So, too, Councillor Benjamin Greenleaf's cousin Jonathan became a senator, the two providing almost continuous service beginning in 1770.[4]

Samuel Holten, on the other hand, was of middle-class origin, and did not become prominent until the Revolution. He was the only son of a Danvers judge. His health did not permit him to attend college, but he studied medicine and practiced until 1775, when public service became his primary occupation. He was a prominent rebel, served in Congress, and sat almost continuously in the Senate.[5]

The new breed of senator is personified even more perfectly by Samuel Baker of Bolton, in Worcester County. Baker appears first in the Provincial Congress of 1774, and though he served for ten years in the Senate, little is known about him. Bolton had a wholly farming population, and it is probable that Baker and his father before him were ordinary yeomen. Amos Singletary of Sutton, in the same county, also began his political career in the first Provincial Congress. He was the first male child born in the town, where his father, a miller and farmer, left a modest estate of £218 11s 6d. Amos never went to school, but learned enough at home so that he could serve as justice of the peace. For that reason local historians refer to him as a lawyer, but actually he was a miller like his father, though perhaps more prosperous. He achieved fame (or notoriety) by vigorously criticizing aristocratic features in the Federal Constitution.[6] Men such as Baker and Singletary had estates somewhat above the average, and were clearly of exceptional ability; yet they must have shared the political views of their fellow farmers. The Senate thus had come to contain both aristocratic and democratic elements.

The history of the Massachusetts Senate unfolds on two different planes: an upper house in its relation to the lower, and a political body divided internally by the political conflicts of the era. In the former capacity, it occasionally performed the anticipated aristocratic function; in the latter, it was unexpectedly democratic. The original intent of the framers of the constitution had been to create a government of checks and balances in which the two houses represented the antithetical principles of democracy and aristocracy. The pre-1780 Council was criticized because it was not chosen independently of the House. Some men would simply have abolished it, but a majority, at least of those in power, sought to render the two branches truly separate. The democratically minded among them wished to eliminate property qualifications, but the

Senate ultimately was designed to contain primarily men of means. On the whole it did so, but, like the prewar Council, from its inception it was internally divided. By 1787 the primary conflict within the legislature was not between the upper house and the lower house but, in the words of one observer, "a jealousy between the Country interest and that of Sea Ports."[7] The opposing forces—whether they be called Shaysites and anti-Shaysites, or other names—competed for dominance in both houses, and the history of the Senate, as in other states, is a part of the larger history of Massachusetts politics. A complete review of the Senate's place in this context is impossible, chiefly because few roll-call votes were taken. Nevertheless, the influence of partisan politics must be briefly discussed.

The elections of 1785, which introduced a number of new men, can be regarded as a turning point. Previously there is no evidence of any important struggle for seats nor of any opposing tickets. There were more candidates than places, of course, but the losers do not seem to have advocated different policies. The number of votes cast remained nearly constant until 1787. In Worcester County, for example, the senators were at first a conservative group, generally well-to-do. Then came the upheaval climaxed by Shays' Rebellion. The county's senators were unsympathetic toward this movement. The result was a political revolution. In Worcester, three-and-a-half times as many men voted in 1787 as in any previous election, and all but one of the county's senators were defeated. The two candidates who received the highest vote had been active Shaysites, one of whom indeed was denied a seat because of his participation in the rebellion, thus clearing the way for the reappointment of a conservative holdover. The new men were small property holders of humble origin who became Antifederalists.

This development horrified many easterners and men of property. They actively worked to get out the vote for the next poll. The election campaign of April, 1788, was therefore exciting and hard fought. Tickets were circulated; in Worcester County the friends of law and order were urged to vote for the 1786 group. Their candidates were uniformly Federalists and had been hostile to the Shays movement.[8] On the other side were most of the incumbents and some additional candidates; they had been closely associated with the rebellion, were Antifederalists, and owned property of moderate size.[9] The latter ticket was victorious in Worcester, though the Federalists succeeded in recovering one seat there; elsewhere the Federalists gained at least a half-dozen seats. The Senate was once again firmly conservative, but clearly it would not now be—as indeed it had never been—an undeviatingly aristocratic body.[10]

Relations between the two houses were determined by the composition of the Senate and the changing constitutional arrangements. The series of events beginning in 1774 left Massachusetts without a legal government. Most of the new states drew up constitutions as quickly as possible in order to prevent anarchy. Connecticut, Rhode Island, and Massachusetts could fall back on their charters, but, whereas in the first two the executive branch and the upper houses continued to exist without interruption, in Massachusetts the executive authority was overthrown by revolutionary action, and the Massachusetts Government Act had legally superseded the charter in substituting the Mandamus Council for the elected upper house. Until a new constitution was adopted, therefore, the state had no legally defined second branch or executive. Under these circumstances the legislature proceeded pragmatically, and the respective powers and functions of the two houses were evolved in the process during 1775 and 1776.

In July, 1775, the legislature met without the governor. The lower house elected a Council in the usual way. That body then assumed executive as well as legislative functions. It first "concurred" with bills and then "consented to" them, the names of the councillors being listed after each such consent just as the governor's had been. This action was always taken at first by fifteen members (a majority), but in later sessions, when fewer than fifteen were present, this requirement was conveniently forgotten. When the Council acted as an executive body the term "Board" was sometimes used, as in colonial times.

Since the Council regarded itself as the executive branch as well as an upper house, it insisted upon performing the functions appropriate to both, thereby inheriting several disputes long characteristic of colonial legislatures. When the representatives adopted a resolution to appoint a committee for handling financial matters during the recess, the councillors unanimously refused to concur.

The representatives then agreed that the Council should be empowered to concur with all such expenditures, provided that the procedure not be considered as a precedent.[11] Thereafter controversies over such matters were avoided by agreements reached through joint committees. The constitution of 1780 gave the lower house exclusive power over money bills, but the Senate insisted that it had an equal right to originate a bill or resolve for granting money out of the treasury. The lower house never conceded this power, and in practice the Senate did not originate such measures; but it never abandoned the claim.[12]

Another debate concerned the power over appointments. The upper house claimed to have inherited all of the powers of the colonial executive, including the authority to make appointments. However, the lower house now attempted to transfer control over appointments from the executive to the legislature, and moreover to choose officials in joint session with the Council. Since the Council was a smaller body, the power over appointments would pass into the hands of the representatives. The lower house took the initiative in 1775 by appointing its share of a joint committee to consider the method of selecting militia officers. The Council at once unanimously dissented. A few days later the House chose General Joseph Frye to be commander of the Cumberland County militia, with instructions to fortify Falmouth. The upper house promptly objected, again unanimously.[13] The next day the Council (acting in its executive capacity) itself appointed Frye, and attempted to define the functions of the two branches by requesting that the representatives consider the plight of the town and grant necessary relief. The representatives replied that they had already done so.[14] The Council insisted that the House had not made adequate provision. The power of appointment, it asserted, was lodged in the Council, and the job of the House was to provide relief by legislation. Because of the emergency, however, the councillors agreed to join in a joint ballot. The House still insisted that executive decisions should be made by joint committee and appointments by joint ballot, a procedure that was in fact usually followed. The Council, however, never conceded the right, and once in a while made an appointment without consulting the lower house.[15]

The peculiar, partly executive character of the pre-1780 Council, and the force of habit, were evidenced in other ways. The

Council, until after independence, opened each session just as the governor had done, with a message: that of March 16, 1776, for example, recommended that the representatives encourage the manufacture of sulphur.[16] The lower house asked the Council to adjourn the legislature or to dissolve it, which was done in the traditional form. When the representatives passed a resolution for a proclamation of general Thanksgiving the Council rejected it, but instead issued one itself.[17] The Council also exercised emergency executive powers during recesses. In doing so it encountered the criticism that it was acting unconstitutionally; but obviously such action had to be taken at times, and the lower house authorized it to act if necessary.[18] As a rule, however, the representatives themselves assumed the functions of an executive body, and conflicts were prevented by frequent conferences, by the extensive use of joint committees, and by the evidently greater prestige of the lower house. The constitution of 1780, by creating an executive branch, put an end to most of these disputes.

The Council, and the Senate even more, favored conservative economic policies, though the difference between the two houses was minor until 1786. The Council supported high taxes and regular collections. Its message of December 4, 1776, is an exceedingly interesting and able argument in favor of a "sound" financial policy on the ground that unless heavy taxes were imposed, the paper money that was issued would have only an "immaginary value," and would depreciate so greatly that additional issues would not supply the state with more goods. The councillors were able, by such urging, to double the tax imposed. The upper house often resisted attempts by particular towns to obtain tax reductions, requests which were too frequently granted by the representatives,[19] and it was generally more careful in both getting and spending funds.[20] The influence of larger property holders was apparent when the Senate twice attempted to increase the poll tax.[21] The upper house at first opposed the regulation of prices, but had to give in.[22] On the other hand the Senate was more anxious than the lower house to sell confiscated estates, even for depreciated paper; some of the senators may have had a financial interest in the transactions.[23]

The most important economic contest concerned the relations between debtors and creditors during the Shays' Rebellion months of 1786–1787. By the autumn of 1786, the lower house had begun to respond to the general pressure in favor of debtors. The difference in attitude had been presaged as early as 1781, when an act making paper money legal tender had been repealed by a large margin in the Senate and by a very small one in the House.[24] Now the Senate defined its position by a series of votes which negatived each of the following propositions: whether a tender act would be compatible with the British treaty if no exception was made for British creditors; whether a law suspending the recovery of debts and the enforcement of court decisions against debtors would similarly be valid; and whether any tender act would be constitutional.[25] Nevertheless, the representatives passed a stay law and a law suspending executions. Both were rejected. Another grievance had been the appropriation of the impost for paying the state debt, instead of lightening the tax burden by using some of the funds for general expenses. The House attempted to divert half of the impost receipts into the public treasury, but the Senate refused.[26] Because of certain Senate opposition, the lower house did not act upon demands that lawyers' fees be reduced.[27] Later in the winter the Senate made itself even more unpopular by refusing to approve an act for the relief of poor men who were imprisoned for debt.[28] Not until the fall of 1787 did the Senate reluctantly allow the debtors some respite, but it continued to insist upon payment of the state debt by the impost and in 1788 put an end to a tender law.[29]

Several political questions also generated disputes within the legislature. The decision of the lower house to frame a new constitution in 1777 filled the councillors with apprehension. Alterations, they warned, should be made only with the utmost caution. The only major fault of the old government was the executive power of the governor, but this was now exercised by the Council, and the Council's interests were identical with those of the people. A new formula might divide the people, as it had in Pennsylvania, when they ought to be united.[30] The representatives disagreed, and claimed to have the support of public opinion; the Council thereupon surrendered.[31]

The next debate of importance concerned the attempt to grant Congress the power to collect a 5 percent tax on imports (the impost), and the payment by Congress to the Revolutionary officers of a lump sum in lieu of half pay for life ("commutation"). The two houses differed over the first impost bill, but eventually reached agreement.[32] By 1783, however, the public distrust of Congress' intentions and of the Army led the representatives to oppose any grant of permanent taxes and any special treatment of the officers. There followed a contest lasting for several months in which the anti-impost men tried first to defeat the impost bill entirely and then to amend it so as to restrict the power of Congress. The Senate journals do not make clear the situation there, but observers agreed that the upper house was almost unanimously in favor of both the impost and the commutation. Probably these measures were disliked by most farmers in the western two-thirds of the state.[33]

The Senate further annoyed western residents by rejecting a number of petitions for the establishment of new towns (though it approved others);[34] but it did not become really unpopular until the events of 1786. A clue to the Senate's position was its refusal, during an earlier disturbance in 1783, to permit the temporary adjournment of the court in Springfield.[35] In the autumn of 1786 the lower house again tried to avoid further disruption of court sessions by postponing them altogether, but the Senate agreed only to postpone the session of the Hampshire court,[36] and took firm steps to deal with the disturbance: it passed a bill authorizing trials for treason to be held in any county, so that Shaysites could be tried in some post-Revolutionary equivalent of Halifax (the House blocked this),[37] and another bill suspending writs of habeas corpus.[38] Public opinion was further affronted when the Senate tried to empower selectmen to draft men into the militia,[39] and pursued unpopular economic policies.

The election of early 1787 wrought something of a revolution even in the Senate, which then adopted a more conciliatory attitude. By a single vote it approved an act permitting legal actions to be taken before a local justice of the peace.[40] It also agreed to a reduction of taxes. However it continued to be basically unsympathetic to the Shaysites. After first approving a stay law for a limited time, and then agreeing (by a vote of thirteen to twelve) to extend the period, it insisted upon so short an extension that the bill failed entirely.[41] Attempts by the lower house first to remit fines imposed upon rebels, and then to pardon Shaysites, were vetoed.[42] These actions elicited considerable criticism and even suggestions that the Senate be abolished.[43] But, conversely, the Senate was vigorously defended as "your great barrier against the overgrown influence of some artful unpopular man."[44] Then in the spring of 1788, after the state had adopted the constitution, the Federalists and anti-Shaysites were victorious in the upper house, even though they were defeated in elections to the lower. The Senate, observed one Bostonian, "will be a very great check to an *Anti* and insurgent lower house."[45] And so, in fact, it proved to be. Indeed, it is remarkable that at a time when the popular majority was clearly Antifederal—as shown in the voting, first for the ratifying convention, and then for the House—the Senate was completely dominated by the opposite party.

No other disagreements were of major importance. The curious action of the Senate in rejecting a bill to repeal all laws respecting Loyalists perhaps was related to the upper house's enthusiasm for the sale of confiscated estates, as one source suggests, or perhaps was due to the absence of many senators at the time, as another commentator believed.[46] The two branches concurred on most measures not involving economic issues. The Senate was willing to grant a high salary to the president of Harvard, whereas the House was not—at least not to that particular president. The upper house was also more willing to spend money for a doctor who would care for the poor in Boston. But these are minor issues and even here the grounds of contention are not clear.

The most valuable function performed by the Senate was not in opposing measures desired by the House but in improving legislation through amendments. Most bills were introduced in the lower house after a joint committee had reported, and were then extensively revised in the upper house, especially after 1780. The journals almost never reveal the nature of these changes, but they were exceedingly numerous and evidently seldom controversial, though the representatives sometimes balked at amendments to money bills.[47] For example, an address to the inhabitants of Massachusetts was accepted with nineteen amendments. The lower house changed one, and submitted a new draft, which was then further amended and accepted.[48] During one day the Senate amended five measures and rejected three.[49] On another occasion it made twenty-six amendments to an excise bill, all of which were accepted.[50] A bill setting fees prompted eighteen changes, of which the representatives agreed to all but one.[51] It seems likely that this increased activity after 1780 reflected the new independence of the Senate, which enabled it to oppose the House on crucial matters of policy and also to act as an equal in the framing of all legislation. Therefore even when the Senate did not act as an aristocracy, it still functioned as a check upon the lower house, playing an important and useful role as a revisory body.

NEW HAMPSHIRE

New Hampshire, like Massachusetts, had two successive governments after the Revolution; but, whereas from as early as 1769 the composition and character of the Massachusetts Council were gradually modified, New Hampshire's upper house remained intact until 1776, and then was abruptly transformed. In that year the colonial Council was replaced by a body of the same name but of entirely different composition, consisting of twelve reputable freeholders chosen by the representatives. This form of government, obviously patterned after that of Massachusetts, continued until the adoption of a new constitution in 1784. The "Council" then became the "Senate" (which word will be used hereafter). It still contained twelve men, who now were required to have been residents of the state for seven years, and to possess a freehold estate worth £200 (the type of money is not specified). According to pre-Revolutionary probate records, slightly over half of the men owned property valued at more than that amount, including about three out of five farmers. Probably the requirement eliminated very few men likely to seek high office.

Beginning in 1776, each of the five counties was represented roughly in proportion to population. Rockingham, which contained Portsmouth, sent five men. Strafford, which included the rest of the maritime towns, had two, as did Hillsboro and Cheshire in the center of the state; but Grafton, along the Connecticut River, was entitled to only one. After 1784, senators were elected by the voters of a county—that is, anyone with town privileges. If the requisite number of candidates failed to win a majority, the senators who had been successful, together with members of the lower house, chose the rest from among the leading candidates in each county.

About half of the senators were elected in that way. The front-runners seem not to have differed significantly from the other principal candidates. Curiously, when popular elections replaced appointment by the representatives in 1784, the composition of the upper house did not change. Individuals were replaced, but the new men were very similar to their predecessors. It is possible that they were more willing to follow public opinion, though the proceedings of the legislature show no such development.

The nature of the New Hampshire Senate, like that of most of the state senates, derived in part from its limited membership and in part from its selection by the counties. To be known throughout an entire county, senators had to be men of prominence; and indeed most of them had established a reputation by serving as representatives or in some other office. Three out of five had been high-ranking officers during the War, and most of the rest had been active in other capacities. The Senate, then, contained many of the state's outstanding citizens. Included were three Wentworths (all wealthy); the Signers Josiah Bartlett, William Whipple, and Matthew Thornton; John and Woodbury Langdon; Wyseman Claggett, formerly the king's attorney; and George King, who inherited the Atkinson estate and took the name. One-third of the members were merchants, another third were lawyers or large landowners, and only a handful were farmers.

Nevertheless, the upper house was not an aristocratic body. Perhaps the House or the voters would have chosen no one but men of wealth and status had they been given the chance; but the opportunity was usually denied them because New Hampshire's small upper class was clustered in a limited area, whereas the senators came from all over the state. New Hampshire did not have great agricultural resources, and wealthy farmers were rare. Commerce was more lucrative, but unfortunately the state has a short coastline into which empties just one river. Only the Piscataqua directly benefited the state's merchants, and even that river, on which Portsmouth and Dover are located, has a small valley and does not give access to the interior. Five of the twelve senators therefore came from areas that simply did not produce men of wealth; besides which, most of the interior towns were of recent origin. Portsmouth, Dover, and the towns dependent on them could and did send members of the colony's established upper class, such as

George Frost, Nicholas Gilman, Pierse Long, John Pickering, Mesech Weare, and the Wentworths, but they could not control even all of the senators from the two southeastern counties. Rockingham County in particular always sent at least one or two men who came from the inland farming communities. The aristocratic element, never very large, had been further weakened by the Revolution; more important, direct, county-wide elections made the upper house a more democratic body than before.

As a result of these changes, the handful of wealthy men were greatly outnumbered by those who were well-to-do, and some senators were even less well off. Nearly one-third were merchants, but inland New Hampshire sent men who practiced various trades. Doctors, lawyers, and shopkeepers served with farmers of substantial means who often surveyed, kept a mill, or were justices of the peace on the side. A remarkably high proportion—about two-fifths —were born out of the state; several were immigrants from Europe. Most of the senators had achieved success with little help from their parents. The dozen who belonged to the colony's prominent old families were outnumbered by entirely self-made men. About half were the sons of respectable farmers or artisans. The typical New Hampshire senator was born in a small agricultural community within the state or in Massachusetts, from which he moved as a young man. The father was a small farmer, but the son, even if he homesteaded, quickly added some other skill and eventually derived most of his income from a nonfarm occupation. In doing so he earned far more than his parent: he became, in fact, well-to-do, one of the prominent men of his community, rising to near the top of the social order. The Revolution gave him a chance to distinguish himself, and he became active as a high-ranking Army officer, a member of the legislature, or an important civil officeholder.

This description is a composite of many quite different sorts of men, some of whom differ from the norm in almost every respect. Benjamin Bellows of Walpole (1741–1802) was such an exception: a representative from the interior but from a wealthy family. His father, Colonel Benjamin, had a large estate in Lunenburg, Massachusetts, where the senator was born. The colonel founded Walpole and owned much of the land; indeed the family was above average not only economically but in their education and style of life. The colonel gave away part of his estate before he died but still left nearly five thousand acres. Senator Benjamin moved to Walpole, where he became a storekeeper, a lieutenant colonel on active service, a justice of the peace, and, later in his career, a major general and a presidental elector for the Federalist party.[52] Another exception was Nicholas Gilman, whose ancestry was even more distinguished. His father, a merchant and a member of an old Exeter family, left an estate of £33,931 (probably equal to less than £5,000 lawful money). Nicholas (1731–1785) continued the family business, was treasurer first of the colony, then of the state, and was a senator from 1776 until his death. His son, another Nicholas, became adjutant general and attended the Federal Convention.[53] Such men as Bellows and Gilman demonstrate the continuity that marked the transition from colony to state.

Other senators typify the revolutionary atmosphere of those years. Jacob Abbott (1746–1821) fits the composite rather well. His father, Jacob (d. 1761), was a farmer and deacon in Hollis who left an estate of £4,908, equal to at most £700 lawful money. Jacob Jr. moved to the frontier, where he became a pioneer farmer. He sold the farm to his brother in about 1776 and concentrated on trade and milling. He served the town as justice, town clerk, and representative before his election to the Senate.[54] John Bell also rose from the status of small farmer. His father, John (1678–1743), immigrated from Ireland and homesteaded sixty acres which he increased to three hundred. The son evidently received some of his talent from his mother, who came from an educated family. John Jr. had only a common school education, but he read widely. He inherited the paternal farm, married a girl from a locally prominent family, and at once became a leading citizen, serving as representative, justice of the peace, town clerk, colonel, and elder of the church.[55]

Among those who were entirely self-made was Robert Means, who immigrated from Ireland with another young weaver and one shilling and sixpence between them. The two became weavers and peddlers in Merrimack, where Robert's partner remained and prospered. Robert moved to Amherst, married a minister's daughter, concentrated on trade, and eventually became wealthy.[56] Matthew Thornton came from Ireland with his parents as a child, studied medicine apparently on his own, moved to Londonderry, and became both a colonel in the provincial militia and a representative as early as 1758. Eventually he was a Signer and a judge.[57]

Although Means, Thornton, Abbott, and Bell were certainly not aristocrats, they did differ from their compatriots in the lower house. Whereas the Senate consisted mostly of merchants, lawyers, and others with nonfarm occupations, the House had a substantial majority of men engaged solely in agriculture. Indeed, most of them were small farmers like most of their constituents. Only one out of eight was a merchant or a lawyer; one out of five was a doctor, artisan, miller, innkeeper, or had some other nonfarm occupation. The senators lived in towns; the representatives in rural villages. Most of the senators were at least well-to-do; most of the representatives were of moderate property.[58] The House contained a few men of upper-class origin, but a very large majority came from humble backgrounds.

Because of their somewhat different make-up, the two houses might be expected to have had frequent disputes. The contrary was the case: relations between the two houses were uniformly harmonious. One practice can be credited with precluding serious disputes: on subjects of major importance all the members convened in a joint committee of the whole and agreed upon the action to be taken. Thus, money bills (which originated in the lower house) were never rejected and almost never amended by the Senate. Debates over the date of adjournment, and many other potential disputes, were avoided by consultation. Indeed, the Senate did not truly fulfill its intended function as a check upon the House of Representatives.

Some disputes did occur which reflected the characteristics of the two bodies. The Senate, in which the eastern counties were especially strong, preferred to meet in Portsmouth on the coast or, as a second choice, in Exeter, a few miles away, whereas the representatives wanted to meet anywhere other than in Portsmouth, preferably in Concord on the Merrimack.[59] Disagreements sometimes arose over the choice of various officials. The Senate always insisted upon its right to vote separately from the lower house lest it be outnumbered and deprived of its rightful equality.[60]

These were minor points. The only issue of any real consequence was economic: the Senate consistently followed a pro-creditor monetary policy. The House tried to maintain artificially the value of the various state and federal certificates and to accept them for taxes at a higher rate than their actual worth, whereas the Senate preferred to let them find their true value and was reluctant to receive them for taxes. The House also sought to issue new certificates for a part of the principle on the old ones; the Senate objected and tried to reduce the amount so issued.[61] The lower house was much more sympathetic toward the general demand for lower taxes and attempted to keep down the costs of government. It tried, on one occasion, to encourage the payment of the federal debt at a depreciated rate; the Senate did not entirely prevent this but adopted a less permissive policy.[62] The Senate was a little more favorably disposed toward nonresident landowners,[63] and tried to repeal an act that had protected debtors from being imprisoned when they offered real or personal property in settlement.[64] On the whole, however, decisions of the two houses, with few exceptions, were identical. The Senate had its functions: it reviewed and sometimes rejected the numerous private bills and resolutions adopted in response to petitions, and it sometimes—though infrequently—made amendments; but its role is best described as innocuous. Newspapers contained no criticisms of the upper house, and there is no evidence that anyone disapproved of its existence or of its policies.[65]

The four major factors that contributed to this harmony have already been analyzed: the state's social structure was democratic rather than aristocratic, and the small upper class, limited almost entirely to the coast, could no longer dominate the state; most of the senators, although they engaged in nonagricultural occupations and were considerably more prosperous than the general populace, belonged by birth and experience to the same class of property holders as did the representatives; the senators were chosen either by the same voters who chose the lower house, or just as often by the representatives themselves; and the similarity of outlook was reinforced by the continuous cooperation between the two branches in making major decisions. There were exceptions to this consensus, and there perhaps were senators who dissented from the majority (the records contain no votes). But most of the members clearly were interested not in checking the popular will as expressed by the House of Representatives, but in furthering policies that were approved by both houses.

CONNECTICUT

Connecticut's legislature was little changed by the coming of independence. The crisis, such as it was, had passed a decade earlier, at the time of the Stamp Act, when the potentially Loyalist element was purged. During the years 1774–1776, when most other councils were being entirely replaced, all of the assistants were reelected regularly except the Anglican William S. Johnson. Nor did the composition of the upper house change significantly during the postwar era. The assistants almost invariably continued to be college graduates and judges. Most of them served in Congress. Lawyers still predominated, comprising three-fifths of the membership. The rest were businessmen, for farmers were rarely chosen. As before, the assistants were well-to-do or, in a few cases, wealthy. The geographical balance of power had shifted slightly eastward and markedly northward, suggesting that the farmers, though still choosing the same sort of men to represent them, had increased their influence. Perhaps a similar trend is discernible in the social origins of the assistants. Before the War, over half were descended from the colony's established upper class. After 1776, a majority were of undistinguished ancestry; their fathers seldom were men of wealth, and more often were ministers or farmers. Roger Sherman had already emerged at the time of the Fitch purge; and others of humble birth were chosen in increasing numbers, such as Oliver Ellsworth and Samuel Huntington, who started as an apprentice to a cooper. On the whole, however, the major characteristic of the upper house was its resemblance to the prewar Council.

Although the citizens of Connecticut did not alter their form of government, not everyone was satisfied with the role of the upper house. The adoption of new constitutions by other states attracted attention. One writer noted approvingly (but erroneously) that Virginia's senators were chosen by counties, and asserted that Connecticut's system was "too much expos'd to the intreagues of designing men" because the voters could not know candidates who lived far away from them. He suggested that each town should nominate one person, and that the General Assembly should then select from that list four of each county.[66] On the other hand, Timothy Dwight believed that the Connecticut system ensured the continuance in office of men with ability and experience;[67] while "A Freeman" agreed that the councillors were men of integrity and patriotism, who truly represented the people and essentially checked the lower house.[68]

No attack of consequence occurred until 1783, when a series of disputes between the two branches led to a protest movement. The controversy developed primarily over relations between the state and Congress. Specifically, as in Massachusetts, the upper house favored, while the lower house opposed, both the impost and the commutation. Moreover, the House of Representatives wanted to retire the entire debt, federal and state, through a state import tax, instead of giving Congress the means to do so. At stake were the amount of authority delegated to Congress, special concessions to an officer class, and local financial policy. The proposed state impost was designed especially to protect Connecticut's manufacturers by taxing such articles as hats and clocks, and also to relieve farmers of the burden imposed by a general tariff or some other state tax. Much of the weight of the 5 percent impost would be borne by trade, but the merchants were so eager to achieve financial stability and a stronger central government that they generally supported the measure. The center of opposition to the impost and commutation lay in the agricultural areas, especially those remote from the coast.

After the assistants had unsuccessfully supported the federal impost and commutation, and rejected the state impost, there were angry attacks against the upper house. Some people even suggested abolishing it through a revision of the constitution.[69] But more immediately an effort was made to elect members who would oppose the impost. In the spring of 1784 a convention of delegates, chosen by many town meetings, met at Middletown, drew up an address to be circulated, and nominated a ticket for the upper house. The convention urged the election of a number of incumbents and several new men. The special favorite was Erastus Wolcott, a well-to-do farmer of distinguished ancestry who had won popular favor as a general during the War. He had only a common school education, but his father had been governor. Wolcott took the popular side, and a few years later was to advocate extensive tax reforms which would shift the burden from the farmers, especially poorer ones, to merchants and others.[70] The convention's candidate for governor, Matthew Griswold, was elected. However, Wolcott and six others backed by the convention were defeated. The election was in fact a victory for the incumbents and their supporters in the lower house. With that victory, opposition to the impost and commutation virtually ceased.[71]

The controversy involving the upper house, however, continued for more than a year. Suspicion of its aristocratic propensities was aroused during 1784 when it passed bills giving to the governor and Council supreme executive authority and repealing a 1779 law that had given freemen the right to elect Connecticut's delegates to Congress. Both measures were rejected by the House of Representatives.[72] In the same year a change of membership was occasioned by a law which prohibited the governor, lieutenant governor, assistants, and other high officials from serving as judges.[73] As a result, which was perhaps intended, four assistants resigned, and among their replacements were two favorites of the Middletown convention, Erastus Wolcott and James Wadsworth.[74] Within the next year William Hillhouse and William Williams, who were of the same political persuasion, entered the upper house. So extensive was the change that now the conservative nationalist Jeremiah Wadsworth was hoping that "our upper House will be purged."[75]

Conflicts between the two houses now seem to have ceased. Perhaps the absence of legislative journals conceals antagonisms, but these cannot have been serious, for no notice was taken of them in other sources. The substitution of the four new men seems to have modified the conservative bias of the assistants. Presumably they continued to act as a check upon a somewhat more democratically inclined lower house, but obviously both houses now represented, as they always had done, much the same interests in society.

RHODE ISLAND

The people of Rhode Island, like those of Connecticut, did not have to wait until 1776 to reform their upper house. The major change, such as it was, occurred during 1774 and 1775 when almost every magistrate was replaced, though only a few of the old members opposed independence. This wholesale displacement did not result from a basic shift of power. The social, economic, geographical, and religious characteristics of the upper house were scarcely different after the Revolution than before it. A few changes did take place, which are evident when the magistrates of 1763–1774 are contrasted with those of 1778–1788. Most marked was a geographical shift: the post-Revolutionary magistrates came less often from the commercial centers bordering Narragansett Bay, and more frequently from the inland, agricultural communities. Newport, in particular, lost its influence. The geographical change was accompanied by a slight reduction in the number of merchants. Fewer Anglicans were chosen, probably due to a decline in the prestige of that denomination.

Far more impressive than these differences, however, was the striking similarity between the upper house before and after the Revolution. In both bodies farmers, though not a majority, formed the largest occupational group. There was no difference in the amount of the magistrates' property: only about one-fifth were wealthy, while almost twice as many had moderate incomes. As before, about a fourth belonged to prominent old families and nearly all of the rest came from ordinary backgrounds. Very few were immigrants. More magistrates now were college men, but this fact is due not to any basic change in their circumstances but to the fact that Rhode Island College had been founded just before the War. On the whole the differences were minor.

Rhode Island's upper house therefore continued to be a relatively democratic body. Although it consisted of only twelve members, the state's population was so small that the number of voters per magistrate was lower than in any other such house. Nowhere else did farmers' sons with little property have so much influence. The average magistrate was not an average Rhode Islander, for although most of the voters were small farmers, they chose townsmen to represent them. Yet it is testimony to the democratic nature of the upper house that a considerable number of its members were so ordinary that almost nothing about them is known. Robert Brown, for instance, who served one year, was evidently a substantial farmer from South Kingston: a man of that name owned seven slaves in 1774. The Browns, who were Presbyterians, had been in the town for several generations. One line produced a governor, but probably Robert's father was John (1696–1764), who is obscure.[76] The Hazard or Haszard family contributed four members to the upper house, who may profitably be contrasted with families in other states—with Wentworths of New Hampshire, Morrises of New York, Carrolls and Lloyds of Maryland, Lees of Virginia, Horrys of South Carolina. The family collectively owned several thousand acres in the rich farm land of South Kingston; but the property had been subdivided so often that the magistrates' fathers, who were of about the fourth generation, were nothing more than prosperous farmers. Thus the magistrate Enoch (1735–1785) was a fourth son who inherited only two hundred acres and had five slaves in 1774.[77] These men were kept responsive to public opinion by annual elections, and indeed they seem to have been remarkably subject to popular control.

During the 1780's, political factionalism in Rhode Island waned while economic conflict flourished. The lines of battle were now debtor *vs.* creditor, merchant *vs.* farmer, urban *vs.* rural. Yet these contests did not greatly affect relations between the two houses because both houses were divided in much the same way. When, in 1786, a political revolution swept paper money forces into power, the upper house was transformed just as much as was the lower: all but four magistrates were displaced by that single election and two others were defeated the following year. The fact that agricultural towns usually controlled both houses meant, as before the War, that controversies between them were seldom serious.

Probably because of this there was no effort to change the procedure by which the magistrates were chosen. Rhode Island cherished its form of government, and although there was an effort to alter the method of representation, no one suggested reforming the upper house. One writer, to be sure, opposed any revision of the government for fear such a revision might lead to an abolition of the House of Magistrates because of a belief that it stood in the way of the House of Delegates;[78] but this fear had no foundation. The method by which the upper house was selected was criticized during 1786 by a writer who felt that nominations were made by "a few Gentlemen" whereas they should be made by the freemen. The Connecticut system, he suggested, would be preferable.[79] This objection can hardly be taken seriously, for a few weeks later the paper money party gained control of both branches of the legislature, and no further criticisms were published.

The position taken on state and national affairs by the two houses depended upon which groups controlled them. When they were in the same hands, matters went along peacefully with minor disagreements on either side. When the two houses were controlled by opposing interests, differences between them grew; but within a year they would either be resolved, or else the two bodies might reverse themselves as their make-up altered. There was little consistency, and it is difficult to identify any distinguishing viewpoint of the magistrates. They were active enough, occasionally initiating legislation, frequently amending measures (including money bills),[80] and rejecting a large number of bills or resolves originating in the lower house; indeed, the magistrates "nonconcurred" with over one hundred votes during the years 1776–1787. They obviously performed a useful function in reviewing legislation; but they can hardly be said to have constituted a check, for rarely was there any basic quarrel between the two branches.

One type of legislation needing careful scrutiny was that granting money to the real or pretended public creditors. These bills were usually sent up by the delegates and then considered by the magistrates, who often reduced the sums granted.[81] Only rarely was the amount increased, though on one occasion a former magistrate received more than the House of Delegates had granted.[82] On the other hand, the delegates sometimes reduced or even rejected sums appropriated by the upper house.[83] The magistrates also reviewed the salaries or expense money granted to various officials, but they did not adopt a consistent policy. When, in February, 1777, the lower house voted four dollars per day to members of Congress, the upper house dissented because "this House do not think it a sum adequate to their services." Yet in 1780 delegates were granted eight dollars by the lower house and only five and one-half by the magistrates. The latter twice reduced the salary of the general treasurer,[84] but their action was not taken because of sympathy for the taxpayers: they tried to raise their own per diem and were prevented by the lower house.[85]

The magistrates showed a similar lack of consistency with respect to other financial affairs. During the War they occasionally cut expenses, as when they twice rejected bounties for the militia;[86]

and once they defeated a lower house resolve for the speedy collection of taxes from delinquent towns.[87] In 1780 they showed themselves more willing than the delegates to assist the poor: when the lower house instructed tax assessors to lower the poll tax "as the Circumstances of the several Towns" seemed to require, the upper substituted the clause "to consider the Circumstances of the Poor in their respective Towns, and not to lay the Poll Tax upon such as they shall think unable to pay the same."[88] After the War, the magistrates, now influenced perhaps by the creditor class, twice permitted payment of interest to public creditors when the delegates had refused.[89] Twice the upper house showed a greater sense of responsibility than the lower by increasing the amount of money provided for Congress.[90] When, in the spring of 1786, the paper money forces gained control of the government, the upper house agreed to an issue of paper money and the postponement of taxes,[91] though it did reduce the amount of money issued from £160,000 to £100,000.[92] The unity of the legislature on these matters is typical: earlier financial affairs and relations with Congress (the 5 percent impost, for example) had been arranged without disagreement.

Magistrates and delegates usually concurred on treatment of Loyalists. The upper house on a few occasions showed a disposition to lenity, but at other times acted with severity.[93] The two houses differed over the proper mode of representation, with the upper suggesting that taxes paid, as well as numbers, should be considered.[94] There was a debate also over who should be permitted to sit in the legislature. When the House of Delegates voted to exclude justices of the superior court (called judges) from the legislature, the magistrates—several of whom were judges—voted to exclude those of the inferior courts (justices of the peace); but the delegates, who either were or hoped to become justices, defeated the amendment. Subsequently, the magistrates tried to prohibit all plural office-holding. The delegates did not reply.[95]

In the May election of 1787 a slight shift of power occurred so that the upper house became somewhat more "federal." The magistrates, who had earlier opposed sending delegates to the Federal Convention, now reversed themselves, and at the same time voted to repeal all acts repugnant to the treaty with England. Both measures were defeated by the delegates.[96] Later in the year the upper house attempted to impose much heavier taxes, and tried also to aid owners of state securities. The delegates rejected both of these proposals.[97] The period thus ended on an unusual note of discord; but even then the magistrates were not successful in their opposition. The relations between the two houses during the period, taken as a whole, demonstrated that, despite the different method of election and the fact that the delegates represented the towns and the magistrates the entire state, the members of the two houses were fundamentally similar and were agreed on almost all basic issues.

New England's senates were the most nearly democratic of all the upper houses, except for that of North Carolina. Only one-fifth of the members were wealthy, less than half as many as in other states. Men of small property were much more numerous, comprising over a third of the whole number compared with less than one-fifth elsewhere. All four upper houses were somewhat more conservative than the lower houses, especially in regard to economic matters; but the difference between them was minor except for a brief period in Massachusetts. All four were divided internally, probably in a way similar to the factional lines elsewhere; but the rather inadequate evidence suggests that the parties were less clearly defined than in such states as New York and New Jersey. Again, Massachusetts may be an exception, but only after 1785.

During the great majority of sessions the New England senates enjoyed power nearly equal to that of the lower houses, and contributed greatly to the legislative process by their careful scrutiny of petitions and expenditures, their extensive revision of bills, and their occasional rejection of bad measures. The aristocratic role was decidedly subordinate to, and even to a great extent replaced by, this important revisory function. The councils had also acted in that capacity; but for them (in most colonies) it was a role of secondary importance. Now it had become primary.

Post-Revolutionary Senates: A Summary

*A*fter the states declared their independence, they re-formed their governments to meet new needs and opportunities. The colonial councils were replaced by radically different bodies, usually called senates. Connecticut and Rhode Island retained their Assistants and Magistrates unchanged. Nine of the other eleven states also established bicameral legislatures. The new upper houses no longer had to defend the prerogative, and were shorn of their connection with the executive branch. They were almost entirely legislative bodies. In general they were equal in power to the lower houses, but seven could not initiate money bills and one could not originate any law whatever.

As a rule they were not intended to be democratic: the lower houses represented the people, so the senates were supposed to represent a different element in society, variously referred to as "property" or the "aristocracy." The senates were to be removed from popular control and brought under the influence of property by various devices. In some instances terms were longer than the annual ones of the lower house. Maryland's senators served for five years, New York's and Virginia's for four, Delaware's for three, and South Carolina's for two. The senates usually were small bodies averaging about fifteen members. With the exception of Maryland, Connecticut, and Rhode Island, they represented districts rather than the state as a whole. In two cases—New York and Virginia—these districts included more than one county. The most common system was for each county to form an electoral unit. Massachusetts and New Hampshire tried to apportion representation according to taxes paid. In the other states—North and South Carolina, Delaware, and New Jersey—each county sent an equal number of representatives.

The proviso most expected to assure aristocratic influence was the property requirement. Its effect, however, has been exaggerated. Probably almost no person who lacked a freehold, and exceedingly few who possessed less than the average amount of property, would be a serious contender for a seat in an upper house. On the basis of this assumption, Virginia, North Carolina, Delaware, New York, Connecticut, Rhode Island, and perhaps New Hampshire excluded few, if any, candidates. Farmers of substantial means could hold office in Massachusetts, while in the other states, though the qualification was more restrictive, one did not have to be rich to serve and some men of small property were chosen without being challenged.

Certain other constitutional provisions may have had more influence than the property requirement. Maryland's electoral college was unique and proved a brilliant success in rendering the Senate a stronghold of conservatism. The system used in New Hampshire and Massachusetts, whereby only the candidates who obtained majorities were successful, with the victorious senators and the representatives filling the remaining places, restricted popular control, as did the practice of filling vacancies by a method other than popular vote. Connecticut's system ordinarily led to the re-election of incumbents. Still, despite these attempts to dilute or —to use a favorite word of the time—to refine the democratic influence, the great majority of senators were chosen for short terms by small property holders.

The composition of the senates testifies to the failure of the upper class to retain its control. Only in South Carolina and Maryland did men of wealth constitute a majority. In Virginia they came close; but elsewhere they formed a proportion as low as one-fifth, averaging certainly less than one-third and probably one-fourth, depending upon the delimitation of "wealth." The occupational groups that made up the colonial "better sort"—large landowners, merchants, and lawyers—contributed barely half of the senators, and, if South Carolina and Maryland are excepted, they could not muster a majority. If social origin rather than wealth or occupation is considered more important in constituting an aristocracy, the elite was even less successful, furnishing only one-fourth of the whole number. Fewer than one in five senators were educated men.

Still, although the senates failed adequately to embody the aristocratic principle, they did protect property rights and the status quo far better than did the lower houses. Like the councils, they opposed paper money and pro-debtor laws; they were more apt to support Congress; they favored higher taxes and regular collections, defended Loyalists, and sided with the eastern, creditor, upper-class, urban elements against westerners, farmers, and debtors. Such an unqualified statement, however, is misleading. Certainly the senates, consisting of the more well-to-do citizens of each state, tended to adopt these policies, but they did so occasionally rather than consistently, and often to little avail. For example, in only one state where the lower house made a determined effort to obtain paper money did the senate successfully oppose it. Even worse, from the aristocratic point of view, the upper houses in Rhode Island and North Carolina almost never played the conservative role; those in New York and New Jersey did so only sporadically; and others were not much more reliable.

A factor of major importance in changing the character of the senates was the development of political alignments. The course followed by the upper houses was determined increasingly not by their kinship to the House of Lords but by the balance of power in party conflicts. Although the emergence of parties was more advanced in some states than in others, their rudiments at least can be discerned everywhere. Sectionalism was almost always a key characteristic; and other economic and social distinctions also seem to have been significant. As a rule, the descendants of the colonial upper class voted together against the men who rose to power during the Revolution; men of large property tended to oppose those of smaller estate; merchants, lawyers, and large landowners joined forces, as did ordinary farmers or their representatives. In each case, the upper-class group was stronger in the senate, and conflicts between the two houses were most likely to occur when the other group controlled the lower house.

The early emergence of opposing groups was significant, but the growth of parties was only just beginning. Most of the time the senators were unaffected by parties; this was especially true prior to about 1783. The senates ordinarily neither defended particular economic interests nor served as the instruments of faction. In fact, they had become almost indistinguishable from the members of the lower houses, except that they were somewhat more conservative and, perhaps, wiser. The senate's primary function was that of a revisory body. This role was old, but its extent and importance were new. As a result, the citizens of the new country eventually found it necessary to re-evaluate the bicameral system. Previously accepted theories no longer fit the conditions, and political thought began to change pragmatically in response to realities.

Part Three

THE UPPER HOUSE
IN REVOLUTIONARY AMERICA

$\mathcal{B}$OTH CONTEMPORARY political thought and custom were available as guides to the American statesmen in remodeling their governments. During the colonial period, certain political ideas of European origin had come to be generally accepted in America. One was the concept of a balanced government, in which power was divided, usually into three parts.[1] One part, which we would call today the executive branch, embodied what was then called the monarchical element, admired for its efficiency. A second part was democratic, necessary to give the government popularity. Finally, an aristocratic influence was needed for its wisdom. The last was usually lodged in an upper house of the legislature, ordinarily modeled on the Roman Senate or the English House of Lords. William Smith's plan for a general government in 1766, calling for an American parliament with a council of at least twenty members appointed by the Crown, was in this tradition. "To preserve their Independency," he observed, the members "ought to be Men of fortune, and hold their Places for Life; with some honorable Distinctions to their Families, as a Lure to prevent the Office from falling into Contempt."[2] A minority view rejected the idea of a balanced government and preferred to concentrate all authority in a single, popular branch, for "a well-regulated Democracy is most equitable."[3] However, in most colonies the councils, though imperfect, had proved their usefulness, and they were retained by the states in the altered form of senates. During the next decade the nature and functions of the upper houses evolved rapidly, and their new character reinforced the belief in their value. The Fathers of the Federal Constitution successfully enshrined the bicameral principle. By 1788 the evolution of council into senate was complete.

CHAPTER 7

THE UPPER HOUSE IN CONTEMPORARY THOUGHT

*D*URING THE COLONIAL PERIOD the colonists had little control over the legal form and designated functions of their upper houses. In the practical conduct of government, however, they were able to exercise considerable influence on all political institutions. They had the ability, if they had so desired, to accord the councils so much respect and authority—to strengthen the aristocratic or even the monarchical elements within them—that they would have become more powerful than the House of Lords. Alternatively, they could have chosen severely to curtail the functions of the upper house, perhaps even to deny the bicameral principle: they might have regarded the councils as exclusively executive bodies, and concentrated all power in the elected assemblies, thus strengthening the democratic element. With few exceptions they followed a middle course. The councils were never permitted to become dominant, nor were they rendered powerless.

The actions and attitudes of the colonists depended partly upon local circumstances and partly upon the political philosophy of influential leaders. The major attacks upon the councils occurred where they were intimately associated with the prerogative, and consequently were antagonistic to the aspirations of the lower houses. The council then became, in the opinion of the colonials, merely an agent of the governor, an arm of the executive authority rather than an upper house.

The influence of the governor over the council was most perva-

sive in the southern colonies, except Virginia, and was symbol-
ized or in some cases was partly caused by plural office-holding.
The placemen, particularly if they were not natives, and despite
any economic and social attachments to the colonies they may have
had, were regarded as alien to colonial society; and the councils in
which they were numerous were therefore looked upon as being
opposed to rather than a part of local institutions. Moreover, in
practice, where the placemen were strong, the prerogative was
effectively defended, and the councils often seemed to have no
value other than the negative one of resisting the lower house.
Even in Virginia, "E. F." felt that the councils served no useful
purpose. They consisted, he wrote, of "only twelve private gentlemen," whose assent to the laws was "merely farcical; for, as they
are creatures of the crown, and removeable at pleasure, they never
can be considered as a separate branch of government from the
crown. Their power is no more than a faint and distant emanation
of royalty, which passes through the obscuring medium of a gover-
nour; and, when it reaches them, is scarcely *darkness* visible."[1]

No attack on the Council's legislative authority developed in
Georgia because there the lower house was too weak effectively to
challenge the royal government. In North Carolina the Council was
accused of being merely an agent of the governor, not an "intermediate body of the legislature," but the issue was not pressed. In
Maryland, in 1762, the Council was denied legislative power, on
the ground that its members owed their existence entirely to the
proprietor, who secured them to his interest by dispensing favors.
After that year, however, the Council acted without challenge as an
upper house.

A more significant attack upon the Council's legislative authority occurred in South Carolina. In that colony the appointment of
placemen in the late colonial period, together with the inactivity of
several native Carolinians, caused the Council to pass under the
control of the governor and to become alienated from the ruling
merchant-planter elite. By 1773, the members of the Commons
were insisting that the Council was not an upper house and never
had been one. The argument, as presented in court by Edward Rutledge and accepted by Judges Rawlins Lowndes and George Gabriel Powell, was based upon the assumption that an upper house
could exist constitutionally only as an independent branch, like the

House of Lords, whereas the Council existed at pleasure. Lowndes agreed that the Council could refuse its assent to laws, but insisted that this power was derived from its association with the governor, who was instructed to approve of laws only if the Council passed them.[2]

The point of this argument was not that the upper house should be abolished, but that the council was not a proper legislative body. During the colonial period there was virtually no objection to a bicameral legislature. In most colonies the existence of the council was not challenged at all; only when its nature and functions departed from the colonists' prescriptions did it encounter serious criticism.

The colonial theorists—the vocal element in society—adhered to the body of political ideas associated with the term "Whig." Unlike the "Tory" concept of government, which concentrated all power in the monarchy, and the "Democratic," which diffused it among the people, Whig theory accepted the British form of government as they understood it. That government the Whigs defined as consisting of three parts, which represented a balance of the three major elements in society and polity: the monarchical, the aristocratical, and the democratical. The colonial councils ought to be the equivalent, as nearly as conditions permitted, of the House of Lords. They should therefore possess the following qualities: independence of the executive, permanence, and upper-class membership.

The basic weakness of the councils, according to the Whig view, was that they depended upon the Crown for their existence, and the members held office at pleasure instead of for life. In England, wrote Richard Henry Lee, the Lords consisted of a "powerful body of Nobles, independent in the material circumstances of hereditary succession to their titles and seats in the second branch of the Legislature." But in Virginia, there was no such "just equilibrium" because the councillors were "appointed by the crown, and their places held by the precarious tenure of pleasure only."[3] The colonial council as a result was only an imitation of the Lords, vastly inferior in "Influence, Privileges and Stability," a mere tool of the ministry.[4] Therefore the upper house, which ought to be a separate branch of government checking both the governor and the lower house, was allied with the former. Its loyalty was cemented by executive and judicial powers and offices, so that it combined the functions of the Lords with those of the Privy Council.

The reaction in Massachusetts to the Mandamus Council suggests that New Englanders shared these ideas. A convention in Middlesex County resolved that "there must be an Equilibrium in the Legislative Body, without which constitutional Check, they cannot be said to be a free People." The new councillors, serving at pleasure, would be nothing but "Tools and Creatures." Other conventions also stressed the need for an independent upper house.[5]

Despite the fact that nowhere outside of New England was the council independent of the executive, there was little demand that it be entirely abolished; and, in fact, the colonists did not have the power to do so. All they could do was to carry on a sporadic fight, where necessary, to reduce its influence. But more important, the colonials did not want to abolish the council, because the dominant minority, perhaps the majority, regarded an upper house as a positive good. Even the South Carolina radical Christopher Gadsden asserted that he was not inimical to the council if it consisted of men "interested in, and connected with, the province"; while in Massachusetts the Mandamus Council was promptly replaced by an upper house chosen in the old way.[6]

Apologists argued that, properly constructed, the council would check both the governor and the people. They insisted that even in Maryland the councillors would protect the welfare of the colony against "any wicked measures of an oppressive governor" and would not countenance "any encroachment of the Proprietor on the liberty, privilege, or property of the people."[7] And in fact the councillors did sometimes side with the lower house against the executive. Perhaps more important in the eyes of colonial aristocrats, the council could check the democratic impulse; for if the prominent colonial leaders were determined to defend their rights against the Crown, they were equally determined to protect their power against popular assault. Democracy they considered commendable—at least in theory—but only when properly confined. In most colonies they had little to worry about until the Revolutionary movement began to poison the people's minds (so they said) with a "levelling spirit,"[8] though in New England the strength of the democratic elements had already caused some alarm and had even occasioned suggestions that a greater admixture of monarchy or aristocracy would be advisable.[9] Elsewhere attention was directed toward the value of the council in checking the "violence of a levelling, popular assembly."[10] Too often, it was feared, the upper house lacked that "Balance against popular Weight, which distinguishes the Parent Kingdom."[11] Above all, an aristocratic council, rendered independent, could exercise a wise and just influence. Its members, conspicuous for "Family Connections, Influence, and Property," would guard against encroachments on property; and as men of liberal education they would guarantee good government.[12]

These considerations explain why, outside of the Carolinas and Maryland, the council was so seldom criticized: in most colonies the councils did consist of men of fortune—and thus did represent the aristocratic element. Moreover, in such colonies as Virginia, New York, and New Jersey, the councillors were by no means subservient to the governor, but reflected the views of the dominant group in colonial society. The same was true in the New England colonies other than New Hampshire. The theory of a balanced government suited colonial political figures because it justified their resistance to both monarchy and democracy, and at the same time it also justified upper-class rule. The councils were subjected to criticism only when they failed to perform their aristocratic function. Therefore when independence came the upper class tried only to purge the councils of their monarchical taint, not to destroy them as houses of the legislature.

Here a qualification must be introduced. These theories of government were held by the articulate segment of colonial society, not by the great majority of citizens. The latter may have felt quite differently; indeed in New England even before the Revolution the upper houses were being shorn of some aristocratic elements and partially democratized. There, demands were multiplying for equal representation of every part of a colony, a principle that circumstances were encouraging in Rhode Island and Connecticut, and that was to some extent legally established in Massachusetts. Plural office-holding was attacked in Massachusetts,[13] and in Connecticut a writer was urging that "every trade, calling, and occupation" be represented.[14] Such ideas probably ran counter to those of most upper-class colonials, but they may have been held by a majority of the ordinary citizens.

THE DEMOCRATIC IMPULSE

The foregoing analysis is based not so much upon statements made during the colonial period, of which few can be found, as upon the actions taken by the legislatures, and even more upon what was said and done during the first years of independence. From 1776 to 1780 most of the states established new governments based upon the ideas and experiences of the colonial past. Since experiences differed from colony to colony and ideas differed within colonies, the result was a good deal of diversity in both thought and action. Some states, in freeing their upper houses from executive control, endowed them with more power than before, while others eliminated the aristocratic element entirely and subordinated the upper house to the lower.

At one extreme were those who wanted a purely democratic government and regarded the upper house as antidemocratic. One of the best expressions of this view was the essay by "Spartanus." Government, he wrote, should represent everyone: farmers as well as merchants, "people in high life" as well as "the poorer sort, who are perhaps nine tenths of the useful part of mankind." There were, he asserted, four types of government: the monarchical, the aristocratical, the democratical, and the mixed. The last had several branches, as in Great Britain, each checking the other. "Proper *Democracy* is where the people have all the power in themselves, choose whom they please for their head for a time, and dismiss him when they please; make their own laws, choose all their own officers, and replace them at pleasure." This is the best form of government. A bicameral legislature must be avoided, "because a plurality causes perpetual contention & waste of time," as the history of Rome, England, and New Hampshire proved.[15] Similarly, "Clitus" from Massachusetts was willing to abolish the posts of governor, lieutenant governor, and Council, which had proved nothing but "a check and clog to business of consequence."[16] "The Considerate Freeman" told his fellow Pennsylvanians that an upper house, "consisting of a small number of grandees, can at any time gratify their ambition, and thirst for power at the expense of the people." Moreover, there was no need of a body to revise legislation or guard against an abuse of power. Annual elections by the free voice of the people, rotation in office, open sessions, the weekly publication of votes, and laws presented for the people's consideration before they took effect, made every freeman a counsellor, so that "the negative lies in the whole body politic." This formed "a council as much to be preferred to the legislative council of these gentlemen, as the wisdom and virtue of the whole state is to be preferred to that of twenty or thirty of our gentry."[17]

Where these ideas were dominant, unicameral legislatures were established. In Georgia, democratic theory was reinforced by colonial experience; in Pennsylvania, by the tradition of unicameralism. In Vermont, the democratic impulse emanating from Connecticut, western Massachusetts, or the New Hampshire frontier may have been aided by disgruntlement with the long Wentworth hegemony.[18]

At the other extreme were opponents of democracy, who advocated a strong aristocratic upper house which would check the more popular branch. Replying to "Clitus," "A faithful friend to his Country" warned that in popularly elected assemblies were found "innumerable legerdemain tricks, and fraudulent devices." Men were basically selfish, savage, cruel, and fierce, and had to be restrained by government. Power should never remain in the people; government derived not from them but from God. The colonists were fighting, he declared, against arbitrary power and oppression on the one hand, and *"popular licentiousness, anarchy, and confusion"* on the other. An independent legislative branch was therefore essential, for a single house led to tyranny.[19] In Pennsylvania, "Addison" feared that an assembly chosen by the people might itself become a House of Lords: "Rich Men in a Legislative Council and an Assembly, mutually controlled by each other, are certainly less dangerous than in an Assembly without any controul."[20] Writing just before independence, "C. X." judged Maryland's upper house defective because its members were removable at pleasure. In order to "form some counterpoise to the democratical part of the legislature," he suggested that "it should be composed of gentlemen of the first fortune and abilities in the Province; and they should hold their seats for life."[21] So also Carter Braxton warned against "the tumult and riot incident to a simple Democracy," and called for a government as much like that of England as possible, including a governor and a council, chosen for good behavior.[22]

Letters exchanged between Edmund Pendleton and Thomas Jefferson shortly after Virginia's constitution was published reveal the attitude of many men of their class. Pendleton felt that the Senate had not been made sufficiently independent, either of the lower house or of the people. He would not object, he wrote on August 10, 1776, to the election of the senators by the people, had they been given life terms and "been chosen out of the people of great property." As it was, "the Delegates will have too much influence in the Senate Elections." He wished that they had been forbidden to hold any lucrative office, and that they were elected only by men with "fixed Permanent property."[23] Jefferson essentially agreed. He had originally suggested that the Senate be chosen by the House; for "a choice by the people themselves is not generally distinguished for it's wisdom. This first secretion from them is usually crude and heterogeneous. But give to those so chosen by the people a second choice themselves, and they generally will chuse wise men." He had hoped, he recalled, to make the senators independent by a nine-year term with no re-eligibility, so that they would never have to curry favor with the electorate. A committee on which Pendleton served had suggested, however, that the people of each district choose electors, who would then choose a senator. Jefferson thought that this had been a good idea, and he would even "submit, tho' not so willingly to an appointment for life, for any thing rather than a mere creation by and dependance on the people."[24]

Such antidemocratic theories were, as Pendleton admitted, "disagreeable to the temper of the times." Similar proposals were made by others, but only in Maryland was the upper class sufficiently determined and powerful to create a truly aristocratic Senate. There, the system of electors was successfully introduced, and was supplemented by a high property qualification and a long term of office (five years) with re-election permitted. South Carolina allowed direct election but, like Maryland, required a large estate. The long background of controversy between royal councils and assemblies in both of these states might suggest that abolition of the upper house would have been welcomed. Actually, even

during colonial times, the councils had demonstrated their usefulness: once divested of royal influence, with the aristocratic element
paramount, they might become valuable instruments for upper-
class rule. Such was the intent of the framers of the Maryland and
South Carolina constitutions. In every other state the conventions
followed a middle course: an upper house was created, but it was
never an entirely aristocratic body and it sometimes had no aristocratic element at all.

The reason for this moderation lies partly in the power structure: neither the democratically inclined farmers and artisans nor
their upper-class opponents had complete control in most states, so
compromise was essential. Moreover, the majority of voters probably adhered to neither extreme but to a middle way, consonant
with colonial experience. Most states therefore retained the upper
house as an important branch of the government, but eliminated
most of its aristocratic features.

The evidence that a majority of politically active citizens wanted
such democratized councils is conclusive. Perhaps most telling is
what the framers produced. Pennsylvania, Georgia, and Vermont,
to be sure, did institute unicameral legislatures. But North Carolina, which designed a government under popular auspices, had a
Senate: while the people of Mecklenburg County preferred a single house, the democratic instructions from Orange called for two
houses, both of which would be responsible to the people.[25] It may
be true that "the Senate of Massachusetts was created in order to
protect property against democracy,"[26] but there were exceedingly
few protests against it even though the constitution was widely debated. Such criticisms as were made in 1778 and 1779 were directed not against the existence of the Senate but against particular
features of it, especially the property requirement. The same was
true in New Hampshire. Rhode Island's farmers undoubtedly
wielded enough influence to have abolished the House of Magistrates
had they wished to do so, but they did not. In general the bicameral
system seems to have suited public opinion.

The need for an upper house, people believed, grew out of the
faults of the lower. John Adams' influential *Thoughts on Government* ably summarized these deficiencies. Adams had been greatly
disturbed by Thomas Paine's advocacy of the unicameral system.
Indeed, he informed Joseph Warren that " 'Common Sense,' by his

crude ignorant Notion of a Government by one Assembly, will do more Mischief, in dividing the Friends of Liberty, than all the Tory Writings together."[27] Adams addressed himself to the subject in a pointed refutation. He gave six reasons why a single assembly was bad. It was, he asserted, "liable to all the vices, follies, and frailties of an individual; subject to fits of humor, starts of passion, flights of enthusiasm, partialities, or prejudice, and consequently productive of hasty results and absurd judgments. And all these errors ought to be corrected and defects supplied by some controlling power." Moreover, "a single assembly is apt to be avaricious, and in time will not scruple to exempt itself from burdens, which it will lay, without compunction, on its constituents." In addition, the members would grow ambitious, and perpetuate themselves in power. If all power were concentrated in one elective house it would not be able effectively to exercise the executive and judicial functions of government. Finally, it would pass arbitrary laws in its own interest. A division of power was therefore essential, necessitating a separate legislative branch between the popular assembly and the executive.[28]

These ideas were widely accepted and quoted without acknowledgment. "A single Assembly," repeated a Connecticut writer, "is liable to all the Vices, follies, and frailties of an Individual—subject to fits of Humor, starts of Passion, flights of Enthusiasm, partialities of Prejudice, & consequently productive of hasty Results and absurd Judgments."[29] This low opinion of the representatives was doubtless most congenial to that large number of well-to-do Americans who were skeptical of pure democracy; but even democrats had to admit that mistakes were probable. Therefore a revisory body was needed to protect the people "from the fatal influences of hasty, incorrect, passionate and prejudiced determinations."[30] Equally serious was the possibility that a single legislature might be corrupted by power. Americans had good reason to know the danger of an excessive concentration of authority without sufficient checks; Adams and other political theorists warned against it, and their own experience both as Europeans and as colonials made the evil manifest. If the legislative power were vested in a single body, warned the Reverend William Gordon, ambitious men would soon be "building up their own particular greatness, upon their country's ruin."[31] A senate was essential not only as a council of revision but as a bulwark of liberty.[32]

These functions of the upper house defined, to some extent, the characteristics desired in senators. They were expected to be independent, particularly of the executive and the lower house. The system in Massachusetts by which the upper house was chosen by the representatives, though advocated by Adams, was generally considered to be faulty, and was abandoned in 1780. Senators also were expected to be the wisest and most virtuous of men, with "a superior degree of acquaintance with the history, laws, and manners of mankind," so that their advice would be excellent.[33] Some men felt that such attributes would most often be found among the well-to-do, who possessed "that Weight which arises from property and gives Independence and Impartiality to the human mind."[34] Probably this conviction, as much as the belief that the senate ought to protect property, accounts for the qualifications written into most constitutions: the senates were to be filled with the natural aristocracy of the new nation. Prevailing opinion elsewhere held that any person with a small stake in society was eligible; therefore requirements were negligible in Delaware, Virginia, and New Jersey. Several states set age requirements—older men in those days evidently being men of twenty-five or thirty.[35]

Other similar features were adopted by the various states. Most of the senates had small memberships, though they were considerably larger than the prewar councils. The senators were almost always chosen by geographical units, which provided a more equitable representation than the councils had furnished. The principal exception was Maryland, where the Senate was not intended to represent the people. Otherwise, either each county had an equal number of representatives (Delaware, New Jersey, North and South Carolina) or an effort was made to allocate senators roughly in proportion to population or taxes paid, either by combining several counties into districts (Virginia and New York), or by adjusting the number of senators chosen by each county (New Hampshire and Massachusetts). Vacancies were almost always filled by popular vote. Only in Maryland did the men who favored indirect election as a means of reducing popular influence have their way.

Opinions on one issue—the senators' terms of office—were divided. If the senators were to be independent not only of the other branches but also of public opinion, as Jefferson and others wished, then long terms of office were desirable. One Virginian, for instance, suggested seven years.[36] Two-year terms were adopted by South Carolina, three in Delaware, four in New York and Virginia, and five in Maryland. Those who preferred a democratic body that would be responsible to the people wanted annual elections. They were successful in North Carolina, New Jersey, Massachusetts, and New Hampshire. Since both Rhode Island and Connecticut continued to have elections every year, the democratization of the senate in this respect was evident. Popular influence was increased by the practice of rotation, followed by every state but two, even where terms were longer, as in Delaware, New York, and Virginia. Although the ideal of the House of Lords still had great influence in 1776, the thinking of most Americans about the proper role of an upper house had radically changed. The desirability of a balanced government, of a separation of powers, led to the retention of a senate in most cases, but it was no longer conceived of primarily as a bulwark of aristocracy. The next decade saw a further development in the direction of democratic control.

Theory Follows Fact

To some extent the experience of each state shaped the citizens' judgments of the upper houses during the 1780's. New Hampshire's Senate, although composed of well-to-do men, seldom opposed the wishes of the people. It represented reasonably well the different parts of the state and reflected the fundamentally democratic nature of the social structure. Until 1784, the councillors were chosen by the House of Representatives, after the Massachusetts pattern. The constitution adopted in that year provided for annual elections by the people. There were two undemocratic features: the property qualification of £200, and the provision that vacancies, including those created when too few candidates received a majority of votes cast, would be filled by joint ballot; but these aroused no opposition. Most farmers, after all, had enough property to qualify for the office.

Massachusetts' Senate under the constitution of 1780 had been designed, as Samuel Adams explained to the French traveller

Chastellux, to represent property and to check the "purely demo-cratical" lower house.[37] The convention, indeed, frankly stated as much in its address to the people. Counties were assigned a num-ber of senators proportionate to their taxes, not their population. The difference was not very great, and the Senate never became a truly aristocratic body. There were no criticisms of it until 1786–1787; the few newspaper comments were favorable.[38] In the spring of 1786 an interesting article by "Scribble-Scrabble" (George Thacher) argued that a single house was competent to legislate, and the Senate only caused delay. If there were but one house, the people would naturally elect to it persons noted for wisdom and virtue. In England the House of Lords was necessary because it represented the nobility, which formed a distinct interest; but in Massachusetts no such nobility existed, so no such house was needed.[39] The article probably was not widely read, and certainly few people in Massachusetts agreed with Thacher. A handful of at-tacks on the Senate emanated from Shaysites angered at the upper house's economic conservatism; but most of their petitions did not even mention the upper house. The few newspapers that discussed the Senate either defended it on the ground that a system of checks and balances was necessary,[40] or urged the people merely to change its personnel. Indeed, this was the solution advocated by most of the discontented citizens. Clearly only a small minority sought to abolish the upper house.[41] The property qualification did not prevent the candidacy of men who were sympathetic with the Shaysites or who were even Shaysites themselves. The election of 1787 demonstrated that the Senate could be brought to heel if peo-ple took the trouble to vote. The upper house did tend to represent property, but it could be made to represent numbers.[42]

Elsewhere in New England the established governments in Con-necticut and Rhode Island seem to have been generally approved. The assistants of the former state were attacked when they favored commutation and the impost in 1783;[43] but as in Massachusetts change was sought not through constitutional reform but through electoral contests. Rhode Island's upper house, as far as is known, was not criticized at all. Such comments as exist favor the bicam-eral system.[44] New York's Senate perhaps was originally designed to protect property rights, but it readily fell under the influence of the Clintonians, and neither party seems to have been dissatisfied

with it. Similarly, in New Jersey, "An Elector" considered both
houses to be equally "creatures of the people." "A True Patriot"
put forward the curious idea (which seems to have been derived
from De Lôme) that there was some advantage in isolating "the
most learned and rich" in the Council, where they would not mis-
lead "the more unlearned though honest" assemblymen.[45] However, few writers agreed with Councillor John Stevens, Jr., that the
state's upper house was designed as a check on democracy.[46] From
every point of view the New Jersey Council was considered a useful
body. Nor was any dissatisfaction evident in Delaware.

In the states thus far surveyed, few objections were raised to the
existence of a senate. In Pennsylvania, its absence was frequently
criticized. From the first, "Republicans" had opposed the constitution of 1776. Benjamin Rush, for example, lamented the lack of
an upper house. Power, he wrote, should never be lodged in a single body. Any analogy with the House of Lords was false, he asserted, for an upper house would be chosen by the people and
would have their happiness as its objective. Rush observed that an
inequality of property had created classes. There existed no check
upon wealth because in a unicameral legislature the "men of middling property and poor men" would be overborne, whereas "by a
representation of men of middling fortunes in one house, their
whole strength is collected against the influence of wealth." A senate was needed not to protect the aristocracy from the democracy,
but to protect the many from the few.[47] Others emphasized the util-
ity of a body to which appeals could be made in case of error, and
warned that a single house tended to become despotic. Members of
the "Republican Society" denied that they intended an aristocratic
branch; both houses were to represent the people.[48]

In 1784 the Pennsylvania Council of Censors recommended
the creation of a Legislative Council of twenty-seven men, chosen
triennially.[49] A minority report, written by the "Constitutionalists," warned that the purpose was to accommodate the "better sort
of people."[50] The Constitutionalists consistently defended the unicameral system against what they termed the "aristocratic nobility."[51] The Republicans countered that a division of power was
essential to guard against the tyrannical designs of ambitious men,
and that an aristocracy might be more dangerous in a single legisla-

tive branch. They pointed out, moreover, that all of the other states except Georgia benefited from their senates.[52]

Despite their protestations that the Senate would not be designed to protect the upper class, the Republicans undoubtedly expected it to do so. Their leaders were well-to-do merchants, lawyers, and landowners who were distressed at the excessive democracy of the existing government and who often found it difficult to control the legislature.[53] To them a single branch became "an engine in the hands of factions," influenced by "the popular phrenzy of the moment, or the selfish views of an interested majority," and lacking stability. A second house would protect property and prevent unwise and unjust laws.[54]

These arguments were occasionally countered,[55] but the Constitutionalists clearly had lost the debate, especially after the adoption of the Federal Constitution. When a constitutional convention met in 1790 the argument was not whether there should be two houses, but how the Senate should be chosen. Most of the Republicans still hoped to make it a bulwark of aristocracy by indirect elections and high property qualifications. But some of their most prominent leaders joined with the Constitutionalists in opposing such a house. Perhaps they believed, as Alexander Graydon did, that the protection of wealth was unnecessary because wealthy men would successfully unite to protect themselves. Others, like James Wilson, abandoned the notion of a check on democracy and called instead for a body which would be popularly elected, but which, through longer terms of office, would create a more stable, balanced government.[56] This view, clearly held by the majority, prevailed.

The other former proprietary colony, Maryland, had established the most manifestly aristocratic of all the senates, and its legislative history was characterized by many conflicts with the lower house. Despite this, criticisms of the upper house as such did not develop. Indeed, the leader of the paper money party, Samuel Chase, had been one of the Senate's creators. Most, if not all, of the principal political leaders favored the constitutional status quo, and economic disagreements rather than challenges to its existence motivated attacks upon the upper house. Whether the majority of Marylanders, who were yeomen farmers, agreed with their leaders is impossible to determine. Their views, if expressed, are not recorded.

Most of the newspaper articles in Maryland accepted the electoral college system and the high property qualification, and regarded the Senate as contributing to good government. "A. B. C." contrasted with satisfaction the 1779 legislature with that of colonial days. The Senate, he believed, was just as representative of the people as the House of Delegates, and had no interests apart from those of the majority.[57] "A Republican" felt that the high property qualification was a mistake, because citizens of the greatest wealth were more likely to be corrupt than some poor men of talent; yet he defended the Senate against attack.[58] Articulate Marylanders agreed that the upper house was a necessary check on the "ebullitions of popular passions or caprice," for it incorporated "virtue, ability, integrity and patriotism."[59] And probably most of the state's powerful citizens agreed with "Marylander" that the ideal senator was "easy in his circumstances, firm and independent in his sentiments and principles, and . . . superior to erroneous popular caprice, or the clamours of faction."[60]

When the important debate over financial policy pitted the Senate against the lower house, the question was not whether the Senate should be abolished or altered, but whether the senators were obliged to follow public opinion. Samuel Chase believed that the sovereign people had a right to instruct both branches and to demand redress of their grievances. The people, he admitted, might become "licentious," but then senators and delegates also might become oppressive and tyrannical. The latter danger history proved to be the greater. The Senate had been created to check the delegates, but it had not been created independent of the people.[61] The Senate's defenders replied that the Senate had been created to represent property and virtue, not the people. If senators were denied the right to exercise independent judgment, good men would never serve, but only compliant men who followed the multitude. In that case the constitutional distinction would vanish and there would be, in effect, only one branch.[62] When legislative power resided in the people, government was strictly democratic. But Maryland's government was representative rather than democratic: men of superior talents were granted the right to govern. The people could indeed dissolve the government, but this should be done only if liberty was endangered and if all means of redress had proved ineffectual. Instructions were to be regarded with respect, but not as commands. "An Elk-Ridger" added that if the Senate obeyed instructions it would no longer be a check on the democratic part of the legislature, "which might create anarchy and confusion."[63] The controversy remained unsettled, but no effective attack was made on Maryland's Senate, which continued to check the more democratic House of Delegates.

Virginia's Senate was not aristocratic enough for men such as Jefferson and Pendleton, and the former, at least, continued to be dissatisfied with it. It was, he wrote, too similar to the lower house to be an adequate check. The purpose of establishing different houses was to represent different interests. In some states the delegates represented persons and the senators property, but in Virginia this was not the case. Jefferson still preferred Maryland's electoral college. Madison agreed with him, and suggested property qualifications for the voters and a six-year term to introduce "system and steadiness."[64] Some Kentuckians, on the other hand, questioned whether an upper house was necessary at all.[65] "Republicus" thought that it was a mere redundancy. A single body contained as much wisdom and virtue as did two houses. The second branch would waste time and money, and since there was only one common public interest—the greatest good of the whole—it could only do harm by delaying or checking necessary measures. Was it not as likely to check a good bill as a bad one? Why do business with the right hand and prevent it with the left? But if the purpose was not to represent the people, then it had no business existing at all.[66] The conduct of the Senate in Virginia merited the criticisms of Jefferson rather than the fears of Kentuckians, for it was certainly not an aristocratic body, and there seems to have been no popular hostility to it.

Carolinians seemed generally content with their upper houses. North Carolina's Senate was so democratic that one would hardly expect objections to it from that side, and none are known to have been made from the other. South Carolina's upper house, though certainly not a democratic body, did not behave as an aristocratic branch even though that was probably the original intent. As in Maryland, the conservatism of the lower house limited the area of possible conflict, and the Senate seems to have won general acceptance. There was some hostility toward it in the mid-1780's, but "Philodemus" (Thomas Tudor Tucker) was probably correct in thinking that the Senate did not have to fear its own demise. An upper house, he wrote, was needed as a check upon hasty proceedings. All men are influenced by interest, passions, and the ideas of a few leaders, he observed, but "two separate bodies of men do not so readily, without good reason, come into each other's opinions, as the same men collected together in one general meeting."[67]

The same view was gaining currency in Georgia, which, like Pennsylvania, had a unicameral legislature. In 1784, the state's only newspaper printed an article which argued that an upper house would prevent the legislature from being "hurried on by the transient gusts of passion and prejudices."[68] Someone wrote at the bottom of the next issue that the author was "a *pretty* Republican! the writer of this—an aristocrat in disguise." The author went on for two more weeks, however, insisting that the benefits of a mixed government, with separation of powers and checks and balances, were universally approved. He did not believe that the Senate should represent the aristocracy, for very wealthy men seldom were patriots, and a state's real riches lay in its "industrious citizens." The Senate, like the lower house, should be chosen in proportion to the taxable inhabitants.[69] These ideas presently became dominant, especially after the federal government was made bicameral. In 1788 the legislature recommended a new constitution which included a Senate. Each county would choose one senator for a three-year term. A senator had to own three hundred acres of land and other property worth £250 sterling, a provision that disqualified well over half of the Georgians but still permitted substantial farmers and artisans to serve. The convention which was then convened adopted this proposal without any known opposition.[70]

By the end of the decade, the senates in most states had proved themselves valuable instruments in a representative democracy. The concept of an aristocratic upper house protecting property rights was still cherished by many men of property, and was still practiced in Maryland and occasionally elsewhere; but this was now a minority view and other functions were considered more important. Sporadic objections to bicameralism were still heard, but they were becoming rare as the senates demonstrated their usefulness. The concept that the lower house should represent numbers and the upper house geographical areas had still not been articulated as a theory, even though it had been introduced as a practical solution to a problem in the Federal Constitution. Instead, the general opinion was that a senate should consist of wise, and preferably disinterested, men and should be modeled after the Roman Senate rather than the House of Lords; the property requirement was justified by the feeling that men of wisdom would most likely be found among property holders who would then quite correctly defend property rights against the onslaught of numbers. An article in a Maine newspaper, for example, observed that the representatives "in the warmth of temper, or inclination for a favourite measure, pass acts which they soon after reprobate themselves, and are glad there is another branch with power to over-rule." Moreover, the lower house was too often composed of "weak and ignorant men," honest, but "not fit to govern a wise and free people," whereas a senate would contain those who possessed the necessary wisdom and skill. Finally, a senate represented "the property" while the lower house represented "the persons" of the state.[71] Originally the primary purpose of the upper house was to represent the aristocracy; now this was only a secondary function.

For other commentators the aristocratic role had ceased to exist. "The Examiner" considered that experience proved two branches of the legislature essential. Time had shown a single body of men to possess "the same passions, whims, and caprice, as an individual," and likely to be led by designing speakers into measures that reflection would prove evil. "The dividing a legislative body into two branches, must therefore be a wise measure, and should never be departed from while human nature remains [as it is] at present."[72] By 1787, Americans had come to agree with this analysis. They were not yet in accord on who should choose the senators, whether they should be selected from counties, other geographical units, or at large, and what qualifications they and their electors should be required to possess. But the basic concept of a second house to check the first in the interest of better government had become an integral part of the American political creed.

CHAPTER 8

The Upper House and the Federal Constitution

*W*HILE THE BICAMERAL PRINCIPLE was being accepted and incorporated into the state governments, Congress continued to have a single house. No objection to this seems to have been made until the movement for a general reform was well under way. As long as Congress lacked the crucial power to levy taxes, maintain armies, and regulate commerce, little needed to be feared from it. The state legislatures checked it effectively, for they chose the delegates (except in Connecticut and Rhode Island, where the democratic method of popular election was adopted), paid them, reviewed their merits annually, and retired them after three years. Apparently everyone agreed that no further check was needed in a confederacy than for power to be withheld and watchfulness maintained, while the issue of aristocracy *vs.* democracy was fought out within the sovereign states rather than in Congress. When a strong national government was proposed, however, the structure of the whole political system had to be reconsidered. It was at this point that the need for a bicameral legislature became apparent to many of the reformers.

The Senate Created

Most members of the Federal Convention, like most critics of the Articles, assumed that a Senate was desirable. The widely quoted newspaper article by "Nestor" asserted that a one-house legislature was a major defect of the Confederation.[1] John Adams was already known as an ardent supporter of the bicameral principle, and his *Defense of the American Constitutions* was a less forceful restatement of his ideas on this subject.[2] As we have seen, Jefferson, Madison, and Pendleton agreed with him. Such influential leaders as James M. Varnum, John Jay, and Henry Knox felt that one branch of the legislature ought to serve for a long period or even for life, supplementing a lower house which would be (as Knox wished) a "consolidated Democracy." All favored a very strong central government.[3] William Grayson reported to Madison that the New Englanders wanted a Senate chosen for "a good number of years,"[4] while Nathan Dane of Massachusetts wrote that a division of powers was intended by nature.[5]

The Virginia Plan incorporated the foregoing ideas. It proposed an upper house which would be chosen by the lower from men nominated by the state legislatures, for "a term sufficient to ensure their independency." Each branch could originate any sort of bill.[6] Edmund Randolph explained that the intent was to provide a check against the democratic element, which he called the "chief danger." None of the state constitutions, he lamented, had been successful in that objective. "The feeble Senate of Virginia," he asserted quite correctly, was "a phantom." The checks in New York and Massachusetts also seemed insufficient, while even in Maryland the "late distractions" had revealed that the Senate was not powerful enough.[7] The bicameral principle was accepted without debate and almost unanimously, with only Pennsylvania demurring—out of respect for Franklin's opinion.[8] Evidently bicameralism was accepted by nearly everyone, including those who opposed a consolidation. The debate which followed concerned not the existence of an upper house but its character.

The first objection to the Senate as proposed in the Virginia Plan was made by James Wilson. He pointed out correctly that the Senate would not be an independent body if it were chosen by the House or, for that matter, by the state legislatures· Indeed, the method called for by the Virginia Plan was a curious one. The only states in which senates had been elected by the lower house were Massachusetts and New Hampshire, where the procedure had been abandoned for precisely the reason stated by Wilson. New York's Council of Revision was chosen by the legislature, but that body did not originate laws. If Randolph really wished his second branch to be independent, it would have to be chosen for a very long period indeed, perhaps for life. (Possibly the Virginians had not quite dared to suggest this.) Both Roger Sherman and George Mason also objected to appointment by the House of Representatives because it would make the senators dependent on the House. On the other hand, Wilson's proposal that the states be united into electoral districts, as in New York, was criticized by Madison on the basis that the large states would dominate the elections (a line of argument which he may later have regretted). He asserted that in Virginia, where counties were combined, larger counties had sometimes obtained the victory of a candidate inferior to one from a smaller county (Virginia's history proved nothing of the sort). The delegates finally rejected the method of election proposed in the Virginia Plan and turned to other matters.[9]

Discussion of the Senate was resumed a week later. The persistent issue was who should select the upper house. Elbridge Gerry and John Dickinson both rose to defend the system of election by state legislatures, arguing that the Senate ought to check the effects of democracy, or, in Gerry's words, "secure more effectually a just preference of merit." Gerry asserted that the people of Massachusetts had wild ideas concerning government, among which was the abolition of the upper house (a statement that was incorrect). In his view, there were four modes of appointment: by the lower house, which would make the Senate too dependent; by the president, which would be too monarchical; by the people, which would result in the domination of the agricultural interest over the commercial; and by the legislatures, which would be preferable in that it would protect the commercial interest.[10] Dickinson felt that the major objective should be to refine the Senate so as to "assimilate it as near as may be to the House of Lords in England." Senators should be distinguished "for their rank in life and their weight of property." Selection by the state legislatures, combined with long terms, would accomplish this end. Moreover, the "sense of the States," Dickinson claimed, would be conveyed by the legislatures more accurately than by the people, although he did not explain why this would be so. His final point was that such a method would be "expedient."[11] George Read then suggested that the president might make appointments from men nominated by the legislatures; but this reactionary idea was not considered worthy of a second.[12]

The major reply to Gerry and Dickinson was delivered by Wilson, who denied that the legislatures would be any less influenced by agricultural interests than the people at large, and claimed that unless both houses were chosen by the people there would be dissension between them. He was wrong on both counts, for the commercial interest, however defined, always was much better represented in the legislatures than among the general populace; and events proved that dissension arose from causes unrelated to the method of election. He was, however, supported by Madison, who added that the function of the Senate should be to legislate with more wisdom, system, and coolness than the representatives.[13]

The next discussion, several days later, concerned the senators' term of office. At this time most of the delegates preferred a seven-year term. Both Randolph and Madison stressed the need for a "firm" government to check the "licentiousness" of the states and the "democratic branch." They pointed out that even Maryland's Senate had been unable to do this, and Madison added that in other states the four-year term had proved inadequate. A few speakers objected to so long a duration, but the seven-year proposal passed overwhelmingly.[14] The next day the question of whether the Senate might originate money bills arose briefly for the first time. Gerry had moved that the lower house should have the exclusive right, because the people ought to hold the purse strings. He was countered by several speakers who observed that in such states as Connecticut where both houses had equal power there had been no problem, whereas in South Carolina, for example, where the lower house had an exclusive right, "pernicious disputes" had arisen. Disputes of this sort were, in fact, uncommon. The true motive of those who opposed the resolution was most likely their desire to increase the power of the Senate. Madison reinforced such a view by observing that the senators would be more capable than the members of the popular branch and just as representative of the people. Gerry's proposal was then defeated by a large majority.[15]

The Convention thereupon turned to a consideration of the New Jersey Plan, which proposed to retain the unicameral system of the Articles. The discussion focused primarily on whether a national government was to be established at all, though Wilson did introduce the more specific issue of what he called the "Legislative despotism" of a single house with no adequate check.[16] He was undoubtedly drawing upon his experience as a Pennsylvania "Republican." While the more basic question was still being argued, Hamilton, in a major address, countered the unicameral idea by advocating an even stronger and more undemocratic Senate than that which had been proposed. The seven-year term, he believed, was too short in view of "the amazing violence & turbulence of the democratic spirit." New York's upper house, despite its four-year term, was "inefficient," while that of Maryland would have yielded to the demand for paper money if the people had been united. He proposed that Maryland's electoral system be adopted and that the senators serve for life or for good behavior. Moreover, they should have the power to declare war, as well as to share in the making of treaties and appointments.[17] This plan seems in retrospect to have offered the best chance of retaining the aristocratic principle, but it was not even considered by the Convention.

The New Jersey Plan was defeated, and the Convention then returned to the Virginia Plan with its bicameral legislature. Sherman, still unconvinced that a confederation had been finally rejected, insisted that a second branch, though necessary in a state legislature, was not needed in the central government. If it were chosen by the people, he claimed, it would serve no useful purpose and would be controlled by a few designing men. He preferred the system provided by the Articles, though if there were no other solution he would agree to two branches, one chosen by the states, the other by the people. Both Wilson and Mason defended a bicameral system, the latter noting that the constitutions which the people had made proved their preference for two houses. This debate was closed permanently when the Convention voted overwhelmingly in favor of a second branch. The opposition to it had come not from those who favored a democracy or opposed a system of checks and balances, but from the "small-state" delegations, who feared that the change might mean domination by the more populous states.[18]

Several weeks elapsed before the other principal issues concerning the Senate were settled. These concerned primarily the term of office, the manner of election, and, in general, the functions of the new upper house. As to the term, three different points of view can be distinguished, though there were individual variants. A few delegates preferred a short term of office either because they themselves wanted the Senate to be responsible to the people or because they felt that the people would insist upon it. Sherman warned that permanency in government was dangerous to liberty, and that frequent elections were necessary to ensure good behavior. Connecticut, he pointed out, had a stable government despite annual elections. He and Gerry were supported, for various reasons, by other delegates, including some of the South Carolinians and Georgians who feared that the senators would be located so far away that if they were chosen for a long period they would lose their attachment to the state.[19]

At the other extreme were the advocates of permanency. These men believed that the Senate could serve as an adequate check only if it were independent. Madison, Hamilton, Wilson, and Gouverneur Morris were the leading spokesmen for that view, which was also supported by Read and Broome of Delaware, by Robert Morris and some of the other Pennsylvania delegates, and probably by all of the Virginians (though Randolph balked at a life term). Previously King and Gorham of Massachusetts had also favored a long term. Madison explained his position by reminding the delegates of the purpose of a second house. The people of the country, he declared, were divided into debtors and creditors, farmers, merchants, and manufacturers, and particularly into rich and poor. There were already symptoms of a levelling spirit, and the minority, he felt, must be protected against the majority. Moreover, when power was granted it ought to be divided. Senators must prevent rash acts; they must be older and more experienced men, of greater knowledge, virtue, and wisdom. A long term, Madison argued, was necessary to obtain this end.[20] Hamilton, too, emphasized that the inequality of property was the "great and fundamental distinction in Society." In his view, the lower house would represent the poorer citizens, and therefore (by implication) the Senate should represent the wealthier.[21] General Pinckney and Abraham Baldwin agreed that the Senate, as Pinckney put it, "was meant to represent the wealth of the Country." Baldwin suggested that for this reason attention should be paid to the relative wealth of the states, as had been done in the counties of Massachusetts.[22] Wilson believed that the Senate, which would have a considerable influence on foreign affairs, would be more respectable in the eyes of foreign nations if its members served for long terms.[23] Gouver-

neur Morris took the same position. The purpose of the upper
house, he observed, was "to check the precipitation, changeable-
ness, and excesses of the first branch." The senator must have
great property, possess an aristocratic spirit, and be independent:
"all the guards contrived by America have not restrained the
Senatorial branches of the Legislature from a compliance to the
democratic." He advocated life appointments made by the executive. Subsequently he added that the Senate would also guard
against "projects of paper money & similar expedients."[24]

This was too much for Randolph, who replied that life terms
would give rise to dissensions such as had occurred in Maryland.[25]
Indeed, most delegates sought a middle course. Neither the shorter
period of four years nor the life term could obtain a majority, and
the final decision in favor of six years represented a compromise.
This moderate position may have been strengthened by the conviction that public opinion was opposed to a long tenure.

The question of who should elect the senators became involved
with and was primarily determined by the conflict between the
small and large states. At first, selection by state legislatures had
been advocated both by those who defended the power of small
states and by those who hoped to preserve a confederation. But
once the idea of a confederation had been abandoned, only a few
die-hards like Luther Martin (who favored a single branch) continued to argue from that point of view.[26] Thus, the method was
now defended primarily by representatives of small states who
wished for an equality of votes in the Senate and accordingly insisted upon election by the state legislatures rather than by the
people, since the latter method would lead to representation by
population rather than by states. One of their arguments was that
the legislatures would choose better men than the people would;
and in this vein John Francis Mercer cited the example of Virginia's Senate as a proof that the people would send the worst men
possible.[27] On the other side, those who advocated a popular vote
were inhibited from arguing that their method was more democratic, because it had already been made clear that the Senate was to
check rather than support democracy.[28] And Maryland's system of
an electoral college, though much admired, was not seriously considered except in connection with the Presidency. The argument
for appointment by the legislatures may have been buttressed by

the idea that the two branches would check each other more effectually if they were differently chosen; but the decisive factor was undoubtedly the desire to preserve equality among the states.

The decision that the senators were to be chosen by the state legislatures reopened the question of control over money bills. The alignment on this issue forecast, to a certain extent, the subsequent division over ratification, for the future Antifederalists Mason and Gerry, together with Randolph, preferred that the power should be lodged in the lower house. So did the delegates from New Hampshire, North Carolina, Massachusetts, and Virginia, which were all states that probably had Antifederal majorities. Their major points on the money issue were the history of their experience under Great Britain and the possibility of losing popular support.[29] Madison, Gouverneur Morris, Wilson, Rutledge, and Carroll, on the other hand, argued that the Senate was more capable of writing a good bill than the House, and cited the histories of various states (such as Virginia, South Carolina, and Maryland) as examples of how restricting the Senate's power caused disputes without offering any compensating advantage.[30] In the end a compromise was reached: the House was given the exclusive right to originate money bills, but the Senate would be allowed to amend them.

Another dispute prophetic of the later Federalist-Antifederalist split arose over the questions of plural office-holding and payment of senators. The future Antifederalists Gerry and Mercer joined Williamson of North Carolina in demanding that plural office-holding be abolished in order to satisfy popular fears and guard against an aristocracy;[31] while Luther Martin sought to keep the Senate subordinate to the state legislatures by requiring that its members be paid by the states. He was opposed in this by Carroll, who insisted that senators should be independent and therefore paid by Congress.[32] The Convention again effected a compromise, by making members of Congress financially independent of the states, but prohibiting them from holding another federal office.

The Convention adjourned with most of the delegates well satisfied with what had been done. Though both Gerry and Mason, who refused to sign, and Martin, who had already departed, remained opposed to certain features of the upper house,[33] the Senate was satisfactory in almost every particular to the great majority of delegates. It was intended primarily as a check against the democratic tendencies of the lower house, and as a bulwark against measures that were unwise or poorly drawn. The Senate would also protect the country from the misuse of power that might characterize a single house. Its independence was assured by the long term of office and, to a lesser degree, by the fact that its members would be somewhat older than the representatives and would be paid by the central government instead of by the states. The small size of the Senate had been found so advantageous in the state legislatures that the question of size was scarcely debated. The equality of votes, two per state, was of course a compromise. It was opposed by the delegates from the large states, and supported by those from the small ones as well as by those few delegates who preferred a confederation. Election by state legislatures followed from that compromise, aided by the additional consideration that indirect elections might result in the selection of wiser men than would be chosen by a popular vote.[34] Thus the Senate combined two major principles. First, the concept of checks and balances included both a recognition of the aristocratic principle and a belief in the division of power. Second, the Senate represented the states, whereas the House represented the people.

THE SENATE ATTACKED

When the Constitution was sent out from the friendly confines of the Federal Convention, it faced a world so hostile that it barely escaped with its life. Antifederalist criticisms were directed primarily at its nationalistic features, and at what some felt to be its threats to liberty and democracy. Attacks on the Senate itself were of relatively minor importance, however; and almost no one objected to the Senate's existence.[35] In view of the situation in some states this seems curious; but there were two good reasons for it. First, the Senate preserved the equality of the states: it was a federal feature in a government otherwise highly centralized, and therefore was approved by the states' rights group. Second, most of the Antifederalists—at least those who were writing and speaking —accepted the bicameral principle. Richard Henry Lee, for example, felt that a "ballanced legislature" would encourage "caution, coolness, and deliberation," while the Senate especially, by supporting the state governments, would lend stability to the new plan. So also, in New York, John Lansing and Melancthon Smith conceded the need for two houses as a check.[36] Only in Pennsylvania was unicameralism seriously supported, and even there the point was not pressed.[37] Similarly, appointment by the state legislature was regarded as preserving federalism and thus was almost never criticized by the Antifederalists, though "Cincinnatus" complained that the Senate was too far removed from the people, and a group of Albany Antifederalists feared that it might become the people's master instead of their servant.[38] Such arguments, however, were most unusual. The critics directed their attacks, instead, not upon the Senate's existence or the method of electing it, but upon its permanency, independence, and power.

Some Antifederalists feared that the upper house might become too aristocratic. "John DeWitt," for example, observed that the passionate thirst for power had led to a general belief in a system of checks and balances, which was especially needed against the aristocracy. But the Constitution provided for an upper house that would be independent of the people during its long term of office; indeed some senators would probably serve for life. Since even the House was not a truly popular body compared with the state legislatures, the aristocratic element, instead of being restrained, would predominate.[39] Similarly the Antifederal minority of Pennsylvania's ratifying convention feared that "men of the most elevated rank in life will alone be chosen. The other orders in the society, such as farmers, traders, and mechanics, who all ought to have a competent number of their best informed men in the legislature, shall be totally unrepresented." They were especially alarmed by the long term and lack of rotation.[40]

These features were particularly disliked because they made the senators independent. Richard Henry Lee recommended a term of three or four years, rotation in office, and recall by the legislatures; for "even good men in office, in time, imperceptibly lose sight of the people."[41] "Brutus" thought the same changes essential, while "A Farmer" insisted that the Senate was not really responsible to the state legislatures because it was not instructed, censured, recalled, or paid by them.[42] A shorter tenure and ineligibility after one term were frequently demanded, while recall (as in the Articles) was mentioned somewhat less often. The Senate's powers were occasionally criticized, though as a rule the issue was

Congress' power as a whole. The most extensive attack was that of "Cincinnatus," who objected to every possible feature, including the close connection between the Senate and the Presidency, the amendment of money bills, and the impeachment process, as well as the term of office; he warned that "aristocratic principles constantly infect the minds of men."[43] On the whole, however, the Antifederalists were much more concerned with other aspects of the Constitution. Only the long term of office and lack of rotation were generally disliked.

The Senate Defended

The Federalists, of course, tried to refute these various criticisms. Several of them insisted that the Senate was not an aristocracy. An aristocracy, "Remarker" observer, was independent, permanent, uncontrollable, and therefore not responsible. The Senate was none of these.[44] "An American Citizen" and Tench Coxe, among others, emphasized that the senators did not constitute an hereditary elite but were a part of the people; they were elected rather than appointed, had no property qualifications, and could hold no other office.[45] Moreover, there were checks upon the Senate's power: every two years some senators were replaced; the state legislatures could and would instruct them; and both the House and the president could prevent any excessive senatorial influence.[46] Another safeguard was the exclusive control of the House over money bills —though Madison admitted that he was still unconvinced that this restriction had been wise.[47]

The Federalists also emphasized that the Senate would protect the small states against the large ones,[48] and that appointment by the legislatures was a federal feature guaranteeing that the states would be represented. Surely if the state legislatures protected the people's liberties, as the Antifederalists claimed, the men whom they chose would have the confidence of the people.[49] The long term was defended partly on the ground that several state senates served for three to five years,[50] but principally because stability and permanence were essential if the Senate was to perform its proper functions.

More important than these particular replies was the Federalists' general affirmation of the need for a system of checks and balances. Especially interesting were the thorough discussions by

Noah Webster and by "Publius"—in this case, Madison.[51] Webster began by explaining the disadvantages of a single house. Men, he asserted, were forever running into the extremes of licentiousness, subject to sudden and violent passions. A single body was often misled by some demagogue. Even in a small republic where men were equal in property and abilities a division of powers was necessary to guard against disorders arising from pride, irritability, and stubbornness. A senate collected men of wisdom, greater age, and experience who were not so liable to the bias of passion. The Senate of Rhode Island seemed an exception to the rule that the upper house would never be governed by passion, but it only proved that the people were corrupt and that the six-year term was essential. "Had the old senate in Rhode Island held their seats for three years; had they not been chosen, amidst a popular rage for paper money, the honor of that state would probably have been saved. The old senate would have stopped the measure for a year or two, till the people could have time to deliberate upon its consequences."[52]

Webster went on to examine the politics of other states for further evidence. Maryland, he said, was saved from the pernicious effects of paper money by its Senate, whose resistance gave people time to think. In Connecticut, when the House, in fits of schoolboyish passion, took offense at commutation, attempted to weaken the Assistants, and tried to rotate the seat of government among all the country towns, the upper house stood firm. Pennsylvania furnished a horrible example of unicameral government, for the legislature changed its policies from year to year; the people of Georgia were also suffering from the inconveniences of such a system. A defect of most state constitutions, Webster claimed, was that the senates were chosen from particular districts, and were inspired with local views. Much better was the policy adopted by Connecticut and Maryland, where senators represented the whole state. He felt that because of the long term of office provided in the Federal Constitution, senators would lose their partiality and act for the general good. "Many plausible things may be said in favor of pure democracy," he warned, "many in favor of uniting the representatives of the people in one single house—but uniform experience proves both to be inconsistent with the peace of society, and the rights of freemen."[53]

Madison based his argument less upon the experience of particular states than upon general considerations. He observed at the outset that the method of choosing senators gave the states an agency in the system and benefited them by "favoring a select appointment." Without elaborating on what that meant—which was perhaps just as well—he proceeded to discuss the equality of voting, which of course he defended primarily on grounds of expediency. The long term of office needed much more explaining, and it was to this that Madison devoted most of his attention. First, he declared, the function of an upper house must be understood. The people needed to be protected against an abuse of power and schemes of usurpation or perfidy. A Senate distinct from the lower house "must be in all cases a salutary check on the government." Such protection, he asserted, would be greater in proportion as the two branches were dissimilar. Moreover, single and numerous assemblies tended "to yield to the impulse of sudden and violent passions, and to be seduced by factious leaders into intemperate and pernicious resolutions." This tendency must be corrected by a body at once less numerous and more stable. In addition, the senators would not only possess greater knowledge than the representatives, but they would correct still another fault of the lower house —its "mutability." Rapid change in membership, argued Madison, meant continual alterations in policy. This, he said, would poison the blessings of liberty by making the law intelligible only to a few, who could then take advantage of their greater knowledge. Further, such inconstancy caused the country to forfeit the respect of other nations, whereas the upper house, unlike the lower, could elevate our national character by attending to the opinion of the world.

Obviously, Madison concluded, a body chosen for a short term could not accomplish all of these ends. The people must be assured of that succession of well-chosen and well-connected measures necessary for good government. A Senate serving for a long term would protect the people from their own temporary errors and delusions, from the tyranny of their own passions. They need not fear, he said, that an aristocracy was being established, for there was more danger from abuse of liberty than from abuse of power. The Senate could not become dangerous until it had corrupted first itself, then the state legislatures, then the representatives, and finally the people. Further assurance against such fears was provided in the next number of the Federalist Papers by Rufus King, who insisted that both history and reason proved the popular branch to be more than a match for every other part of the government.[54]

THE SENATE RATIFIED

No one can tell how effective these arguments were with the Antifederalists. Probably they needed to be reassured not about the desirability of an upper house, which most of them acknowledged, but about the aristocratic tendencies of so permanent a body. Undoubtedly they were less influenced by "Publius" than by such writers as "A Democratic Federalist," who came more directly to the point, admitting openly that the friends of democracy were alarmed by the Senate because of its appearance of aristocracy. He argued, however, that in England the upper house had "often been useful in checking the encroachments of the crown, and the precipitation and inadvertence of the people: In that country they have really held the balance between the king and the commons." A second house, he felt, had real advantages if these could be obtained without departing "from the real principles of liberty"; and he believed that the Constitution had done just this. Seats in the upper house were not hereditary, no property qualifications were fixed, no distinctions of rank existed. The Senate had no interests which differed from those of the people, it was merely a representative body "without one distinction in favor of the birth, rank, wealth or power of the senators or their fathers." It was just as democratic a body as the House of Representatives. This situation, he claimed, was fundamentally unique. The upper house provided for by the Constitution was not designed to be aristocratic but rather to represent the sovereignty of the states. It was a novelty in the history of the world.[55]

Novel it was. Many people continued to have their doubts concerning the democratic quality of the Senate. But clearly it was a body quite new, representing not population, not an upper class, but the states. Thus the Senate took its place as an essential element in the new government.

CHAPTER 9

The Upper House in Review

*A*NY ASSESSMENT of the upper house during the Revolutionary period must include both an analysis of the personnel of these councils and senates and a description of the functions they performed. The important effects of the Revolutionary movement must also be considered, as well as the ideas that were developing about the role the upper house was expected to play.

The Colonial Councils

The councils during the colonial period were usually composed of members of the upper class. Over 60 percent of their members were wealthy; and if we exclude the three "chartered" colonies the proportion reaches 85 percent. Almost all of the rest were well-to-do. However, while most Americans were farmers, fewer than one-third of the councillors drew their principal income from land. Many, of course, who acquired a fortune through trade or a profession invested in real estate; indeed most of the colonial upper class were landowners. But the primary economic interest of the councillors was commerce or the closely related legal profession. Naturally in the south planters were better represented, controlling about half of the seats; but in the north the agricultural interest of the councils was minor, in the chartered as well as in the royal colonies. As a result the councils were not representative even of the colonial upper class, to say nothing of the people generally.

For one thing, the councillors were much better educated than most colonials, more than a third having had a college education or its equivalent. A majority were members of the Church of England. And they were for the most part men of wider experience than the ordinary citizen: they were better travelled, had extensive connections in other colonies and in the Old World, and occupied a variety of civil and military offices. In addition, whereas most Americans lived in the country, the councillors were townspeople, residing either in or near the major urban center of the colony or in some other principal trading town. Almost all lived within a few miles of the coast or along a major navigable river. Their constituencies—if the term may be used—therefore included a very limited segment of colonial society.

What distinguished the councils most significantly, however, from both colonial society in general and its upper class in particular was that they represented in most colonies the long-established, stable upper class. While the colonial upper class was becoming increasingly stable by 1763, it was still basically new. And though the proportion of self-made men was low in the older rural areas, probably at least a third of the well-to-do townsmen were *nouveaux riches*. Class lines were even more fluid in those regions just emerging from the frontier stage, such as Georgia and the Carolina upcountry. In the councils, however, only 28 percent of the members had surpassed their fathers economically. While European aristocrats would have considered this proportion far too high, by colonial standards it was much too low. Indicative of these standards is the fact that more than a third of the members of the elected councils were economically mobile, as compared with fewer than a fifth of the appointed councillors. Finally, taking all the councils together, we find that half of their members belonged to the first families and another important group were known from birth as reputable, if not outstanding, residents of the community. And in several colonies, notably New Hampshire, New Jersey, Maryland, Virginia, and South Carolina, political influence and control were concentrated in a few large, extended families.

Insofar as the colonies had developed an aristocracy, then, it was to be found in these councils. Had they perfectly represented the colonial elite they would have been regarded, by most influential men, as excellent. Unfortunately they did not do so. In the first place, the councillors were too aristocratic: they did not include enough new men to mirror accurately the local upper class. Moreover, too many merchants and lawyers and not enough farmers, too many townspeople and not enough country gentlemen, were members. In the north there were too many Anglicans; in the south, and to some extent everywhere, there were too many royal officials. Although placemen dominated only two or three councils they were generally more numerous than most colonials thought they ought to be. Finally—and this came to be the most important factor—they were too conservative in their political attitudes. There were too many Tories and not enough Whigs, too many Loyalists and not enough rebels, to reflect even the conservatively inclined upper class. Excluding the elected bodies, more than three-fourths of the councillors became Loyalists or neutrals, and even in the three exceptions the proportion—well over one-fourth—was much higher than in New England's society generally. The fact that most of the councillors were prerogative men of course was responsible for their appointment; but it was also responsible for most of the trouble that followed.

The most important function assumed by the councils was their defense of royal authority. The New England "assistants" were seldom cast in that role (though there were exceptions, especially in Massachusetts). Similarly, in Virginia, New York, and New Jersey the moderate policy followed by the lower house seldom made such a defense necessary, and when some issues did arise, as in Virginia, the council generally followed a conciliatory course. In the other five colonies, however—all peculiarly distinguished by the presence of many royal officials who, even when they were not strictly speaking "placemen," represented a point of view quite different from that of most colonials—the councils became increasingly Loyalist in sentiment while the lower houses grew more rebellious. In New Hampshire, for example, the kinship of most councillors with the Wentworth family led them to support the governor, as well as to protect the royal authority in such affairs as the king's woods, the governor's salary, control over excise collectors, and representation. The four "placemen" councils were even more vigorous in upholding Parliament, king or proprietor, and governor. For this reason, Georgia's weak lower house could make little headway until the very end of the period; while

North Carolina's Assembly was too divided to obtain more than a draw. And a number of exciting combats took place in the legislatures of Maryland and South Carolina, most notably the Wilkes case and the tobacco bill affair.

The presence of placemen was an equally important factor in controversies over the rights of the upper house; for those councils which had few or no placemen almost never found their powers questioned. During the preceding century the rights of each house had been defined and an equilibrium achieved. The distribution of powers vested the right to originate money bills, including the levying of taxes and appropriation of funds, unquestionably in the lower house; and in practice that house originated most measures. Trouble developed only when the council energetically opposed the pretensions of the assembly to greater power, or where the dividing line of authority was disputed in connection with major issues. Thus the legislatures of the three southernmost colonies all argued over who should control the colony's agent; and here, as well as in Maryland, the lower house attempted to dominate the appointment of officials, and the councils resisted in the name of king or proprietor. The placemen councils also tried to limit the financial power of the lower houses, especially the expenditure of money—an issue so vital that the legislature of South Carolina was paralyzed by it, and the Commons there became so enraged that it challenged the very existence of the Council as an upper house.

Yet, despite these conflicts over the royal authority and the rights of the upper house, when we turn our attention to other issues the differences between the two houses are seen to be relatively minor. In South Carolina and Virginia there were no disagreements at all concerning economic policies, and such matters were seldom debated elsewhere. The councillors naturally defended their own property rights, as when they protected absentee proprietors in North Carolina, New Jersey, New Hampshire, and Massachusetts. But even in these colonies the councillors' estates were rarely threatened, and in other colonies not at all. The insignificance of such incidents may best be understood by considering what might have happened had the land engrossers in Georgia or New York been seriously challenged. Similarly, there were times when the councillors favored the creditor over the debtor, and merchants over farmers, and supported the prompt collection, in money, of higher taxes; but these indications of economic differences are isolated and exceptional. Disputes of a social, cultural, or political nature, other than those described, are also rare. One finds the upper house occasionally protecting Anglicans (or in Maryland the Catholics), once in a while defending Indians, perhaps a bit more inclined to support education and social welfare measures when these did not infringe upon some property rights, and somewhat unsympathetic with the political aspirations of westerners. But that is nearly all.

In attempting to account for this harmony, the obvious answer is that the lower houses seldom passed measures with which the upper house disagreed. Where the council, influenced by placemen or other factors, adopted a vigorous pro-British policy, bitter conflicts occurred whenever the lower house was strong enough to fight. Otherwise disputes were avoided because there were no reasons for disagreement. The two houses did not differ enough in their composition to create disparities in policy; and what differences there were are far less striking than the resemblances. The lower houses, for example, like the upper, were usually controlled by men of the economic upper class. Thus in South Carolina wealthy members constituted about 70 percent of the whole number, in Virginia 54 percent, in Maryland 40 percent, in New Jersey about 35 percent, in New York at least 43 percent, and in New Hampshire over 30 percent. Further, almost all the representatives of these colonies and of the other provinces were well-to-do, belonging to that 10 percent who stood at the top economically and who owned, incidentally, nearly half of the property. As in the councils, the nonfarm interest was heavily represented, always, by a large minority, and sometimes by a majority. Prominent old families furnished between 30 and 50 percent of the membership in the lower houses, and these characteristically supplied much of the leadership. Easterners dominated everywhere.

Had the people chosen a majority of Bacons, Husbands, Leislers, or Shayses—had, say, the New York Clintonians or the Pennsylvania Constitutionalists of the postwar years dominated these assemblies—there would have been turmoil indeed. As it was, the two branches differed principally on the political issue of whether power lay with the king or with the commons, and even on that question the council, as in Virginia, sometimes remained neutral. Controversies were also avoided or minimized by local circumstances and practices. The fact that the councillors in Massachusetts were chosen by the representatives and that Connecticut's assistants and Rhode Island's magistrates were elected by the people, the system of joint committees used in those legislatures, and the reduction of the Council's power in Virginia to a revisory role only— all these factors kept disputes to a minimum.

The upper houses, however, were by no means merely negative bodies which occasionally thwarted the colonials' drive for liberty. On the contrary, the councillors were usually men of exceptional ability, education, and experience, and their activities seem, on the whole, to have been beneficial. Most of their time was spent improving, not obstructing, legislation; and their amendments—often numerous—were usually accepted. They frequently took great care in their review of bills, of resolves, and of legislative business generally. As a result the colonials, even when most bitterly struggling with the councils, proposed not their abolition but only their reform. There were exceptions, as later developments made obvious, but in general the upper houses were criticized only when they ceased to perform their proper legislative functions and acted instead as agents of the executive.

Therefore, when independence made possible the adoption of new governments, the usefulness of the councils guaranteed their survival. Most of the upper class expected only to free the councils from their dependence upon the king, making them into aristocratic and independent senates. But the upper class was in for some surprises, for two unanticipated developments took place: the senates became increasingly democratic bodies, and political parties were born.

THE NEW SENATES

The new state constitutions incorporated both the old aristocratic assumptions and the new democratic directions. The conservatives tried to establish senates through which the elite could protect themselves, but they failed almost everywhere. In Virginia, for example, some of the most respected leaders hoped for life terms and indirect elections, and the plan presented to the convention by George Mason called for the voters to choose "deputies" who would then appoint senators possessed of £2,000 worth of land.[1] Instead, the convention eliminated all property qualifications and provided for direct elections. The first draft of the New York constitution, drawn by conservatives, included an electoral college, but this was eliminated by the convention. North Carolinians like William Hooper, who referred to a one-house legislature as a "many-headed monster," retired from that state's convention discomfited by its establishment of a Senate nearly as democratic as the House.[2] In Massachusetts, Theophilus Parsons advocated in his *Essex Result* the use of special county conventions to choose senators who would be "gentlemen of education, fortune and leisure,"[3] but he did not win his point. Conservative Pennsylvanians tried but failed to establish a second branch, while elsewhere the new governments either were unicameral or included a democratically chosen upper house.

Only Maryland's constitution was really satisfactory from the aristocratic point of view; for although high property qualifications were established in South Carolina, that Senate proved unreliable in practice. Every senate except Maryland's was elected by the voters. In six of the eleven states that had bicameral legislatures senators were chosen annually, and nowhere for as long a period as under the present Constitution of the United States. Property qualifications were often minimal, and probably only in Maryland and South Carolina did they exclude likely candidates for office. Thus, although many historians have felt that the Revolution was primarily a conservative movement, independence had actually brought a resounding conservative defeat.

The defeat was not, however, a rout. While the senates did not become elite bodies, they did contain strong aristocratic elements that occasionally succeeded in checking the more popular branch. They were no longer councils, yet they had not been totally transformed. In contrasting them with their predecessors we see the leaven of change; but in comparing them with the representatives, we see the persistence of the old.

The senates differed from the councils in almost every respect. First, they were larger bodies: during the dozen years before 1775 there had been fewer than three hundred councillors; during the next dozen there were nearly nine hundred. Most people at the time agreed that the senates were more representative as a result.

They were also more representative geographically. Whereas two-thirds of the councillors had resided in coastal commercial centers and three-fourths lived near the sea, over half of the senators came from interior districts and less than one-fourth lived in the large towns. The balance of power, then, even in the upper house, had shifted westward and become decisively rural; while the constituency of a councillor was a group of upper-class townspeople, that of a senator was a community of middle-class farmers. The occupations of the members had also changed. There were still fewer farmers than there ought to have been, but their proportion had increased markedly from about 30 percent to over half. The proportion of merchants was correspondingly cut in half, and lawyers suffered nearly as great a loss. Power also shifted downward economically. There were half as many wealthy men and three times as many men of moderate property; these were now, in fact, equal in number to the rich. The social origins of the senators contrasted just as sharply. Whereas extensive, powerful families had dominated many of the councils, this was not true of any senate except Maryland's, where the Lloyds still were influential. Men of the elite families—those known to be the sons of the merchants, lawyers, large landowners, and other men of means—now held one-fourth of the seats instead of one-half. Their places were taken, in the post-1776 upper houses, by men of humble origin—self-made men—whose numbers had now nearly doubled. For among the wealthy councillors, 24 percent had surpassed their parents' economic rank, as compared with 45 percent of the wealthy senators—a remarkably high rate of mobility, incidentally, in a political elite. The less aristocratic nature of the senates is further evidenced in the fact that only half as many senators were college men —scarcely more than one in six. Perhaps the increase in the number of dissenters at the expense of Anglicans would have been regarded, at least in Tory circles, as a turn for the worse. On the other hand, if Federalism equals conservatism the senators merited high marks, for two-thirds favored the ratification of the Constitution, and if North Carolina is omitted the proportion rises to more than three-fourths.

But while the senates obviously cannot be called aristocratic bodies, they were not, on the other hand, democratic, if to be so requires that they accurately reflect their society. The evidence for this has already been supplied: most senators were at least well-to-do, of good family; merchants and professional men furnished a third of the members, large landowners another third; and of course as a group they were still better educated and far more experienced politically than most of their countrymen. If the elite had been rendered nearly powerless in Georgia and North Carolina, and seriously weakened in New Hampshire and New Jersey, they still dominated the senates of South Carolina and Maryland.

The survival of upper-class influence—of what was then called the aristocratic principle—is especially obvious when the senators are compared with the representatives. There is no need to recapitulate here the facts already detailed. In general, an examination of the lower houses of New Hampshire, New York, New Jersey, Maryland, Virginia, and South Carolina shows that farmers (including large landowners) held between half and two-thirds of the seats and that men of wealth were outnumbered by majorities ranging from two-to-one to as high as eight-to-one.[4] Of course farmers and men of moderate property dominated the lower houses of the other states as well. Such controversies as developed between the two houses, and such attacks on the senates as occurred, were due to these contrasts.

THE RISE OF POLITICAL PARTIES

The process by which the upper houses were losing, though incompletely, their aristocratic qualities was accomplished by a change, fully as significant, in which they became the arenas for disputes between incipient parties. The development seems to have been unexpected and much lamented, although there had already been clear indications of it in various legislatures before 1776. No confident discussion of these emerging alignments is possible until a full analysis of the votes in the lower houses has been completed. However some generalizations can be risked. The divisions grew primarily out of political and economic rather than cultural issues, and are found in half to two-thirds of the votes recorded. There are sufficient votes in New York, New Jersey, Maryland, and North Carolina for us to draw satisfactory conclusions, and there are enough in several other states to be suggestive. The lines of division seem to have been similar everywhere. A sectional alignment was always present, but no simple terms such as east versus west are adequate. In New York, the City and its environs opposed the interior counties except for Albany. East and West Jersey took different sides. Sussex County, Delaware, furnished most of one party there, and Maryland's Eastern Shore was a center in that state. The principal antagonists in Virginia were the Northern Neck and the southwestern Piedmont. The northeastern counties of North Carolina obtained occasional support from the southeast against a nearly solid west, while low country and upcountry are fairly accurate terms for the division in South Carolina.

Differences in occupation are also discernible. Most evident is the consistent alignment of farmers—but not of large landowners —on one side. They were generally opposed by the large landowners and those with a nonfarm occupation, though the division is erratic. Much clearer is the class basis. Senators who were well-to-do were found in equal numbers on both sides, but the wealthy senators and those of moderate property were consistently opposed to one another (except in Virginia). An alignment even more significant statistically was that in which senators from the prominent old families voted by a margin of fifty-six to twenty against the self-made men; among the latter only thirteen out of sixty-seven deserted their side.[5] Finally, the tendency for Presbyterians and Anglicans to vote against one another continued. Most of the latter preferred the wealthy, eastern, old families who supported policies favorable to the aristocratic element; whereas the Presbyterians, along with the new men, joined the western, farmer, small-propertied, "popular" party. This description is certainly incomplete and may be inaccurate in its details, but several facts are indisputable. Most, perhaps all, of the senates witnessed the emergence of a popular party whose members cooperated in practice, though rarely in an organized way, in support of measures favorable to debtors, westerners, lower-income groups, and small farmers. They were often provincial rather than national in their outlook and were usually anti-Loyalist and anti-aristocratic. They generally favored the bills passed by the lower houses, since these houses were under a similar influence. As a rule they formed a minority element in the senates. But in North Carolina, Rhode Island, New Hampshire, and Delaware they were usually in control; in New York they were equal to their opponents; while in Massachusetts and New

Jersey they scored occasional victories. Most of them became Antifederalists.

On the other side was the conservative, "federal," or aristocratic
party. This party was originally intended to dominate all of the
senates, but it was secure only in four. It was sometimes able to
prevent or modify measures unfavorable to its interests, but the
senates proved increasingly unreliable in this respect. In the years
following independence, these factions or parties gradually became more cohesive, until by the end of the decade they had become major political forces. As this happened, the purely aristocratic role of the upper house became subordinate and its other
functions grew more conspicuous.

Controversies between the two houses developed most often when
the country or popular party controlled one house and its opponents the other. Each state therefore had its peculiar legislative
history. In Rhode Island, farmers held power in both houses, so
that the upper challenged the lower only on such rare occasions as
when the former became momentarily "federal" in 1787. Connecticut was peaceful except for two years when the impost and commutation were favored by the assistants but not by the deputies.
Relations were similarly harmonious in New Hampshire, though
the Senate did defend the creditor interest and oppose inflationary
measures. In New England generally, the two houses worked very
closely together through committees which reconciled their
differences in advance. Virginia's Senate also accepted most major
bills, despite its somewhat upper-class composition. Three probable reasons for this are that the Senate was not truly aristocratic
and the delegates were not as democratic as in some other states;
political alignments were less consistent here and parties more ru-
dimentary than in a state such as New York; and the Senate had
been deprived of its due influence by the constitution, which assigned it only a revisory power. North Carolina's Senate was equal
to the lower house in authority but did not differ from it in principle, so disagreements in that state followed no pattern. Thus in five
of the eleven bicameral legislatures the senates did not act as a
check upon democracy and did not adopt any specific policies
which would lead to disputes.

In several other senates, where emerging parties played a more prominent role, the situation was not so peaceful. In Massachusetts, where joint committees settled most issues, differences between the two houses were minor until the mid-1780's, when the upper house took the aristocratic side in defense of creditors, lawyers, sound money, and the strict collection of debts. It also manifested at this time a pro-eastern bias. In 1787, however, the Shaysite sympathizers made such gains as to cause a partial reversal of these policies. In New York, New Jersey, and Delaware, where the Clintonians and their equivalents managed to capture both houses, parties were even more important. Their control over the senates was uncertain, however, and disputes sometimes developed as a result, though these were minimized in New Jersey by numerous "free conferences," and in Delaware by the use of joint committees.

Only in South Carolina and Maryland were the senates truly aristocratic bodies; and even in the former a group of westerners formed a strong minority element that, during 1787, actually defeated the easterners on several votes. The influence of eastern planters was nevertheless strong enough in the lower house so that with the aid of frequent conferences most questions were settled amicably. Maryland, then, remains the one exceptional case; for here the House was sufficiently democratic and the Senate so aristocratic that prolonged and bitter disputes could not be avoided. Yet even in that stronghold of conservatism a minority faction took form which sided with the delegates.

Viewed as a whole, the senates had either ceased entirely to represent the aristocracy or did so only sporadically and imperfectly. By far their most important activity was the amending, rejecting, originating, and perfecting of bills and resolves. In almost every state the senate was equal to the lower house except in the initiation of money bills, which frequently was reserved for the representatives. And many instances can be cited in which the upper house was highly useful: it was more responsible financially, more careful in granting money, more inclined to support Congress, and sometimes more favorable to humanitarian and educational measures. The senators' superior education and experience —and perhaps, too, their superior ability—were unquestionably responsible for the passage of better laws and the rejection of unwise bills.

Senates in the New Nation

Thus not only the councils themselves but the very basis for an evaluation of the upper house had been revolutionized; and the senates were justifying themselves, even from a democratic point of view, as instruments of better government. They had come to perform functions scarcely different from those of the representatives, and they were now almost as much democratic bodies as they were aristocratic ones. Instead of uniformly reflecting the desires of a stable social or intellectual class, they were becoming the scene of political conflicts among men who represented a variety of interests. And the emergence of "factions" represented the beginning of popular parties, which were becoming the vehicle for majority rule in both houses. These important developments were, however, either unrecognized or opposed by most political writers of the period. On the one hand, theorists in the Whig tradition continued to think of the upper house as a stronghold of the elite whose task was to check democracy and monarchy. They regarded the factions as evil, resulting from the depravity of the people and the ambitions of demagogues. On the other hand, more democratically inclined writers sometimes continued to advocate the abolition of the senate; thus the Pennsylvania Constitutionalists opposed bicameralism in the fear that the upper house would represent property instead of people. Such attacks, however, were becoming increasingly infrequent, as senate after senate demonstrated its usefulness for a democratic government. While democrats had not yet articulated a defense for the new developments, except in a tentative way, they might well have regarded them as excellent.

The rapid decline of the aristocratic element in the senates, and the rise instead of parties, make the debates in the Federal Convention seem curiously anachronistic and unreal. When Randolph asserted that the chief danger lay in the democratic part of the Constitution, the delegates from most of the states might well have asked him what part he referred to. The idea that a senate must be independent of popular control was already outmoded. The delegates were indeed correct in noting that only Maryland's upper house successfully checked the lower; but instead of perceiving that the concept of an aristocratic "balance" was obsolete, many of them tried to resurrect the old system. The addresses of such men as Hamilton, Madison, Gouverneur Morris, C. C. Pinckney, and Randolph all stressed the Whig theory and the colonial tradition rather than the realities of the 1780's. Indeed the fact that the national Senate, as created, was something other than a frankly aristocratic body was to some extent unintentional, growing out of the conflict between the large and small states as well as from the need to conciliate public opinion.

Similarly, the later debate over ratification focused on what senates had been rather than on what they were becoming. Noah Webster's long dissertation on the corruption of the common people and the need for checks on democracy was reactionary. Madison's discussion of the checks and balances principle was more to the point, though his hatred of "factions" showed that, unless he is to be considered antidemocratic, he did not fully grasp what was taking place. On the other hand the idea of a division of powers, divested of its aristocratic aspects, was relevant and acceptable to the Antifederalists and Federalists alike. Moreover, most of the voters probably understood what was rarely expressed: that the senates were useful in a democracy and that factions could be beneficial. A Bostonian predicted, in the fall of 1787, that there would always be two parties: the party of the populace, of the levellers and democrats, consisting of debtors and men with small property; and that of the rich men and those with austere political principles, who sought to "subject the people to a rigid aristocracy." These parties, he felt, were good rather than bad.[6] The factions of the eighteenth century were becoming the parties of the nineteenth; aristocracy was yielding to democracy; and the councils, revolutionized, were metamorphosed into senates. The Federal Constitution, forward-looking as it was in many ways, curiously preserved in the Senate many features of the council: the long term, executive and judicial powers, and indirect election. These qualities were essentially European in concept rather than American. On the other hand, the Senate as a protector of state sovereignty—of the federal principle; the Senate whose members needed to have no property; and the Senate that was as representative of the majority will as the lower house, was an entirely new body. Within a few years it, too, was to become, like the state senates, the vehicle of party. When that occurred the transformation of the councils was completed.

Reference Matter

Notes

INTRODUCTION TO PART ONE

1 The exceptions were Pennsylvania and Delaware. See the general discussion of the council in Leonard Woods Labaree, *Royal Government in America* (New Haven, 1930), Chap. IV.
2 The surveyor general of customs for the southern district and (after 1770) the superintendent of Indian affairs for the southern department were members of the southern councils, but in practice they never attended any sessions except in South Carolina, where the superintendent occasionally was present.
3 Labaree, *Royal Government*, 136.
4 For an example, see New Jersey Historical Society, *Collections*, V (New York, 1858), 410–411.
5 By 1763 the governors had ceased to attend legislative sessions except in Massachusetts.
6 Thirty-two percent of the councillors held important offices. The proportion varied greatly from a high of four-fifths in Maryland to a low of one-sixth in Virginia and one-tenth in Rhode Island. But many of these officials had independent fortunes.

CHAPTER 1

THE PLACEMEN

1 Lawrence Henry Gipson, *The Coming of the Revolution* (New York, 1954), 150–152.
2 Kenneth Coleman, *The American Revolution in Georgia* (Athens, 1958), 27–28.
3 The salaries and perquisites are given in Percy Flippin, "The Royal Government in Georgia," *Georgia Historical Quarterly*, IX (1925), 215–216n.

4 Notably Henry Yonge and James Read. Joseph Gaston Baillie Bulloch, *A History and Genealogy of the Habersham Family* . . . . (Columbia, S.C., 1901), 137–138; Allen Johnson and Dumas Malone, eds., *Dictionary of American Biography* (22 vols., New York, 1928–1944), XV, 425.

5 William J. Northen, *Men of Mark in Georgia* (6 vols., Atlanta, 1907–1912), I, 23–31.

6 *D.A.B.*, VII, 476, VIII, 68–70; *The Georgia Gazette* (Savannah), May 9, 1770, July 13, 1768.

7 Allen D. Candler, comp., *The Colonial Records of the State of Georgia (1732–1782)* (26 vols., Atlanta, 1904–1916), VII, 155, 346, 377, 445, 454, 483, 633, VIII, 595, 603, IX, 513, X, 42, 160, 279, 882, 969–970, XI, 86. Another councillor, James MacKay, was a captain of "easy fortune" who received 500 acres. A few years later, it seems, having risen to the Council, he was granted another 700 acres, and then within a few years obtained at least 3,000 acres and several town lots. There were at least two men of the name, however, so precision is impossible. *Ibid.*, VI, 215, 226, VII, 265, 790, 820, IX, 315, X, 41, 395, XI, 323, XII, 121, 145, 311–312.

8 Wilbur Henry Siebert, *Loyalists in East Florida* (2 vols., DeLand, Florida, 1929), I, 80, II, 37; *Col. Rec. Ga.*, XI, 412, XII, 13, 52, 313; Lorenzo Sabine, *Biographical Sketches of Loyalists of the American Revolution* (2 vols., Boston, 1864), II, 534.

9 *South Carolina Historical and Genealogical Magazine*, XVII (1916), 148; Alexander A. Laurence, "Anthony Stokes," *Georgians in Profile: Historical Essays in Honor of Ellis Merton Coulter* (Athens, 1958), 61–88; Bulloch, *Habersham*, 137–138; C. L. Mowat, *East Florida as a British Province, 1763–84* (Berkeley, 1943), 125–127. Francis Harris' wife had a valuable estate in England. *Georgia Historical Quarterly*, XV (1931), 198–199. Lewis Johnston's father was a doctor in the royal navy, while Clement Martin's was a West Indian planter. Bulloch, *Habersham*, 177; *Col. Rec. Ga.*, VI, 443, X, 260, 402.

10 Grey Elliott, who had a mercantile firm with John Gordon, was probably a member of a prominent South Carolina family; James Read certainly was. Noble Jones was already a doctor when he came to Georgia with his intimate friend James Oglethorpe, and James MacKay may have had connections in Jamaica. Northen, *Men of Mark*, I, 195–207; *Col. Rec. Ga.*, VI, 215, 226. James E. Powell was a merchant when he arrived and almost immediately was appointed judge advocate of the Admiralty court. Siebert, *Loyalists*, I, 182; *Col. Rec. Ga.*, VI, 401, 429. Hume and Habersham, whose families may have been inconsequential, improved their position by fortunate marriages.

11 All but two or three of the councillors remained loyal during the Revolution. Bryan was a rebel. The positions of Martin and Read are un-

certain. They clearly played no prominent role on the rebel side, but their property was not confiscated.

12 *Col. Rec. Ga.*, XVII, 199–200.

13 *Ibid.*, 263.

14 William W. Abbot, *The Royal Governors of Georgia, 1754–1775* (Chapel Hill, 1959), 113.

15 *Ibid.*, 137; Coleman, *Revolution*, 27–28; *Col. Rec. Ga.*, XVII, 340, 342, 353, 357, 360.

16 *Ibid.*, 362–364.

17 *Ibid.*, 365–366.

18 Abbot, *Royal Governors*, 109–113, 135–136; Coleman, *Revolution*, 24–26; Jack P. Greene, *The Quest for Power: The Lower Houses of Assembly in the Southern Royal Colonies 1689–1776* (Chapel Hill, 1963), 425–426; Ella Lonn, *The Colonial Agents of the Southern Colonies* (Chapel Hill, 1945), 105–107.

19 *Col. Rec. Ga.*, XVII, 372–373.

20 Abbot, *Royal Governors*, 139.

21 *Col. Rec. Ga.*, XVII, 437.

22 For example, one measure concerning the regulation of slaves was rejected because it lacked a "suspending" clause (suspending its execution until the king approved of it). The lower house evidently gave in, and after several conferences an agreement was reached. *Ibid.*, 405, 509, 524, 551.

23 *Ibid.*, 763–764; see also *Georgia Gazette*, Mar. 23, 1774.

24 *Col. Rec. Ga.*, XVII, 774–779; Abbot, *Royal Governors*, 160; Coleman, *Revolution*, 26; Lonn, *Colonial Agents*, 108–109; *Georgia Gazette*, Jan. 26, Mar. 9, 1774.

25 Peter Force, ed., *American Archives*, 4 ser. I (Washington, 1837), 1154–1155, 1159.

26 Coleman, *Revolution*, 72.

27 Technically, £1,000 currency in other real estate. Material on the social structure of the colonies throughout this book has been drawn principally from a study of probate and tax records. See my book, *The Social Structure of Revolutionary America* (Princeton, 1965).

28 William Wragg, a wealthy planter, had been a member earlier, and in 1769 was appointed chief justice and councillor, but he rejected both offices and served instead in the lower house. *The South Carolina Gazette*, May 25, 29, Sept. 14, 1769. Daniel Moore, collector of the customs, arrived from Barbados in the spring of 1767 and was in theory a councillor, but he seems never to have attended, spent part of his brief term in England, was removed from the office of collector in 1769, and resigned from the Council in 1771. He has not been included. *Ibid.*, Oct. 18, Nov. 2, 1769, Sept. 19, 1771; *The South Carolina Gazette, and Country Journal*, Mar. 24, 1767.

29 *D.A.B.*, III, 252–253; *S.C. Hist. and Gen. Mag.*, I (1900) 76–90.

30 *Ibid.*, XX (1919), 11; *D.A.B.*, V. 448–449.
31 *D.A.B.*, XII, 600; *S.C. Hist. and Gen. Mag.*, I (1900), 153–161.
32 Colonial Society of Massachusetts, *Publications*, XIII (1910–1911), 195–196; *S.C. Hist. and Gen. Mag.*, XXI (1920), 15n, 63; Fielder M. M. Beall, *Colonial Families . . . Bell, Beal, Bale, Beale, Beall . . .* (Washington, D.C., 1929), 250–252. See also information of M. Eugene Sirmans, "The South Carolina Royal Council, 1720–1763," *The William and Mary Quarterly*, 3 ser. XVIII (1961), 378.
33 Bernard Elliott's grandfather founded the family fortune; Sir John Colleton's father had been a councillor; and John Guerrard's father was an eminent merchant as early as 1700. Henry A. M. Smith, *The Baronies of South Carolina* (Charleston, 1931), 131; *S.C. Hist. and Gen. Mag.*, I (1900), 335–338, XLIII (1952), 10–11.
34 H. Hale Bellot, "The Leighs in South Carolina," Royal Historical Society, *Transactions*, 5 ser. VI (1956), 161–187. Thomas Skottowe, one of the placemen, married into the wealthy Bellinger family (his wife's father was a Landgrave). John Stuart, the superintendent of Indian affairs, also married a prominent Charleston girl and acquired a beautiful home in the city. His brother, moreover, was a Beaufort merchant. John Burn, a Scot, held no office other than that of councillor. He married the widow of a Charleston minister and had at least 2 wharves, 2 schooners, 30 slaves, 2,750 acres, 2 lots in Charleston, and money out at interest, so that he was a part of the colony both socially and economically. J. Skottowe Wannamaker, *The Wannamaker, Salley, Mackay and Bellinger Families* (Charleston, 1937), 26–27; *D.A.B.*, XVIII, 172–173; *S.C. Gazette*, Oct. 6, 1766; *S.C. Hist. and Gen. Mag.*, XX (1919), 259; *The South Carolina and American Gazette*, Nov. 16, 1769.
35 Sirmans, "S.C. Royal Council," 392. See also, for Elliott, Smith, *Baronies*, 143; for Guerrard, Arthur Henry Hirsch, *The Huguenots of Colonial South Carolina* (Durham, 1928), 24–25; for Skottowe, *S.C. Hist. and Gen. Mag.*, VI (1905), 124–125.
36 Sirmans, "S.C. Royal Council," 390; W. Roy Smith, *South Carolina as a Royal Province 1719–1776* (New York, 1903), 87; Edward McCrady, *The History of South Carolina under the Royal Government* (2 vols., New York, 1899), II, 712.
37 *S.C. Gazette*, June 22, 1769.
38 Journal of the Upper House, July 5, 16, 1764.
39 Smith, *Royal Province*, 325.
40 Journal of the Upper House, July 17, Aug. 7, 1764.
41 Smith, *Royal Province*, 166–168; Sirmans, "S.C. Royal Council," 388–389; Lonn, *Colonial Agents*, 76.
42 Journal of the Upper House, Aug. 21–24, 1764.
43 *Ibid.*, Oct. 3–5, 1765.
44 *Ibid.*, Jan. 15, 1765. See Beale's protest of Jan. 31.
45 Smith, *Royal Province*, 293–294, 302–303; Frederick C. Bowes, *Cul-*

tural Life in Early Charleston (Chapel Hill, 1942), 125; Greene, *Quest for Power*, 53–60.

46 Journal of the Upper House, Aug. 22–23, 1764.

47 *Ibid.*, Mar. 20, 1767. A similar measure passed two years later.

48 *S.C. Gazette,* Dec. 3, and supplement, Oct. 1, 1764.

49 Journal of the Upper House, Mar. 25, 1768.

50 Journal of the Lower House, July 19–22, 1769, Feb. 23, 1771; Greene, *Quest for Power*, 382–383, 400.

51 Technically, the Commons had already ordered the money to be paid from the treasury, and the tax bill now replaced the money that had been spent. This practice, which originally had been followed only in emergencies, had become usual.

52 McCrady, *South Carolina,* II, 683–688; Journal of the Lower House, Apr. 7, 10, Aug. 22, 29, Sept. 7, 1770; Jack P. Greene, "Bridge to Revolution: The Wilkes Fund Controversy in South Carolina, 1769–1775," *Journal of Southern History,* XXXIX (1963), 19–52.

53 Journal of the Lower House, Nov. 4, 1771; John Drayton, *Memoirs of the American Revolution from its commencement to the year 1776 . . .* (2 vols., Charleston, 1821), I, 65–70.

54 Journal of the Upper House, Mar. 26, Aug. 13, 21, 24, 1773.

55 Drayton, *Memoirs,* I, 103–107, 214–215.

56 Journal of the Upper House, Aug. 26, 1773.

57 McCrady, *South Carolina,* II, 715–723; Smith, *Royal Province,* 389–393; Journal of the Upper House, Aug. 26, 31, Sept. 2–3, 6–7, 11, 1773.

58 *S.C. Gazette,* Sept. 13, 1773.

59 *Ibid.*, Sept. 15, 1773.

60 *Ibid.*, Nov. 5, 1772.

61 Drayton wrote: "A Man, who *can* 'boast of having received a liberal Education,' and Men who have *read a little,* whether their Knowledge is acquired from *Compendiums,* or the *Embellishments of a Map,* it matters not; I say, I think such Men should make a proper use of such Advantages, and not have consulted *de arduis respublicae,* with Men who never were in a Way to study, or to advise upon any Points, but Rules how to cut up a *Beast in the Market* to the best Advantage, to *cobble* an old Shoe in the neatest Manner, or to build a necessary House. Nature never intended that *such Men* should be *profound Politicians,* or *able Statesmen. . . ." Ibid.,* Sept. 28, 1769.

62 *Ibid.*, Sept. 21, 1769, Oct. 18, 1770.

63 For the artisans' counterattack, see *ibid.*, Oct. 5, 1769.

64 Letters of Governor Bull, Sept. 13, Oct. 8, 1764, Colonial Office Records, 5 ser., 378. I am grateful to Merrill Jensen for bringing this reference to my attention.

65 *S.C. Gazette,* May 3, 1764.

66 The paper noted that the business of the superintendent had been shifted to other individuals, so that he had little to do except dis-

tribute presents to the Indians, yet his salary had just been increased. He was reported to have left town, "but whether he is gone farther than his Plantation we do not presume to know." *Ibid.*, July 23, Aug. 1, 1768.

67 *Ibid.*, Apr. 4, 1774.

68 *Ibid.*, Mar. 6, 1775.

69 Drayton, *Memoirs*, I, 246.

70 *North Carolina Historical Review*, X (1933), 279.

71 *Ibid.*, II (1925), 351.

72 Colonial Society of Massachusetts, *Publications*, VI (1899–1900), 385–393; Edward A. Jones, *The Loyalists of Massachusetts, Memorials, Petitions and Claims* (London, 1930), 166–167.

73 *S.C. Hist. and Gen. Mag.*, XIX (1918), 60–64, XX (1919), 47–48, XXXVII (1936), 21–22. Robert Palmer, the surveyor general, was born in Pasquotank County, where his father was a prosperous farmer. Robert O. DeMond, *The Loyalists in North Carolina during the Revolution* (Durham, N.C., 1940), 179; J. Bryan Grimes, *North Carolina Wills and Inventories* (Raleigh, 1912), 278.

74 DeMond, *Loyalists in North Carolina*, 159–160; *N.C. Hist. Rev.*, X (1933), 279; Charles G. Sellers, Jr., "Private Profits and British Colonial Policy: The Speculations of Henry McCulloh," *Wm. and Mary Qtly.*, 3 ser. VIII (1951) 535–551. Lewis Henry De Rosset may have been born in the colony, though it is more likely that he was already a few years old when his father, a doctor, left Basle, Switzerland, for Wilmington. De Rosset was a respected and wealthy merchant who, though accused of currying favor with the people, became a Loyalist. William L. Saunders, ed., *The Colonial Records of North Carolina* (10 vols., Raleigh, 1886–1890), IX, 973; DeMond, *Loyalists in North Carolina*, 56–57; Marshall De Lancey Haywood, *Governor William Tryon* . . . . (Raleigh, 1903), 47; Kemp B. Battle, *Letters and Documents, Relating to the History of the Lower Cape Fear*, James Sprunt Historical Monographs, No. 4 (Chapel Hill, 1903), 21. Nathaniel Dukenfield's great uncle had been a landowner in Chowan County. Haywood, *Tryon*, 50.

75 *Col. Rec. N.C.*, VI, 1130–1132.

76 *Ibid.*, 1255.

77 *Ibid.*, 1133–1137. See for background, Lonn, *Colonial Agents*, 78–85.

78 *Col. Rec. N.C.*, VI, 1287–1288.

79 *Ibid.*, VII, 337, 347–350.

80 *Ibid.*, 918, VIII, 98. See Tryon to Hillsborough, Feb. 25, 1769, VIII, 11.

81 *Ibid.*, VII, 55–56.

82 *Ibid.*, 312, 314, 324, 328, 330–331. See the discussion in Greene, *Quest for Power*, 234–243.

83 *Col. Rec. N.C.*, VI, 1235, 1246.

84 *Ibid.*, 1142.

85 *Ibid.*, 1122, 1243, 1256.

86 *Ibid.*, 1252, VII, 334–335; Greene, *Quest for Power*, 292–294.

87 *Col. Rec. N.C.*, VII, 272.

88 To Dartmouth, New-Bern, Apr. 6, 1774, *ibid.*, IX, 971.

89 *Ibid.*, VII, 919–920.

90 *Ibid.*, VIII, 357–377.

91 *Ibid.*, VII, 338, 341, 620.

92 *Ibid.*, VIII, 375–377.

93 *Ibid.*, 376; Dobbs to the Board of Trade, Mar. 7, 1763, *ibid.*, VI, 970.

94 *Ibid.*, IX, 732, 781–782.

95 *Ibid.*, 844–846, 853–854.

96 *Ibid.*, VI, 1234.

97 *Ibid.*, IX, 434–438, 721–723. The Council finally surrendered on the latter issue, however, despite the royal allowance of a previous law.

98 *Ibid.*, VII, 911–915.

99 Martin to Dartmouth, Dec. 24, 1773, *ibid.*, IX, 792.

100 The law that passed was unsatisfactory because it included provisions for the attachment of foreign property; moreover it did not set adequate fees for the chief justice, and limited the superior court's jurisdiction to creditors of "Inferior types," as Governor Martin put it. *Ibid.*, 404–406, 412, 416–417, 830, 844–871, 973. Rutherford, wrote the governor, was a bankrupt (he was not); De Rosset sought applause, and Sampson followed De Rosset; Dry was a republican (he did, in fact, become a rebel); and Cornell, who had no education but had acquired a fortune "from the lowest beginning" (actually his father was a well-to-do farmer), was good at trade but knew nothing else.

101 *Ibid.*, VII, 912.

102 *Ibid.*, 915–922.

103 *Ibid.*, IX, 119.

104 *Ibid.*, 222, 233.

105 *Ibid.*, VII, 329, 352, 598, 600, VIII, 372.

106 *Ibid.*, VII, 605.

107 *Ibid.*, VI, 1102, 1107, 1109, 1202, 1115, 1137–1138.

108 *Ibid.*, VII, 325, 561, 600, 915, VIII, 352, 360, IX, 113, 116.

109 *Ibid.*, VII, 911, IX, 855.

110 *Ibid.*, IX, 866–867. The Council's veto accorded with British policy.

111 *Ibid.*, VI, 1240.

112 *Ibid.*, VII, 58, VI, 1246, IX, 433, 547, VIII, 349.

113 *Ibid.*, VII, 1104, 1116–1118, 1122–1125, 1111, 1121, 1126, 1239, 1244, 1257, VIII, 325–327, 606, 614, 616–617, 620, 652, IX, 425, 433, 427, 435, 438, 547. One bill thus vetoed would have pardoned certain Regulators.

114 *Ibid.*, VI, 1122, VII, 54, VIII, 352, 357, IX, 115, 418.

115 This group contained the following men: Benedict Calvert was the bastard son of the fifth Lord Baltimore; John Ridout came over as private secretary and heir of Governor Sharpe and married a daughter of Governor Ogle; George Steuart was a relative of the Calverts, and was entrusted with the care of Benedict when the latter first arrived. Benjamin Tasker's sister married Governor Bladen and his daughter married Governor Ogle (so that Ridout married Tasker's niece). Daniel and Walter Dulany were allied politically with this group, and the former married Tasker's daughter. R. Winder Johnson, *The Ancestry of Rosalie Morris Johnson* (n.p., 1905), 22–24, 30; Donnell MacClure Owings, *His Lordship's Patronage: Offices of Profit in Colonial Maryland* (Baltimore, 1953), 77, 129, 132; Lady Matilda Ridout Edgar, *A Colonial Governor in Maryland* (London, 1912), 2, 10n; Hester Dorsey Richardson, *Side-lights on Maryland history, with sketches of early Maryland Families* (Baltimore, 1913), 192; Aubrey C. Land, *The Dulanys of Maryland* (Baltimore, 1955), 50–52; *Maryland Historical Magazine,* IV. (1909), 191–192.

116 The Lloyd family tree is a complex affair, interlocking especially with the Tilghmans, the Hollydays, and the Rousbys. Colonel John Rousby's sister Elizabeth married Richard Bennett. Their son took as his second wife the widow of Philemon Lloyd, progenitor of the family. Philemon's grandson Edward Lloyd (who became Richard Bennett's heir) married one of Colonel Rousby's daughters. Other daughters married Councillor R. J. Henry and the future senator, Richard Barnes. Colonel Rousby's widow married George Plater, and their son, Councillor George, married Colonel Rousby's granddaughter, the daughter of John Rousby, whose widow married George Fitzhugh of the Council. Meanwhile a granddaughter of Philemon Lloyd wed the Honorable J. B. Bordley, brother of the Honorable Stephen Bordley; another granddaughter married the Honorable Samuel Chamberlaine; and a great-great-granddaughter married the Honorable William Hayward. See John Bozman Kerr, *Genealogical Notes of the Chamberlaine Family* (Baltimore, 1880), 8–23; William Henry Eldridge, *Henry Genealogy* (Boston, 1915), 193–194; *D.A.B.*, XI, 330–331; Richardson, *Side-lights,* 14–15, 128, 217.

117 For Key, see *Md. Hist. Mag.*, V (1910), 194–199.

118 For Hammond, see Rosamond Randall Beirne and Edith Rossiter Bevan, *The Hammond-Harwood House* (Annapolis, 1914). William Hayward's origins are not known. Ridout had attended Oxford and presumably came from a family of means, and perhaps was a relative of Governor Sharpe. George Steuart apparently belonged to a Scottish family of some importance.

119 Charles A. Barker, *The Background of the Revolution in Maryland* (New Haven, 1940), 181.

120 Elizabeth Bordley Gibson, *Biographical Sketches of the Bordley Family, of Maryland* (Philadelphia, 1865); E. Alfred Jones, *American Members of the Inns of Court* (London, 1924), 26–27; for Goldsborough, see *Md. Hist. Mag.*, X (1915), 100–107, XXXVI (1941), 315–335.

121 See Owings, *Patronage, passim;* Newton D. Mereness, *Maryland as a Proprietary Province* (New York, 1901), 182. All of the councillors were justices of the peace. Land, *Dulanys,* 355.

122 For additional information on the councillors see: for Henry Hooper, Elias Jones, *Revised History of Dorchester County, Maryland* (Baltimore, 1925), 350–356; for the Lees, Margaret Brown Klapthor and Paul Dennis Brown, *The History of Charles County, Maryland* (La Plata, Maryland, 1958). 98–100; and for the Lloyds, Oswald Tilghman, *History of Talbot County, Maryland* (2 vols., Baltimore, 1915), I, 164–176.

123 If the division within the 1765 legislature was typical, the difference between the members of the two parties was not economic or social, but geographical. Delegates from the Eastern Shore and the counties of Calvert and St. Mary's on the lower Chesapeake almost invariably adhered to the court party, while those from other counties of the upper Chesapeake (Baltimore and Anne Arundel) and the Potomac (Prince Georges, Charles, and Frederick), which also included the "west," were almost without exception part of the country party.

124 Evarts Boutell Greene, *The Provincial Governor in the English Colonies in North America* (New York, 1898), 88n.

125 Barker, *Background,* 248–249.

126 William Hand Browne, J. Hall Pleasants, Raphael Semmes, and Elizabeth Merritt, eds., *Archives of Maryland* (65 vols. to date, Baltimore, 1883–1952), XIV, 25, 53.

127 *Ibid.,* LIX, 392–395, 412–413.

128 *Ibid.,* LVIII, 280–283, 405–406.

129 *Ibid.,* LXIV, 79–80.

130 *Ibid.,* LXI, 127–128, 209–210. The Council's objection sounds like a legalistic argument to justify what was really a defense of royal authority, but since the Council had approved of the Stamp Act Congress, its stated reason may have been the true one.

131 *Ibid.,* 126–130.

132 *Ibid.,* LXII, 354, 407–408.

133 *Ibid.,* 364.

134 *Ibid.,* LXIII, 25.

135 *Ibid.,* 28, 33–35. See also LVIII, 265, for an instance of successful amendment.

136 *Ibid.,* XVIII, 244.

137 There is an excellent account in *ibid.,* LIX, lvi–lvii; see also Lonn, *Colonial Agents,* 102–105.

138 "A Friend," Sept. 26, 1768. The Council amended the bill so as to suspend its operation for nine months. Ultimately it became law. *Archives of Maryland,* LXI, lxxi–lxxii.

139 *Ibid.,* LXIII, 326. See for other examples *ibid.,* LXII, 28, 202, LXIII, 330, LXIV, 286, 325.

140 *Ibid.,* LXI, xxiii, civ–cv, 8, 25, 32, 53.

141 *Ibid.,* LVIII, 268; Land, *Dulanys,* 250–251; Barker, *Background,* 332–333.

142 *Archives of Maryland,* LXIII, 286, 411–412, LXI, xxii, cii–cvi, l.

143 *Ibid.,* LXIV, 58, 285.

144 Owings, *Patronage,* 12–13n.

145 £500 sufficed to enable one to live like a gentleman. Moreover the men concerned usually had other sources of income.

146 Mereness, *Maryland,* 389. See also Barker, *Background,* 345–349.

147 *Archives of Maryland,* LXII, 200, 370, LXIV, 297. One-third of the councillors were lawyers. Other instances in which the will of the proprietor and councillors prevailed over that of the delegates are documented in *ibid.,* LVIII, 252, 255–256, 364–365, LIX, xxxvii, xxxv, LXI, xxxiv–xxv. A debate occurred over an Act for Issuing Writs of Replevin Out of the County Courts of this Province. These writs could be obtained only from the Chancellor's office in Annapolis, where he extracted a fee, and were therefore expensive and inconvenient for most people. The Council defended the Chancellor, and asserted that it would not submit to an attack which might set a precedent. The bill was defeated on three different occasions and never became law. *Ibid.,* LXII, xxxi, 26–28, 201, LXIII, 31.

148 *Ibid.,* XVIII, 246, LXII, 46, 163–165. Note that the lower house here recognized the Council as part of the legislature.

149 *Ibid.,* LVIII, 223–224, 228–231, 333–338, 238–241, 348–350, 245–247; LXII, xxvii–xxxi and references given; LXIII, 18, 42–65, 331; LXIV, xvii–xviii, xx, 12, 38, 45. See the account in Barker, *Background,* 345–358.

150 *Archives of Maryland,* LXI, 8, 10, 124–126, 247–252, LXII, 28–29, LXIII, 29, 328–329, LXIV, 12, 61, 66–68, 291–292. Bills were defeated in 1773 but passed in 1774. For additional instances of the Council's defense of property rights, see *ibid.,* LIX, 57, 62, 68, LXIV, 64, 290.

151 *Ibid.,* LIX, xxvii, lix-lx, 49, 161, 181–182, 194–195, LXII, 353–354, 360, 362.

152 *Ibid.,* LVIII, 253–254, 260, LXIV, 289.

153 *Ibid.,* LXI, 75–82, LXII, 15. This involved certain proprietary rights.

154 *Ibid.,* LXIII, 23, 26–27.

155 *Ibid.,* LXI, 118, 307, LXIII, 29.

156 *Ibid.,* LIX, xxv.

157 *Ibid.,* LXII, xxiii–xxiv.

158 *Ibid.,* LVIII, 261, 382, 402–403; Land, *Dulanys,* 248–249, 360. Bark-

er feels that the delegates really wanted a college, but obviously they were unwilling to pay for one themselves. *Background*, 330.

159 *Archives of Maryland*, LXII, 201, 358.

160 *Ibid.*, LXI, 114, 154, 187, 190, 235, 238.

161 *Ibid.*, LXIII, 323–324. The Council's acceptance of a law that regulated clerical incomes was a victory for the delegates over the proprietor. There is a good account in Barker, *Background*, 360–366.

162 *Archives of Maryland*, LXII, 304, LXIII, 31, 329, 381–382.

163 *Ibid.*, LXIV, 295–297, 355.

164 *Pennsylvania Chronicle*, Mar. 23, 1772.

165 Matthew Tilghman and Charles Carroll, Barrister, both refused appointments in 1768. *Archives of Maryland*, LXIV, 550–551, 557.

CHAPTER 2

THE ELITE

1 For Camm see Allen Johnson and Dumas Malone, eds., *Dictionary of American Biography* (22 vols., New York, 1928–1944), III, 440–441; *William and Mary College Quarterly*, 1 ser. XIX (1910–1911), 28–30. Technically Stuart was a member of all of the southern councils, but I have treated him as a member of South Carolina's upper house because he made his residence in that colony and attended meetings nowhere else. Earlier in the colonial period Virginia's councillors had held many high offices. See Percy Scott Flippin, *The Royal Government in Virginia 1624–1775* (New York, 1919), 154, 159–160.

2 Gawin Corbin's father Richard and grandfather Henry had both been councillors. The Corbins were related to the Lees, Tayloes, and Wormeleys. The Carters had intermarried with the Burwells, Nelsons, Pages, and Byrds, while the Pages brought in the Randolphs, Wormeleys, and Tayloes from the first group. Presly Thornton married an adopted daughter of Colonel John Tayloe. The councillors were related to the Harrisons, Grymes, Griffins, Armisteads, Braxtons, Fitzhughs, Turbervilles, Bassetts, and Ludwells. See especially references in Earl G. Swem, comp., *Virginia Historical Index* (2 vols., Roanoke, 1934–1936); Louis Morton, *Robert Carter of Nomini Hall* (Princeton, 1941).

3 *Virginia Magazine of History and Biography*, IV (1896–1897), 102–104, XXXIV (1926), 29–48.

4 *D.A.B.*, II, 337.

5 With few exceptions, councillors educated in England became Loyalists. Those educated in the colonies divided about as did the non-college men.

6 Jackson T. Main, "The One Hundred," *William and Mary Quarterly*, 3 ser. XI (1954), 354–384.

7 The statements in the text are based on an examination of the 1773

Burgesses using the references in Swem's *Index,* local histories, genealogies, tax lists, and probate records.

8 Jackson T. Main, "Sections and Politics in Virginia, 1781–1787," *Wm. and Mary Qtly.,* 3 ser. XII (1955), 96–112.

9 An excellent analysis of the power structure within the Burgesses is Jack P. Greene, "Foundations of Political Power in the Virginia House of Burgesses, 1720–1776," *ibid.,* XVI (1959), 485–506.

10 H. R. McIlwaine, ed., *Legislative Journals of the Council of Colonial Virginia* (3 vols., Richmond, 1919), III, 1332–1334 (hereafter referred to as *Council Journals*).

11 *Ibid.,* 1383–1384.

12 Byrd had opposed the resistance movement but took no open stand. Richard Corbin remained loyal but retired and was not molested. Fairfax went to England in 1773 and died there. Philip Ludwell Lee might have become a Tory or a neutral, but he died in 1775. Cazenove Gardner Lee, Jr., *Lee Chronicle* (New York, 1957), 72. Ralph Wormeley was arrested as a Loyalist and confined until 1778, but his property was not touched. *Va. Mag. Hist. and Biog.,* XVIII (1910), 373–375. Camm, of course, was a thoroughgoing Loyalist. On the other hand, Robert Carter, Gawin Corbin, the three Nelsons, the two Pages, and John Tayloe were all Whigs. There remains only Robert C. Burwell among the contemporary councillors whose position is not clear. He certainly was not an active Tory. Thus there was a clear majority on the rebel side.

13 H. R. McIlwaine and John P. Kennedy, eds., *Journals of the House of Burgesses of Virginia* (13 vols., Richmond, 1905–1915), 1769, 304, 322–323; 1770, 103–104; 1775, 276 (hereafter referred to as *Journals of the Burgesses*).

14 *Ibid.,* 1770, 36, 54.

15 *Ibid.,* 82–83.

16 *Ibid.,* 1765, 351–354; 1770, 104–106.

17 *Ibid.,* 1763, 189.

18 *Ibid.,* 1767, 129; *Council Journals,* 1375–1376.

19 *Council Journals,* 1384; *Journals of the Burgesses,* 1764, 308; 1772, 306–307.

20 *Journals of the Burgesses,* 1772, 254, 266–268; *Council Journals,* 1465.

21 *Council Journals,* 1319.

22 *Journals of the Burgesses,* 1770, 82–84.

23 *Ibid.,* 1772, 260–261.

24 *Council Journals,* 1335.

25 *Journals of the Burgesses,* 1770, 12.

26 Supplement Extraordinary to the *Virginia Gazette,* Oct. 25, 1765.

27 *Council Journals,* 1373–1374, 1402.

28 *Ibid.,* 1421, 1464.

29 *Journals of the Burgesses,* 1772, 301; 1773, 34–35.

30 *Council Journals*, 1341, 1374, 1417.

31 *Ibid.*, 1319, 1335, 1337, 1346, 1374.

32 *Ibid.*, 1405–1406; *Journals of the Burgesses*, 1770, 55–56.

33 *Va. Gazette* (Purdie and Dixon), July 18, Aug. 29, 1766; see also July 25, 1766.

34 North had proposed that Parliament refrain from taxing any colony that adequately provided for the common defense and the civil government. The colonies uniformly rejected the plan.

35 *Va. Gazette* (Purdie), June 2, 1775.

36 Lucille Blanch Griffith, *The Virginia House of Burgesses, 1750–1774* (Northport, Alabama, 1963), 14.

37 The relationships were through the Skinner, Kearney, Johnstone, and Parker families, and included councillors Peter Kemble, Robert Lettice Hooper, John Lawrence, John Stevens, Stephen Skinner, and James Parker. Other relatives were the attorney general, Cortlandt Skinner, John Watts of the New York Council, the New York manor lord Stephen Van Cortlandt, Treasurer John Smyth, and General Thomas Gage. Several other councillors, though not, strictly speaking, members of the Perth Amboy family, were connected with it, including William Alexander, David Ogden, Richard Stockton, and the East Jersey Proprietors Robert Hunter Morris and Lewis Morris Ashfield. See Edgar Jacob Fisher, *New Jersey as a Royal Province 1738–1776* (New York, 1911), 58–71; William A. Whitehead, *Contributions to the Early History of Perth Amboy and Adjoining Country* . . . (New York, 1856), 99–120, 129–136; Leonard Lundin, *Cockpit of the Revolution: The War for Independence in New Jersey* (Princeton, 1940), 13n, 45–47, 78–80; James Parker, *The Parker and Kearney Families of New Jersey* (Perth Amboy, 1925); W. Northey Jones, *The History of St. Peter's Church in Perth Amboy, New Jersey* (New York, 1925), 340–349.

38 Donald L. Kemmerer, *Path to Freedom: The Struggle for Self-Government in Colonial New Jersey 1703–1776* (Princeton, 1940), 310n; *Documents relating to the Colonial History of the State of New Jersey* (Newark, Trenton, 1880 to date), n.s., IX, 475–477n (hereafter referred to as *New Jersey Archives*).

39 Frederick Smyth may have had some property in England, but all that is certain about his economic status is that as chief justice he was paid £120 or so annually, plus fees, and that as a Loyalist he received a yearly allowance of £400. John Lawrence was certainly well off, but there is no evidence of real wealth, and he was not a great landholder. On the other hand, William Alexander, to give a single example, left legacies of £6,300. New Jersey Historical Society, *Collections*, IX (Newark, 1916), 156–157; *New Jersey Archives*, X, 302–303, XXXIII, 20.

40 Fisher, *New Jersey*, 67.

41 *New Jersey Archives*, XVII, 344–356.

42 *Ibid.*, XVIII, 97, 99.

43 Fisher, *New Jersey*, 308–317.

44 *New Jersey Archives*, XVIII, 95, 100; *Journals of the New Jersey House of Representatives*, Oct.–Dec., 1769 (hereafter referred to as *Journals of the House*).

45 *Journals of the House*, Feb. 15, 21, 1769.

46 *Ibid.*, Mar. 3, 5, 1774.

47 *New Jersey Archives*, XVII, 369–377; *Journals of the House*, Feb., 1764.

48 *New Jersey Archives*, XVII, 380.

49 *Ibid.*, 492–495.

50 *Ibid.*, XVIII, 84–89; *Journals of the House*, Oct.–Dec., 1769.

51 *New Jersey Archives*, XVIII, 333, 427; *Journals of the House*, Feb. 14, 1775.

52 *New Jersey Archives*, XVIII, 241, 245.

53 *Ibid.*, 246–251.

54 The Council adopted the following amendment to a bill for the protection of cattle, to which the Assembly objected: "Provided always, That nothing in this Act shall be construed to extend or give Relief to any Person or Persons making a Practice of driving Horses, Cattle, Sheep and Hogs into the Counties of Bergen, Morris and Sussex, from any other County in this Province, or from either of the said Counties into the other, with an Intention or Design of pasturing the same in the Ranges or Outlets of unimproved Lands within either of the three Counties aforesaid, unless every such Person be an Owner and Proprietor in his or her own Right of a Freehold of at least Three Hundred Acres of Land within the particular County to which he or she shall drive the said Horses, Cattle, and Sheep as aforesaid, or Hogs for Range or Pasture." *Journals of the House*, Feb. 28, 1774.

55 I have here omitted Sir William Johnson, the Indian agent, who never attended after 1753, and Cadwallader Colden, the lieutenant governor.

56 Charles W. Apthorpe, William Axtell, Henry and John Harris Cruger, James Jauncey, Jr., Joseph Reade, Hugh Wallace, William Walton II, John Watts, and Henry White owed their fortunes to trade, not to their landed estates, while the two William Smiths and Horsmanden derived their principal income from the law. Therefore only William Alexander and Oliver DeLancey, both of whom were merchants, and Roger Morris, who had been an army officer, can be considered true representatives of the manor lords.

57 Carson A. Axtell, *Axtell Genealogy* (New Bedford, 1945), 12–13.

58 Virginia Harrington, *The New York Merchant on the Eve of the Revolution* (New York, 1935), 29, 115, 143–144, 218–219; Lorenzo Sabine, *Biographical Sketches of Loyalists of the American Revolution* (2 vols., Boston, 1864), I, 170; Alexander C. Flick, *Loyalism in New York during the American Revolution* (New York, 1901), 156.

59 *Va. Mag. Hist. and Biog.*, XXXV (1927), 229–230; *D.A.B.*, IX, 237–

238; E. Alfred Jones, *American Members of the Inns of Court* (London, 1924), 100–101; New York Historical Society, *Collections*, 1897, 238–284; 1900, 57.

60 *D.A.B.*, XIII, 226.

61 *Magazine of American History*, VI (1881), 272–273.

62 *The Providence Gazette*, Mar. 23, 1771; *Colonial Records of the New York Chamber of Commerce, 1768–1784, with historical and biographical sketches by John Austin Stevens Jr.* (New York, 1867), 19–26.

63 *Ibid.*, 35–40; Sabine, *Biographical Sketches of Loyalists*, II, 417–418.

64 George Joseph Ruppel, "The Council and Its Activities in Business, Politics, and Law in New York, 1600–1760" (diss., University of Pittsburgh, 1955), especially 8, 287.

65 *New York Journal*, Supplement, Dec. 7, 1769.

66 *New York Gazette and Weekly Mercury*, Apr. 23, 1770.

67 *Journal of the Legislative Council of the Colony of New-York, Begun the 8th Day of December, 1743; and Ended the 3d of April, 1775* (Albany, 1861), 1558 (Oct. 19, 1764).

68 *Ibid.*, 1932–1936 (Mar. 15–18, 1774).

69 *Ibid.*, 1525, 1529, 1530, (Dec. 15–20, 1763).

70 *Ibid.*, 1580 (Dec. 20, 1765).

71 *Ibid.*, 1555 (Oct. 15, 1764).

72 *Ibid.*, 1703–1705 (May 18–19, 1769).

73 *Ibid.*, 1698–1699 (May 11, 1769).

74 *Ibid.*, 1736 (Jan. 18, 1770).

75 *Ibid.*, 1706, 1736, 1738–1739 (May 19, 1769, Jan. 18, 23, 1770).

76 Colden to Hillsborough, Feb. 21, 1770, N.Y. Hist. Soc., *Collections*, 1877, 211.

77 See Lawrence Shaw Mayo, *John Wentworth* (Cambridge, 1921).

78 See the account in Leonard Woods Labaree, *Conservatism in Early American History* (New York, 1948), 19–20.

79 John L. Sibley and Clifford K. Shipton, *Biographical Sketches of Those who Attended Harvard College* (in progress, Boston, 1873–), III, 221–231; Nathaniel Adams, *Annals of Portsmouth. . . .* (Portsmouth, 1825), 269; *The New-Hampshire Gazette, and General Advertiser* (Portsmouth), Nov. 3, 17, 1769; clipping, n.p. n.d., New Hampshire Historical Society; Nathaniel Bouton *et al.*, eds., *New Hampshire Provincial, Town, and State Papers* (40 vols., Concord and Nashua, 1867–1943), VIII, 832 (hereafter referred to as *N.H. Prov. Papers, N.H. Town Papers*, or *N.H. State Papers*).

80 Henry Harrison Metcalf, ed., *Laws of New Hampshire . . .* , Vol. III 1745–1774 (Bristol, N.H., 1915), 508; Charles Warren Brewster, *Rambles about Portsmouth* (2 vols., Portsmouth, 1859, 1869), II, 65; Lawrence Shaw Mayo, *John Langdon* (Concord, 1937), 13-14. Councillors John Rindge and Ann (Jotham) Odiorne had a number of children including Elizabeth, who married Councillor Mark H. Went-

worth, Ann, who married Councillor Daniel Peirce, Mehitable, who married Councillor Daniel Rogers, and Councillor Daniel Rindge. James Creighton Odiorne, *Genealogy of the Odiorne Family* (Boston, 1875). The Odiornes were wealthy merchants and large landowners.

81 Nathaniel Barrell's father John was a wealthy Boston merchant. His brother William was also a prominent merchant, first in Portsmouth, later in Philadelphia; while brothers Joseph, Coburn, and Walter also were merchants in Portsmouth and Boston. Nathaniel spent some years in York (now Maine), where he married the only daughter of the town's richest merchant. He acquired a large amount of land in both Maine and New Hampshire. By 1760 he was engaged in trade in Portsmouth, but he left in 1766, evidently because he obeyed the Stamp Act out of religious, if not political, convictions. He became a Loyalist and lived quietly in York. After the Revolution he was chosen as an Antifederalist to the Massachusetts ratifying convention. George Ernst, *New England Miniature: A History of York, Maine* (Freeport, 1961), 170–177; Charles Edward Banks, *History of York, Maine* . . . (2 vols., Boston, 1931), II, 60–63; advertisements in the *N.H. Gazette*, July 15, 29, 1763, Feb. 24, Dec. 28, 1764, Jan. 25, 1765, July 11, 1766.

82 Lawrence S. Mayo, "Peter Livius the Trouble-Maker," Col. Soc. Mass., *Publications*, XXV (1922–1924), 125–129; *N.H. State Papers*, XVIII, 623–625.

83 The *N.H. Gazette* complimented his daughter, on her marriage, as having a "handsome fortune" (Jan. 12, 1770), but his estate was worth only £641. *N.H. Prov. Papers*, VII, 198n; *N.H. State Papers*, XXXVIII, 301–304.

84 Brewster, *Rambles*, I, 163n, 164–166; *N.H. Gazette*, Apr. 29, 1774.

85 Gilman's father was the town's wealthiest citizen, leaving nearly £10,000 at his death. Peter Gilman became a brigadier general and married the daughter of Samuel Wentworth. Arthur Gilman, *The Gilman family* . . . (Albany, 1869), 67–69; *N.H. State Papers*, XXXII, 709–713.

86 *New England Historical and Genealogical Magazine*, LVIII (1904), 227–233.

87 The Reverend Dr. Alonzo Hall Quint *et al.*, *Historical Memoranda Concerning Persons and Places in Old Dover, N.H.* (2 vols., Dover, 1900), 405–406.

88 The excerpts from the Council Journals that have been published in the *N.H. Prov. Papers* are very incomplete. Citations here are to the manuscript journals in the New Hampshire State Archives. The manuscript journals of the lower house were also examined.

89 Journal of the New Hampshire House of Representatives, June 5, 1765 (hereafter referred to as Journal of the House).

90 *Ibid.*, Mar. 1, 1768. The practice of blatantly demanding alterations

because the governor proposed them was also adopted on other occasions. See *ibid.*, Jan. 19, 1771, May 26–27, 1774.

91 See Leonard Woods Labaree, *Royal Government in America* (New Haven, 1930), 346–350.

92 Journal of the House, June 25–28, 1765.

93 *Ibid.*, Aug. 24, Sept. 25 to Oct. 1, 1767, Aug. 25, 1768, Feb. 28, 1769.

94 *N.H. Prov. Papers*, VII, 130–144, 154–155, 161–162, 215–219; Labaree, *Royal Government*, 378–379.

95 Journal of the House, June 11, 1764.

96 Message of July 14, 1775, in Journal of the House.

97 *Ibid.*, May 9, 1764.

98 Journal of the House, Oct. 26, 1768.

99 *Ibid.*, June 8–9, 1768. The Council added that such a request had always been granted.

100 "Reipublicae Amicus," Apr. 1, 1774.

CHAPTER 3

THE ELECTED

1 Henry S. Burrage, "Colonel Nathaniel Sparhawk of Kittery," Maine Historical Society, *Collections and Proceedings*, 2 ser. IX (1898), 225–264.

2 This statement is based upon records of Suffolk and Worcester counties. They are probably fairly representative of the colony as a whole.

3 Ellen Elizabeth Brennan, *Plural Office-Holding in Massachusetts, 1760–1789* (Chapel Hill, 1945).

4 See the extremely valuable account by Leslie J. Thomas, "Partisan Politics in Massachusetts During Governor Bernard's Administration 1760–1770" (diss., University of Wisconsin, 1960).

5 James H. Stark, *Loyalists of Massachusetts . . .* (Boston, 1910), 402–404; Lawrence S. Mayo, ed., *History of the Colony and Province of Massachusetts-bay, by Thomas Hutchinson* (3 vols., Cambridge, 1936).

6 Francis G. Wallett, "The Massachusetts Council, 1766–1774," *William and Mary College Quarterly*, 3 ser. VI (1949), 609–610.

7 Worcester County Probate Records, Will #44820.

8 Whitcomb's father was a cordwainer, tanner, currier, blacksmith, coffin-maker, and lime kiln owner, who left an estate of £2880, or £720 money. Charlotte Whitcomb, *The Whitcomb Family in America* (Minneapolis, 1904), 188–197; Worcester County Probate Records, II, 278. Woodbridge's father was a minister. Electa F. Jones, *Stockbridge, Past and Present . . .* (Springfield, 1854), 133–134.

9 Brennan, *Plural Office-Holding*, 17n.

10 Wallett, "Massachusetts Council," 606.

11 Thomas, "Partisan Politics," 251–253.

12 *Journals of the Massachusetts Council,* Jan. 29, 1766, Mar. 3, 1768 (hereafter referred to as *Council Journals*).

13 Thomas, "Partisan Politics," 444.

14 Wallett, "Massachusetts Council," 612.

15 *Ibid.,* 613–620.

16 *Massachusetts Spy,* Feb. 3, 1773.

17 Abijah P. Marvin, *History of the Town of Lancaster, Massachusetts* (Lancaster, 1879), 221, 297–300.

18 Jonas Reed, *A History of Rutland* (Worcester, 1836), 156–157; Edward A. Jones, *The Loyalists of Massachusetts, Memorials, Petitions and Claims* (London, 1930), 216–217.

19 *Mass. Spy,* Aug. 18, 1774.

20 Thomas, "Partisan Politics," 112, 305–306, 431–432, 711–712.

21 See, for example, *Council Journals,* Jan. 26, July 9, 11, 1772.

22 *Ibid.,* June 7, 1764, Mar. 8–9, 1765.

23 *Ibid.,* Nov. 6–7, 1765.

24 See for instance *ibid.,* Apr. 15, 1772.

25 *Ibid.,* June 15, 1763, Feb. 2, 1764.

26 *Ibid.,* Mar. 5, 1765.

27 *Ibid.,* Oct. 18, 23, Nov. 8, 1770.

28 *Ibid.,* July 14, 1772.

29 See also July 5, 1773, when the upper house insisted that the printing of the provincial laws be done under the direction of the governor and the Council.

30 Thomas, "Partisan Politics," 72, 79, 96–100, 354–378; *Council Journals,* June 14, 1764, Dec. 6–8, 1766, Mar. 19, June 20, 1767, June 21, 1768, July 12, 1769, Apr. 26, 1770, Apr. 24, 1771.

31 *Council Journals,* June 11–14, 1764, July 12–13, 1769.

32 *Ibid.,* Mar. 1, 1765, Jan. 31, 1766. But one finally passed in the latter year.

33 *Ibid.,* June 2, July 16, Dec. 31, 1763, June 21, 1767.

34 *Ibid.,* Jan. 18, 1765, June 23, 1768.

35 *Ibid.,* Dec. 29, 1763, Feb. 16, 21, 1765.

36 *Ibid.,* June 28, July 3, 1771, Apr. 23, June 25, 1772.

37 *Ibid.,* Jan. 3, 1764, Mar. 4, 1768, Feb. 4, 1773.

38 See, for example, *ibid.,* Jan. 16, 1764, Feb. 28, 1765, Feb. 4, 1773.

39 *Ibid.,* Feb. 18, 1765.

40 *Ibid.,* Mar. 13, 1767, Feb. 26, 1768, Apr. 17, 1770, Apr. 12, June 6, 1771, June 30, 1772.

41 *Ibid.,* June 16, 1763.

42 *Ibid.,* Feb. 17, 1767.

43 *Ibid.,* June 19, 1766. See also June 7, Oct. 25, 1764, Nov. 6, 8, 1765, Jan. 7, 1766, Feb. 19, Mar. 17, 1767, Nov. 8, 1770, Apr. 22, 177, June 17, 26, July 1, 2, 4, 1771, Apr. 14, 15, 1772. However the Council did allow some such sales.

44 *Ibid.*, Jan. 31, 1764, Apr. 25, 1771.

45 *Ibid.*, Feb. 2, 15, 16, 1765, Feb. 20, June 27, 1766.

46 *Ibid.*, June 2, Dec. 30, 1763, Feb. 17, June 2, 1768, Apr. 26, 1770, July 1, 1771, Feb. 3, 6, 10, 1773.

47 *Ibid.*, Feb. 15, 1765, Feb. 14, 1766, June 28, 1768.

48 For example, see *ibid.*, Mar. 1, 1765, Nov. 4, 1766, Feb. 11, 1767, June 7, 9, 1768, Oct. 30, Nov. 2, 1770, Apr. 14, 1772.

49 For example, the Council at first rejected a bill that permitted stage plays. On another occasion after a fire in Boston, the Council tried to delay for a number of days the construction of wooden buildings, but the House would not agree. *Ibid.*, Feb. 14, June 19, 1767.

50 Whereas ordinary farmers made up 15 percent of the Council between 1763 and 1774, they comprised about 47 percent of the lower house. Furthermore, 42 percent of the councillors had some higher education, as compared with only 27 percent of the representatives.

51 *The Connecticut Journal; and New-Haven Post-Boy*, Jan. 13, 23, 1769. Charles Grant asserts that the name of the person who had served longest was called first. In either case the effect was to name, in nearly the same order each year, the twelve incumbents. *Democracy in the Connecticut Frontier Town of Kent* (New York, 1961), 126.

52 Frederick Odell Conant, *A History and Genealogy of the Conant Family* (Portland, Me., 1887), 195–196; Franklin B. Dexter, *Biographical Sketches of the Graduates of Yale College with Annals of the College History* (6 vols., New York and New Haven, 1885–1912), I, 442–443.

53 Samuel Orcutt, *A History of the Old Town of Stratford and the City of Bridgeport, Connecticut* (2 vols., New Haven, 1886), I, 428–429, II, 1322–1333; Dexter, *Yale Graduates*, I, 418–419.

54 Charles Burr Todd, *A General History of the Burr Family* (New York, 1902), 7–32.

55 Allen Johnson and Dumas Malone, eds., *Dictionary of American Biography* (22 vols., New York, 1928–1944), XIV, 640–641; E. B. Huntington, *A Genealogical Memoir of the Huntington Family* (Stamford, 1863), 80–81; Edward Elbridge Salisbury and Evelyn McCurdy Salisbury, *Family Histories and Genealogies* (3 vols., 1892), II, 16–69. Huntington and the Pitkins were not lawyers but businessmen.

56 *D.A.B.*, XVII, 88–89.

57 Charles Henry Stanley Davis, *History of Wallingford, Conn.,* . . . (Meriden, Conn., 1870), 769.

58 *D.A.B.*, XVII, 450–451.

59 Loren P. Waldo, *The Early History of Tolland* (Hartford, 1861), 115; Dexter, *Yale Graduates*, II, 390.

60 With allowance for guesswork, the economic status of the fathers was as follows: wealthy, 6; well-to-do, 10; moderate, 6 or 7; poor, 1 or 2.

61 Thirteen graduated from Yale and two from Harvard; one attended Yale but did not graduate; and eight had no college education.

62 Despite the upheaval of 1765, when five of the assistants were displaced, the median term in office was seventeen years.

63 *The Connecticut Courant* (Hartford), Sept. 24, 1771.

64 See the account in Oscar Zeichner, *Connecticut's Years of Controversy 1750–1776* (Chapel Hill, 1949), 55–57, 267.

65 *The New-London Gazette*, Jan. 23, 1767; *The Connecticut Gazette* (New Haven), Mar. 28, Apr. 11, 1767; *Conn. Courant*, Apr. 4, 1767 (several articles).

66 *New-London Gazette*, Apr. 10, 1767; *Conn. Gazette* (New Haven), Mar. 28, 1767; *The Connecticut Gazette; and the Universal Intelligencer* (New London), Apr. 11, 1767. The Fitch group indeed had not altered their opinions. See Ebenezer Silliman to Thomas Hutchinson, Dec. 8, 1768, Connecticut Historical Society, *Collections*, XIX, 155–157, and Silliman to Hutchinson, Aug. 11, 1770, Conn. State Lib.

67 *New-London Gazette*, Feb. 20, Mar. 20, Apr. 3, 1767; *Conn. Gazette* (New London), Apr. 11, 1767; *Conn. Gazette* (New Haven), Feb. 28, 1767.

68 *New-London Gazette*, Sept. 9, Nov. 4, 1768.

69 *Conn. Courant*, May 9, 1768, Jan. 23, 1769; *New-London Gazette*, Sept. 29, 1769; Zeichner, *Connecticut*, 122.

70 *Conn. Courant*, Supplement, Apr. 6, 1767. The New Lights, Congregationalists who had been influenced by the religious revival called the "Great Awakening," were especially numerous in the eastern part of the state, which also was the stronghold of those interested in Connecticut's claim to the upper Susquehanna Valley. Resistance to British measures centered in the same area. See the account in Zeichner, *Connecticut*, Chap. V.

71 James H. Trumbull and Charles J. Hoadley, eds., *Public Records of the Colony of Connecticut 1636–1776* (15 vols., Hartford, 1850–1890), XIV, 347–350, 412–413. These records contain such proceedings of the legislature as have survived. No minutes have been preserved and disputes can be discovered only through newspapers or letters.

72 Lawrence H. Gipson, *Connecticut Taxation 1750–1775* (New Haven, 1933), 34.

73 *Coun. Courant*, Mar. 11, 21, 1768.

74 Both terms were used. The lower house was the "House of Delegates." "Upper" and "lower" were also employed.

75 David S. Lovejoy, *Rhode Island Politics and the American Revolution 1760–1776* (Providence, 1958), 15. I have relied heavily upon this excellent monograph. At the same time I am not convinced that the Ward-Hopkins parties were exclusively factional. Lovejoy underestimates the extent of sectionalism; moreover, as will become clear, there were distinct differences in political and economic attitudes.

76 Quoted in *ibid.*, 164.

77 Caroline E. Robinson, *The Gardiners of Narragansett* (Providence, 1919), 7, 24; John Osborne Austin, *The Genealogical Dictionary of Rhode Island* (Albany, 1887), 82; *Newport Historical Magazine*, IV (1883–1884), 83; *Rhode Island History*, IV (1945), 63; George Champlin Mason, *Annals of the Redwood Library and Athenaeum, Newport, R. I.* (Newport, 1891), 46, 52.

78 Austin, *Geneal. Dict. R. I.*, 238–239; ms. notebook, Rhode Island Historical Society.

79 Frank Alfred Randall, *Randall and Allied Families* (Chicago, 1943), 39–48.

80 Journal of the House of Magistrates, Sept. 11, 1765, Sept. 9, 1766, Feb., 1768; see also Sept. 14, 1769 (hereafter referred to as Journal of the Magistrates). These journals have never been published but are available on microfilm.

81 *Ibid.*, Mar. 5, 1765; see also "A Freeman," *The Providence Gazette*, Apr. 16, 1763.

82 Journal of the Magistrates, Oct. 28, 1763.

83 *Ibid.*, January session, 1764.

84 *Ibid.*, Oct. 27, 1769.

85 *Ibid.*, June 13, 1774.

86 *Ibid.*, Apr. 25, 1775.

87 *Ibid.*, Sept. 10, 1766. Old Tenor referred to paper money, previously issued, which had greatly declined in value. Lawful money was imaginary money which served as a unit of account, the value of which was set by law.

88 *Ibid.*, Nov. 1, 1765, Feb. 27, 1766, Oct. 30, 1767.

89 *Ibid.*, Sept., 1762, June 12, 1766.

90 *Ibid.*, Aug., 1762, May 5, 1775.

91 *Ibid.*, June 10, 1766, June 15, 1768, Feb. 28, 1769.

92 *Ibid.*, June 11, Sept. 10, 1766, Aug. 21, 1772.

93 *Ibid.*, June 11, 1766.

94 *Ibid.*, July 2, 1767, Mar. 9, 1769, Sept. 14, 1770.

95 *Ibid.*, Aug. 13, 1773.

96 *Ibid.*, June 16, 1768.

97 *Ibid.*, Mar. 9, 1769. The Wards were responsible for these amendments.

98 *Ibid.*, June 13, Nov. 1, 1764.

99 *Ibid.*, Feb. 7, 1770, Nov. 1, 1771.

100 *Ibid.*, June 16, 1764.

101 One other dispute deserves notice. When the lower house voted that no appeals to the king in Council should be allowed for less than £300 sterling, the upper house reduced the figure to £300 lawful (equal to £225 sterling). This of course greatly increased the number of permissible appeals. The Hopkins faction was in control at this point. *Ibid.*, June 12, 1771.

CHAPTER 4

THE ARISTOCRACY

1 Beverly W. Bond, Jr., *State Government in Maryland 1777–1781* (Baltimore, 1905), 11; Philip A. Crowl, *Maryland during and after the Revolution* (Baltimore, 1943), 31, 38–40.
2 *Maryland Historical Magazine*, XXXVI (1941), 315–336.
3 Allen Johnson and Dumas Malone, eds., *Dictionary of American Biography* (22 vols., New York, 1928–1944), VII, 366–367; Donnell MacClure Owings, *His Lordship's Patronage: Offices of Profit in Colonial Maryland* (Baltimore, 1953), 132.
4 *D.A.B.*, VIII, 549; J. Winfield Henry, *Letters and Papers of Governor John Henry of Maryland* (Baltimore, 1904); tax list for 1783, Sharf Collection, Maryland Historical Society.
5 Walter Worthington Bowie, *The Bowies and Their Kindred* (Washington, 1899), 431–437; Hester Dorsey Richardson, *Side-Lights on Maryland History* (Baltimore, 1913), 71–73; *Maryland Gazette* (Annapolis), Oct. 30, Dec. 1, 1766, Aug. 20, 1767, Oct. 6, 1774, Apr. 1, 1775, May 17, 1785, Sept. 27, 1787; Jane Baldwin, ed., *The Maryland Calendar of Wills* (8 vols., Baltimore), VIII (1928), 131.
6 Accomac and Somerset tax records, Virginia State Library; Clayton Torrence, *Old Somerset on the Eastern Shore of Maryland* (Richmond, 1935), 468n; Baldwin, ed., *Maryland Wills*, VI (1925), 246; William Hand Browne, J. Hall Pleasants, Raphael Semmes, and Elizabeth Merritt, eds., *Archives of Maryland* (65 vols. to date, Baltimore, 1883–1952), LVI, liii–lv, LXI, xliii, XLVII, 342, 470.
7 Thomas Johnson, who was left a poor orphan by his father's early death. Johnson was a native. None of the immigrants were self-made men, for all were given a good-to-excellent start by their parents.
8 Stone's great-grandfather had been a governor, but Thomas was descended from the governor's youngest son, and the family was respectable rather than prominent. In 1783, he owned 887 acres and 21 slaves, and therefore was well-to-do but not wealthy. Harry Wright Newman, *The Stones of Poynton Manor* (n.p., 1937); tax list for 1783, Sharf Collection, Md. Hist. Soc.
9 Thomas J. C. Williams, *A History of Washington County, Maryland* (Hagerstown, 1906), 247; J. Thomas Scharf, *History of Western Maryland* (Philadelphia, 1882), 1011.
10 The following table, though limited in scope, summarizes some of the contrasts among the various Maryland bodies described in the text. The House of Delegates in 1785 contained fewer prominent men than was usually the case. The figures are approximate percentages.

	Council	1765 Delegates	Senate	1785 Delegates	1786 Electors
Occupation					
Merchant	0 %	2 %	6%	4 %	6 %
Merchant/planter	18	0	11	5	8
Lawyer	4.5	5.5	11	4	10.5
Lawyer/planter	27	7.5	22	4	8
Planter	45.5	57	39	38	26.5
Doctor	4.5	0	3	7	5
Other nonfarm	0	4	8	1.5	0
Large farmer	0	2	0	5	8
Farmer	0	16.5	0	28.5	23.5
Unknown	0	5.5	0	3	10.5
Economic Status					
Wealthy	91	37	58	20	29
Well-to-do	9	39	36	46	34
Moderate	0	19	3	34	32
Unknown	0	5	3	0	5
Social Origin					
Prominent old family	82	30	42	21.5	26
Old family	4.5	56	47	59.5	66
New resident	13.5	15	11	19	5
Unknown	0	0	0	0	3

11 Alexander Graydon, *Memoirs of His Own Times,* John Stockton Littell, ed. (Philadelphia, 1846), 346.

12 One writer believed, "there can be no doubt that a well regulated democracy is most equitable. . . . We should by all means avoid *several* branches of legislature, . . . because a plurality causes perpetual dissension." *Md. Gazette* (Annapolis), Aug. 15, 22, 1776; see also July 8, Oct. 31, 1776.

13 For example, *Senate Journals,* Mar. 31, 1777.

14 *Ibid.,* Apr. 7, June 15, 1773.

15 On another occasion the senators asserted that the formal amending process was "a way more consistent with the independence of the senate, and the spirit of our constitution, than those private negotiations which have sometimes heretofore taken place, and most commonly to very little purpose." *Ibid.,* Jan. 10, 1783.

16 See the explanation given in *ibid.,* Mar. 9, 1786.

17 *Ibid.,* Apr. 3, 1777.

18 *Ibid.,* Mar. 20, 23, 1779.

19 *Ibid.,* May 6, 1780.

20 *Ibid.,* May 10–12, 1780.

21 *Ibid.,* Jan. 20–22, 1785.

22 *Ibid.,* Mar. 5, 9, 1786.

23 *Ibid.*, Dec. 30, 1786, Jan. 5, 6, 15, 16, 1787; Crowl, *Maryland*, 105–106

24 *Senate Journals*, Mar. 24, Dec. 13, 1779, May 6, 16, 1780, Dec. 4, 1781.

25 *Ibid.*, Dec. 26, 1785, Dec. 30, 1786; Crowl, *Maryland*, 90–92, 102.

26 *Senate Journals*, Jan. 5, 1787.

27 See, for example, *Maryland Chronicle* (Fredericksburg), supplement, Feb. 14, 21, 1787.

28 *Ibid.*, Jan. 31, Feb. 28, 1787; William Kilty, *History of a Session . . .* (Annapolis, 1786).

29 *Md. Gazette* (Annapolis), Feb. 22, 1787.

30 *Ibid.*, Feb. 15, 1787, May 10, 1787. See also for this view *Maryland Gazette* (Baltimore), Feb. 13, 1787; *Md. Chronicle*, supplement, Feb. 21, 1787.

31 *Md. Gazette* (Annapolis), Apr. 19, 1787.

32 *Maryland Journal*, May 1, 1787.

33 *Md. Gazette* (Annapolis), Feb. 8, Mar. 8, Apr. 5, 26, 1787; *Md. Chronicle*, Feb. 28, 1787; Kathryn L. Behrens, *Paper Money in Maryland 1727–1789* (Baltimore, 1923), 84. See also the long, impressive statement by "Aristides" (Judge A. C. Hanson) in *Md. Gazette* (Annapolis), June 14, 1787, and the reply by "Publicola" (William Paca) in *ibid.*, June 28, 1787.

34 *Senate Journals*, Feb. 18, 1786.

35 *Ibid.*, Jan. 6, 16, 20, 1787; Crowl, *Maryland*, 104–105.

36 *Senate Journals*, Apr. 19, May 4, 11, 17, 21, 25, 1787; Crowl, *Maryland*, 109. For other examples, see *ibid.*, 90–92; *Senate Journals*, Mar. 21, 1777, Apr. 13, 1778, Mar. 20, 1779.

37 Technically a proxy could not be purchased by any one person, but only by two persons acting jointly, one of whom was rich and the other poor. *Senate Journals*, July 2, 1781.

38 *Ibid.*, Dec. 23, 25, 1783, Jan. 17, 20, Apr. 24, 1787.

39 *Ibid.*, Apr. 16, 1777.

40 *Ibid.*, Apr. 18, 1777.

41 *Ibid.*, Apr. 17, 1777.

42 *Md. Gazette* (Baltimore), Apr. 9–18, Aug. 27, 1777. See also *Md. Journal*, July 27, 1777; *Md. Gazette* (Annapolis), July 17, 1777.

43 *Senate Journals*, Dec. 16, 1777, Apr. 15, 1778.

44 *Ibid.*, Jan. 15–22, 1785.

45 *Md. Chronicle*, Dec. 19–30, 1779, Apr. 14, May 5, 14, 1780; *Md. Gazette* (Annapolis), Feb. 18, Mar. 31, 1780, June 7, 1781; *Md. Journal*, Mar. 21, 28, 1780; Crowl, *Maryland*, 42–44, 71: *Senate Journals*, Jan. 29–30, 1781. For other illustrations of the senators' defense of property, see *Senate Journals*, Nov. 15, Dec. 12, 1777, June 5, 1782.

46 *Senate Journals*, Aug. 15, 1779.

47 *Ibid.*, Jan. 12, 1782.
48 *Ibid.*, May 27, 1782.
49 *Ibid.*, Dec. 30, 1784.
50 *Ibid.*, Nov. 30, 1778.
51 *Ibid.*, May 2, 1787.
52 *Ibid.*, May 24, 1782.
53 *Ibid.*, Dec. 16, 1777.
54 See, for example, *ibid.*, Dec. 23, 1777.
55 *Ibid.*, Jan. 21, 1785.
56 *Ibid.*, Dec. 28, 1785.
57 See, for example, *ibid.*, Dec. 16, 1777, Feb. 20, 1786.
58 *Ibid.*, Dec. 11, 1778, Jan. 11, 1785, Feb. 16, 1786, Jan. 18, 1787.
59 *Ibid.*, Apr. 5, 1777.
60 *Ibid.*, Nov. 25, 1777, Aug. 7, Nov. 24, 1779, Apr. 8, 1780; *Md. Gazette* (Annapolis), May 17, 1781.
61 *Senate Journals*, Dec. 14, 1778.
62 *Ibid.*, Dec. 13–15, 1778.
63 *Ibid.*, Dec. 13, 1778, Mar. 21, 1779, Jan. 9, 1783, Jan. 19, May 3, 1787.
64 *Ibid.*, Dec. 10, 1778, Dec. 21, 1779, Dec. 11, 1782.
65 *Ibid.*, Dec. 11, 1782–Jan. 14, 1783.
66 *Ibid.*, Nov. 24, 1785, Jan. 5, 1786, Jan. 15, 1787.
67 *Ibid.*, Jan. 21, 1785.
68 *Ibid.*, Mar. 10, 1786.
69 *Ibid.*, Mar. 11, 1786.
70 Crowl, *Maryland*, 106.
71 John A. Chapman, *History of Edgefield County from its earliest settlements to 1897* (Newberry, S.C., 1897), 130–133; Emily Bellinger Reynolds and Joan Reynolds Faunt, eds., *Biographical Directory of the Senate of the State of South Carolina 1776–1964* (Columbia, S.C., 1964), 230. This exceedingly useful work furnishes a great deal of information, although it provides little idea of the economic or social status of the senators and their fathers. Unfortunately it has no footnotes.
72 Thomas J. Kirkland and Robert M. Kennedy, *Historic Camden* (2 vols., Columbia, 1905–1925), I, 376–378.
73 He is to be distinguished from his cousins Stephen, son of Barnaby, and Stephen, son of Stephen, both of whom were also wealthy planters.
74 *South Carolina Historical and Genealogical Magazine, II* (1901), 50–55.
75 *Ibid.*, XXIX (1928), 78–79, XXXI (1930), 12, 133.
76 *Ibid.*, XI (1910), 225, 247; tax lists, Archives of South Carolina; Reynolds and Faunt, eds., *Biog. Dir. S.C.*, 299.
77 *S.C. Hist. and Gen. Mag.*, XVIII (1917), 188; *The South Carolina*

Gazette, July 11, Oct. 1, 1768, Jan. 11, Mar. 15, 1770; probate records, Archives of South Carolina.

78 The following table shows the composition of the South Carolina legislature before and after the War (in approximate percentages). Most of those who are unknown were probably farmers of moderate means.

	Council	1766 Commons	Senate	1785 House
Occupation				
Merchant	13%	12%	11%	7%
Merchant/planter	0	10	10	2
Lawyer	7	2	1	1
Lawyer/planter	0	10	8	5
Other nonfarm	7	6	7	7
Planter	73	49	46	37
Farmer	0	2	15	10
Unknown	0	9	2	30
Economic Status				
Wealthy	80	68.5	59	36
Well-to-do	20	19.5	21	24
Moderate	0	0	14	27
Unknown	0	12	6	13
Social Origin				
Prominent old family	80	47	36	22
Old family	0	18	31	14
New resident	20	14	31	20
Unknown	0	21	3	44

79 To be precise: ten lived on or near the coast, three in the transition area, and one in the west.

80 Journal of the House of Representatives, Sept. 1–3, 1779 (hereafter referred to as House Journal). These journals were never published but are available on microfilm. The only earlier session for which the journals are preserved is that of March–April, 1776. None exist until January, 1783, after which date the Senate Journal is complete except for the July, 1783, session.

81 House Journal, Sept. 6–9, 1779.

82 Journal of the General Assembly, Apr. 2, 1776.

83 Senate Journal, Feb. 10, 12, 1783.

84 House Journal, Aug. 9–10, 1783.

85 Senate Journal, Feb. 2, 17, 27, 1784.

86 *Ibid.*, Feb. 25, 1785.

87 "Philodemus," *Conciliatory Hints* . . . (Charleston, 1784). His arguments were repeated in the *State Gazette of South Carolina*, Sept. 7, 1786.

88 *Columbian Herald*, Mar. 28, 1785.

89 House Journal, Mar. 14–15, 1787; and see *State Gazette of S.C.,* Mar. 19, 1787.

90 John Drayton, *Memoirs of the American Revolution from its commencement to the year 1776* . . . (2 vols., Charleston, 1821), II, 177.

91 To Benjamin Rush, Aug. 16, 1784, Rush Papers, Philadelphia Library Company.

92 Senate Journal, Feb. 4, Mar. 1, 5, 23, 1784, Feb. 25, Mar. 1, 2, 1785, Mar. 16, 1787; *Columbian Herald,* Mar. 28, 1785, Feb. 27, 1786.

93 Senate Journal, Feb. 28, Mar. 9, 17, 1786. See the speeches given in the *Charleston Evening Gazette,* Mar. 11, 1786.

94 Senate Journal, Mar. 15, 21, 1784, Oct. 4, 1785, Feb. 21, 1786, Mar. 7, 1787, Feb. 18, 29, 1788.

95 E.g. House Journal, Aug. 6, 8, 1783; Senate Journal, Feb. 9, 15, 1787.

96 Senate Journal, Feb. 15, 1785, Feb. 21, 1786.

97 Senate Journal, Mar. 5, 14, Aug. 9, 1783, Mar. 25, Feb. 12, 1785, furnish examples; see generally those sessions. A disagreement occurred in 1779, the nature of which is not revealed by the records. House Journal, Sept. 6–7.

98 Senate Journal, Feb. 28, 1783, Mar. 12, 1784, Mar. 10, 21–22, 1785, Mar. 13, 17, 1787.

99 *Ibid.,* Mar. 1, 1783.

100 *Ibid.,* Oct. 1, 1785.

101 *Ibid.,* Mar. 21–24, 1787.

102 *Ibid.,* Feb. 18, 1788.

103 *Ibid.,* Oct. 8, 1785.

104 *Ibid.,* Mar. 21–24, 1787.

105 *Ibid.,* Mar. 16, 1784, Oct. 10–11, 1785.

106 Bond Books A, B, C, and D, Archives of South Carolina. The inventories of merchants' estates during the 1780's also show a very large quantity of outstanding debts. No doubt the western farmers owed considerable sums, as they did elsewhere, but South Carolina's paper money program seems to have been inspired by the planters.

107 For other illustrations of the Senate's accepting economic measures desired by the House, see House Journal, Mar. 27, 1787, Oct. 11–12, 1785.

108 *Virginia Gazette* (Purdie), June 7, May 10, 1776.

109 Peter Force, ed., *American Archives,* 4 ser. VI (Washington, 1846), 748–755; Julian P. Boyd, ed., *The Papers of Thomas Jefferson* (14 vols., in progress, Princeton, 1950–date), I, 341–370.

110 Earl G. Swem, comp., *Virginia Historical Index* (2 vols., Roanoke, 1934–1936) ; tax lists, Virginia State Library.

111 *Virginia Magazine of History and Biography,* XXXIV (1926), 212; tax lists, Va. State Lib.

112 *Va. Gazette* (Purdie), June 12, 1778; *Journal of the House of Delegates*

of the Commonwealth of Virginia (Richmond, 1778), Nov. 13, 1778 (hereafter referred to as *Journal of the House*). Another estimate of the firm's damages was £3670. *Ibid.*, May 29, 1778.

113 *Va. Mag. Hist. and Biog.*, IV (1896–1897), 380, XV (1907), 155, XXIII (1915), 411, XXIX (1921), 519; *Lower Norfolk County Virginia Antiquary*, I (1895), 108, IV (1902–1903), 165; tax lists, Va. State Lib.

114 *Va. Gazette* (Purdie), May 10, June 7, 1776; Edmund Pendleton to Thomas Jefferson, Aug. 10, 1776, in Boyd, ed., *Papers of Jefferson*, I, 489; Jefferson to Pendleton, Aug. 26, 1776, *ibid.*, 503–504; Jefferson and Madison in *ibid.*, VI, 280, 296, 308.

115 Archibald Stuart to Jefferson, Oct. 17, 1785, *ibid.*, VIII, 645.

116 Some two dozen votes are preserved, a third of which show no consistent pattern. On the remainder, one group of men voted consistently (five to one) together. Four were from the Northern Neck and five were from the Tidewater. Opposing them (five and one-half to one) were one from the Northern Neck, four from the Tidewater, six from the Piedmont, and three from the west. There were probably other differences than this sectional one, but the number both of individuals and of votes is too small for analysis.

117 *Journal of the House*, Oct. 30, Nov. 30, 1776.

118 *Ibid.*, June 3, 9, Dec. 1, 4, 9, 1777, Jan. 9, June 1, Nov. 26, 1779, and other instances.

119 Va. State Lib., *Bulletin*, XVII (1928–1930), 23–28.

120 *Journal of the House*, Nov. 25–27, 1783.

121 Archibald Cary to Wahington, Nov. 21, 1785, Washington Papers, Vol. 234, #48, Library of Congress; *Journal of the Senate* (Williamsburg, 1776), Jan. 5, 1787.

122 *Journal of the House*, Jan. 4–5, 1785.

123 *Journal of the Senate*, Jan. 3, 1788.

124 Joseph Jones to Jefferson, Richmond, Dec. 21, 1783, in Boyd, ed., *Papers of Jefferson*, VI, 414.

125 *Ibid.*, May 21, 1777.

126 *Journal of the Senate*, Nov. 11, 1776; *Journal of the House*, Dec. 11, 1776; Archibald Cary to Jefferson, June 19, 1781, in Boyd, ed., *Papers of Jefferson*, VI, 96.

127 *Journal of the Senate*, May, 1779, 65–66.

128 *Ibid.*, Dec. 9, 1776, Nov. 20, 1778.

129 Edmund Pendleton to James Madison, Richmond, Dec. 13, 1782, Madison Papers, Vol. 3, Library of Congress.

130 *Journal of the House*, June 4, 1777.

131 *Ibid.*, Dec. 29, 1785, Jan. 13, 16, 1786; Madison to Jefferson, Richmond, Jan. 22, 1786, in Boyd, ed., *Papers of Jefferson*, IX, 196.

132 Stuart to Jefferson, Richmond, Oct. 17, 1785, *ibid.*, VIII, 645.

133 Thomas Jefferson, *Notes on the State of Virginia* (London, 1787), 194.

CHAPTER 5
DEMOCRACY: THE FACTIONS

1 Elisha P. Douglass, *Rebels and Democrats* (Chapel Hill, 1955), 63–64.
2 Only two councillors, William Alexander and Henry Cruger, were rebels. The members of the lower house chosen in 1769 were equally divided. Representatives from New York City, Kings, Queens, and Richmond counties were Loyalists (eight to two, with one neutral).
3 Allen Johnson and Dumas Malone, eds., *Dictionary of American Biography* (22 vols., New York, 1928–1944), XI, 232; *New York Genealogical and Biographical Record,* II (1871), 1–7; Benjamin F. Stevens, *Facsimiles of Manuscripts in European Archives Relating to America 1773–1783* (24 vols., London, 1889–1895), XII (1892), 1233.
4 *History of Greene County, New York, with Biographical Sketches of its Prominent Men* (New York, 1884), 93.
5 William H. Hill, *History of Washington County, N.Y.* (Fort Edward, N.Y., 1932), 127–134.
6 To Marbois, New York, Mar. 10, 1784, Livingston Papers, New York Historical Society.
7 Newton Reed, *Early History of Amenia* (Amenia, N.Y., 1875), 71–73, 102–103; H. D. Paine, *Paine Family Records* (2 vols., New York, 1883), II, 205–206; *New York Mercury,* Feb. 10, 1766; *New-York Packet,* Apr. 11, 15, 25, 1782; *New York Assembly Journal,* Mar. 5, 1784. The *New York Journal* published a long eulogy at his death, praising his democratic ideas and Clintonian persuasion (Aug. 25, 1785).
8 Franklin Ellis, *History of Columbia County* (Philadelphia, 1878), 319–322.
9 Exceptions were Lieutenant Governor Pierre Van Cortlandt, Sir James Jay (based upon a few votes), and Volkert P. Duow, who was a neutral.
10 One exception was John Laurence, New York City lawyer and large landowner, born in England. He married the daughter of Alexander McDougall, merchant, son of a milkman, another exception. I have been unable to identify Stephen Townsend, unless he was the son of a small Oyster Bay farmer.
11 The following table shows the composition of the New York legislature before and after the War (in approximate percentages):

	Council	*1769* Assembly	Senate	*1785* Assembly
Occupation				
Merchant	31 %	28.5%	12.5%	14 %
Merchant/large landowner	44	7	9	1.5
Lawyer	12.5	3.5	11	12
Lawyer/large landowner	6	11	7	0
Other nonfarm	0	3.5	12.5	21.5
Large landowner	6	18	16	8
Farmer	0	25	32	43
Unknown	0	3.5	0	0
Economic Status				
Wealthy	94	43	39	11
Well-to-do	6	50	36	46
Moderate	0	7	25	43
Unknown	0	0	0	0
Social Origin				
Prominent old family	75	36	28.5	15
Old family	0	57	44.5	51
New resident	25	7	25	34
Unknown	0	0	2	0

12 *New York Senate Journal,* Oct. 23, Nov. 4, 1778.

13 *Ibid.,* Feb. 23, 25, 1779.

14 *Ibid.,* Sept. 15, 1779.

15 *Ibid.,* Jan.–Feb., 1785; Charles Tillinghast to Hughes, Feb. 28, 1785, and Hughes to Tillinghast, Mar. 7, 1785, John Lamb Papers, N.Y. Hist. Soc.

16 *New York Senate Journal,* Nov. 6, 1778, Nov. 19, 1784, Apr. 14, 1785, Mar. 17, 1788.

17 *Ibid.,* Oct. 25, 1779, Mar. 13, 1780, Nov. 23, 1781, Apr. 27, 1785, Mar. 13, 16, 1788.

18 *Ibid.,* Oct. 27, 1778, Apr. 20, 1784, Apr. 8, 1785; see also June 21, 1780.

19 Staughton Lynd, *Anti-Federalism in Dutchess County, New York* (Chicago, 1962), 70–72.

20 For example, *New York Senate Journal,* Feb. 12, 1784, June 30, 1781, Mar. 31, 1787.

21 *Ibid.,* Feb. 22–25, Oct. 16, 1779.

22 Thomas Tillotson to Robert R. Livingston, May, 1784, R. R. Livingston Papers, N.Y. Hist. Soc. See votes in *New York Senate Journal,* Mar. 10, 1779, Mar. 24–25, 1783, Nov. 15, 1784, Apr. 17, 1787.

23 *Ibid.,* Mar. 29, 1786.

24 *Ibid.*, Apr. 1, 1784, Apr. 4, 1785.

25 *Ibid.*, Oct. 3, 1777, Apr. 13, 1782.

26 E.g., *ibid.*, Feb. 23, Mar. 29, June 30, 1778, Oct. 10, 1780, Mar. 5, 1783.

27 *Ibid.*, June 20, 1780, Nov. 16, 1784.

28 *Ibid.*, Feb. 27–28, Apr. 18, 1787, Feb. 2, 1788.

29 Hamilton to Gouverneur Morris, May 19, 1777, in Harold C. Syrett and Jacob E. Cooke, eds., *The Papers of Alexander Hamilton* (in progress, New York), I (1961), 255.

30 *Pennsylvania Magazine of History and Biography*, XXXIV (1910), 480–483; Illinois Historical Society, *Journal*, VII, no. 2 (1914), 41–59; *Documents relating to the Colonial History of the State of New Jersey* (Newark, Trenton, 1880 to date), XL, 232 (hereafter referred to as *New Jersey Archives*).

31 *New Jersey Archives*, XXXIII, 218; *Cape May County Magazine of History and Genealogy*, I, no. 3 (June, 1933). He left £17,154 when he died in 1779, but this is a much inflated figure. *New Jersey Archives*, XXXIV, 271.

32 Frank H. Stewart, comp. and ed., *Notes on Old Gloucester County New Jersey* (3 vols., Woodbury, 1936), III, 109, 131; *New Jersey Archives*, 2 ser. II, 592, 2 ser. III, 2, XXXII, 60, XXXVI, 73.

33 Jotham H. Condit and Eben Condit, *Genealogical Record of the Condit Family* (Newark, 1916), 198–200; *New Jersey Archives*, XXXIII, 86–87, XXXIX, 91.

34 "A True Patriot," *New Jersey Gazette* (Trenton), May 12, 1779.

35 Jesse Hand, for example, was a Baptist of Cape May County. His father left a personal estate of £500, which Jesse doubled. Lewis Townsend Stevens, *The History of Cape May County, New Jersey . . .* (Cape May City, 1897), *passim; New Jersey Archives*, XXXVI, 98–99, XXXVII, 161; *Cape May County Mag. of Hist. and Gen.*, I, no. 4 (June, 1934). Similarly, Nathaniel Scudder's father was a miller who apparently had only a modest amount of property but who sent his son through the College of New Jersey. Nathaniel became a doctor, a colonel, a member of Congress, and the owner of a substantial estate. *D.A.B.*, XVI, 524–525; *New Jersey Archives*, XXXIV, 448–449, XXXV, 343. Abraham Van Ness's family were small farmers but he himself acquired a considerable amount of land and served as justice of the peace. *Somerset County Historical Quarterly*, VI (1917), 212–213; James P. Snell, comp., *History of Hunterdon and Somerset counties, New Jersey . . .* (Philadelphia, 1881), 654; *New Jersey Archives*, XXXV, 414.

36 The following table shows the composition of the New Jersey legislature before and after the War (in approximate percentages):

Occupation	Council	1761 Assembly	Leg. Council	1785 Assembly
Merchant	44%	30%	13 %	8 %
Lawyer	50	15	14.5	5
Other nonfarm	0	0	22.5	20.5
Large landowner	6	20	19.5	5
Farmer	0	30	26	59
Unknown	0	5	5	2.5
Economic Status				
Wealthy	90	30	31	10
Well-to-do	5	30	40	23
Moderate	5	25	21	59
Unknown	0	15	8	8
Social Origin				
Prominent old family	83	35	32	15.5
Old family	17	50	43.5	55.5
New resident	0	5	17.5	10
Unknown	0	10	7	8

37 These conclusions are based on nearly one hundred votes. The nature of the issues is seldom evident, and I have not undertaken the considerable research that would be required to discover their character. However, it is clear enough that the group composed of farmers and northern men of moderate property and humble origin was generally anti-Loyalist, favored paper money, tender laws, and relief to debtors, and usually took the side of the Assembly when differences arose. The nature of the division is rooted, to some extent, in historical factors differentiating the two Jerseys. In general, East Jersey was a small farmer stronghold whereas West Jersey contained many large estates. The following table shows the composition and political alignment of New Jersey's Senate (in approximate percentages). The two men whose occupation is given as "unknown" were both judges and probably should be considered either lawyers or "other nonfarm."

Occupation	Northern Group	Southern Group
Merchant/lawyer	30%	21.5%
Other nonfarm	10	28.5
Large landowner	30	14.5
Farmer	20	35.5
Unknown	10	0
Economic Status		
Wealthy	45	14.5
Well-to-do	50	53.5
Moderate	5	32
Social Origin		
Prominent old family	60	14.5
Old New Jersey family	25	57
New or unknown family	15	28.5

38 *New Jersey Assembly Journals,* Mar. 8–11, 1777; *N.J. Gazette,* Mar. 14, 1778.

39 *Journals of the Legislative Council,* Dec. 6–19, 1780.

40 *Ibid.,* Mar. 23, 1786.

41 *Ibid.,* Dec. 17, 1782, Mar. 23, 1786.

42 *Ibid.,* Sept. 21, Nov. 23, Dec. 6, 1781.

43 *Ibid.,* Mar. 14, 15, 23, May 26, 1786; *N.J. Gazette,* Mar. 27, 1786, contains a summary totally at variance with the evidence presented.

44 *Journals of the Legislative Council,* June 1, 1781, amending an act that repealed the legal tender character of the state's bills of credit in such a way as to limit the scope of the act. However, the bill itself, which was favorable to creditors, was then passed but was later rejected by the lower house. June 21, Oct. 6, 1781.

45 *Ibid.,* Nov. 14, 1778. But see Nov. 27, 1780, and June 27, 1781.

46 *Ibid.,* May 27, 1779.

47 *Ibid.,* Oct. 3, 1781.

48 *Ibid.,* Oct. 28–30, 1782.

49 *Ibid.,* Dec. 19, 1782.

50 John Baning, Thomas Collins, George Read, Thomas McDonough, and William Polk were elected three times; Richard Bassett, William Conwell, John Clowes, Joshua Polk, and Nicholas Van Dyke were chosen twice.

51 Assessment lists, Hall of Records, Dover. The median is of course reduced by the large number of people who had almost no taxable property. Apparently the assessors were supposed to estimate the annual income of each taxpayer.

52 *Pa. Mag. Hist. and Biog.,* XXII (1898), 103; William T. Read, *Life and Correspondence of George Read* (Philadelphia, 1870), 458–459.

53 *Biographical and Genealogical History of Delaware* (2 vols., Lancaster, 1899), I, 92–93, II, 100–103, 234.

54 *Genealogical and Biographical Records of the Banning and Allied Families* (n.p., 1925), 31.

55 James Geddes Craighead, *The Craighead Family* (Philadelphia, 1876), 41, 57–59.

56 Will, Delaware Archives.

57 *D.A.B.,* XVIII, 550–551.

58 For Collins, see H. C. Conrad, *History of the State of Delaware* (3 vols., Wilmington, 1908), III, 825–826; for Read, see Read, *Read,* 431–432; for Bassett, see *D.A.B.,* II, 39–40; for Van Dyke, see *ibid.,* XIX, 189–190.

59 *Minutes of the Council of the Delaware State from 1776 to 1792* (Papers of the Historical Society of Delaware, VI, Wilmington, 1887), 50–52, 187–188 (Jan. 29, 1777, Feb. 25, 1778).

60 *Ibid.,* 269–270.

61 *Ibid.,* 616–617.

62 *Ibid.,* 22–23, 80–84, 236.

63 *Ibid.*, 249.

64 *Ibid.*, 161, 388–389.

65 *Ibid.*, 90.

66 *Ibid.*

67 *Ibid.*, 226–227, 232–233; see also 252–254.

68 *Ibid.*, 256.

69 *Ibid.*, 252.

70 *Ibid.*, 118.

71 *Ibid.*, 253. The *Minutes* record the following statement: "The Council apprehend it necessary to strengthen the hands of the Executive Department, to render it useful, and give a necessary influence for the due execution of the laws."

72 *Ibid.*, 911.

73 *Ibid.*, 504–505, 514.

74 *Ibid.*, 780–806, 836–839.

75 *Ibid.*, 827. In these votes Read, McDonough, Grantham, Collins, Bassett, and Cook were opposed by William Polk, Joshua Polk, and Baning.

76 "Timoleon," in *The Delaware Gazette; or, the Faithful Centinel* (Wilmington), July 4, 1787.

77 *Minutes of the Council*, 975.

78 *Ibid.*, 1006, 1057.

79 See especially Emma Morehead Whitfield, *Whitfield, Bryan, Smith, and Related Families* (Westminster, Maryland, 1950); J. Bryan Grimes, *North Carolina Wills and Inventories* (Raleigh, 1912), 45, 53; Johnston and Jones County tax lists, N.C. State Lib.; Johnston County Records, Inventories . . . , 1781–1795, N.C. State Lib.; Zella Armstrong, *Notable Southern Families* (Chattanooga), II (1922), 50–55.

80 Walter Clark, ed., *The State Records of North Carolina* (16 vols., Winston, Goldsboro, Charlotte, 1895–1905), XII, 8–18, 20–25, 98–99, 109–111.

81 *Ibid.*, XIII, 725–726.

82 *Ibid.*, XII, 622, 787.

83 *Ibid.*, XIII, 762–764, XVII, 859–862.

84 *Ibid.*, XII, 97, 104–105, 257–259 XX, 183–184.

85 *Ibid.*, XII, 152, 227, 298–299.

86 *Ibid.*, XIX, 434, XVIII, 417, XX, 473.

87 *Ibid.*, XVIII, 160–161, XX, 430.

88 *Ibid.*, XIX, 459–460, XX, 379–380.

89 *Ibid.*, XII, 219–224, 409.

90 *Ibid.*, XVIII, 115, 47.

91 *Ibid.*, XIX, 121, XX, 82–83, 102, 347–348, XII, 156.

92 See, for example, Samuel Johnston to Thomas Burke, Edenton, June 26, 1777, Thomas Burke Papers, University of North Carolina Library; Archibald Maclaine to George Hooper, Wilmington, May 19 or 29, 1783, *State Rec. N.C.*, XVI, 962–963; Maclaine to Iredell,

Wilmington, Mar. 6, 1768, Griffith J. McRee, *Life and Correspondence of James Iredell* . . . (2 vols., New York, 1858), II, 138.

93 *State Rec. N.C.*, XII, 91–92, XIII, 586.
94 *Ibid.*, XIII, 553, 650. For the vote on the original act, see XII, 252.
95 McRee, *Iredell*, I, 419.
96 *State Rec. N.C.*, XVII, 825, 834–835, XIX, 215, 226, 435, XX, 71, XVIII, 199, XIX, 210.
97 *Ibid.*, XII, 798, 806.
98 *Ibid.*, XVII, 642–643.
99 *Ibid.*, XIX, 435.
100 *Ibid.*, XX, 30.
101 *Ibid.*, XIII, 578, 847, 858–859, XIX, 45, 70, 195.
102 *Ibid.*, XVII, 847, 850, 865.
103 *Ibid.*, XII, 633, XIII, 592.
104 *Ibid.*, XII, 83, 99, 102–103, XIII, 763.
105 *Ibid.*, XVII, 377, XVIII, 185–186.

CHAPTER 6

DEMOCRACY: NEW ENGLAND

1 Ellen Elizabeth Brennan, *Plural Office-Holding in Massachusetts, 1760–1789* (Chapel Hill, 1945), 112–117.
2 Robert J. Taylor, ed., *Massachusetts, Colony to Commonwealth* (Chapel Hill, 1961); Samuel Eliot Morison, "The Struggle over the Adoption of the Constitution of Massachusetts, 1780," Massachusetts Historical Society, *Proceedings*, L (1916–1917), 353–412.
3 For the Pittses, see John Langdon Sibley and Clifford K. Shipton, *Biographical Sketches of Graduates of Harvard University* (13 vols., Cambridge and Boston, 1873 to date), IX, 76–81; Brother Anthony of Padua, *The Tyng Family in America* (Poughkeepsie, 1956), 21–23. For the Woodbridges, Electa F. Jones, *Stockbridge, Past and Present* (Springfield, Mass., 1854), 133–138.
4 James Edward Greenleaf, *Genealogy of the Greenleaf Family* (Boston, 1896), 132–133, 150–151, 427.
5 Allen Johnson and Dumas Malone, eds., *Dictionary of American Biography* (22 vols., New York, 1928–1944), IX, 184–185.
6 William A. Benedict and Hiram A. Tracy, *History of the Town of Sutton* . . . (Worcester, 1878), 527, 726–728; *Centennial History of the Town of Millbury* (Millbury, 1915), 457; Worcester County Probate Records, XII, 229.
7 Samuel Breck to Henry Knox, Boston, July 14, 1787, Knox Papers, XX, 131, Mass. Hist. Soc.
8 Prominent among them were Timothy Paine, the wealthy landowner and Mandamus councillor who had managed to save his property by resigning and remaining neutral; General Artemas Ward, a well-to-do

merchant and Harvard man; Moses Gill, a wealthy merchant and large landowner of prominent family; and John Sprague, a prosperous Harvard-educated lawyer.

9 Their leaders were Singletary; Dr. John Taylor, a former senator and onetime well-to-do trader and land speculator, who had been jailed for a debt of £900 in 1784; Jonathan Grout of Petersham, a lawyer though not a college man, who was an enthusiastic Shaysite and later went to Congress; and Timothy Fuller, a former minister, teacher, farmer, Antifederalist, and longtime opponent of Gill in Princeton.

10 To illustrate: Thomas Dawes, a Boston merchant and Federalist, replaced Benjamin Austin, Jr., ropemaker, Antifederalist, and later Republican; Azor Orne, a Federalist merchant, replaced Aaron Wood, a well-to-do Antifederalist farmer; General Eleazer Brooks, a Federalist, succeeded Walter MacFarland, a poor farmer, Shaysite, and later Jeffersonian; Samuel Thompson, a wealthy Antifederalist trader and general from Maine, gave way to the Federalist miller, Dummer Sewall, of a prominent family; and Federalist Nathaniel Wells, a Harvard graduate, farmer, and judge, replaced Tristram Jordan, a Maine trader.

11 Senate Journals, Oct. 31, Nov. 10, 1775. These journals were never published but are available on microfilm.

12 *Ibid.*, June 13, July 4, 1783, Mar. 11, 1785.

13 *Ibid.*, Nov. 1, 7, 1775.

14 *Ibid.*, Nov. 8, 10, 1775.

15 *Ibid.*, Nov. 14, 1775, Apr. 17–20, 1776.

16 The same wording was used as during colonial times: e.g., "The importance of this matter ought to engage the most serious attention of this Colony. We therefore most earnestly recommend the same to your farther consideration, and that you will take such measures as to you shall appear proper for the obtaining that necessary article." See also *ibid.*, Mar. 29, Apr. 27, May 4, 1776.

17 *Ibid.*, Oct. 24, 1777, Oct. 9, 1778, Feb. 1, 1779.

18 *Ibid.*, Sept. 6, 11, 1776, Feb. 8, Mar. 22, Apr. 5, Oct. 17, 1777.

19 *Ibid.*, Dec. 2, 1777, Mar. 5, July 3, Oct. 5, 1782, July 13, 1785; *The Boston Magazine*, Nov. 1784, 580.

20 Senate Journals, June 22, 1779, Apr. 20, June 28, Sept. 28, 1781, Feb. 19, Mar. 14–15, 20, 1783, Feb. 25, Mar. 1, July 4, 1784.

21 *Ibid.*, May 3, 1781, July 1, 1785.

22 *Ibid.*, Apr. 17, 1778.

23 *Ibid.*, Sept. 30, 1782, Mar. 18, 1783.

24 *The Boston Gazette*, Feb. 5, 1781; *Massachusetts Spy*, Jan. 11, 1781.

25 Senate Journals, Oct. 17, 1786.

26 *Ibid.*, Nov. 4, 9, 1786, House Journals, Oct. 26, Nov. 6, 1786; *Boston Magazine*, Mar. 1784, Dec. 1786.

27 See, for example, *The Hampshire Gazette* (Northampton), Oct. 25, 1786.

28 Senate Journals, Feb. 20, 1787.
29 *Ibid.*, Mar. 31, 1788. The impost had been the subject of frequent disagreements earlier. For other testimony to the conservative bias ot the Senate see Caleb Strong to Theodore Sedgwick, June 27, 1786, Theodore Sedgwick Papers, Vol. A, Mass. Hist. Soc.; Samuel Henshaw to Nathan Dane, May 21, 1786, Nathan Dane Papers, Library of Congress; Marquis de Chastellux, *Travels in North-America, in the Years 1780, 1781, and 1782* (2 vols., London, 1807), I, 273–274.
30 Senate Journals, Apr. 14, 1777.
31 *Ibid.*, Apr. 21, May 5, 1777.
32 *Ibid.*, Mar. 5 to May 4, 1782.
33 *Ibid.*, July 5, Oct. 1, 2, 20, 1783; Joseph Pierce to Henry Knox, Oct. 7, 1783, Knox Papers, XV, Mass. Hist Soc.; William Hull to Knox, Oct. 14, 1783, *ibid.*; Stephen Higginson to an unidentified correspondent, Oct. 14, 1783, Etting Collection, Autograph Letters, Vol. VI, Hist. Society of Pennsylvania.
34 Senate Journals, Mar. 17, June 4, 9, July 3, Oct. 17, 1783, Feb. 6, 1784.
35 *Ibid.*, June 26, 1783.
36 *Ibid.*, Sept. 29, Nov. 8, 9, 1786.
37 *Ibid.*, Oct. 30, Nov. 9, 1786.
38 *Ibid.*, Oct. 30, 1786.
39 *Ibid.*, Feb. 6, 1787.
40 James Sullivan to James Duane, Apr. 16, 1787, Duane Papers, New York Historical Society.
41 *Boston Gazette*, Nov. 12, 1787; *The Massachusetts Centinel* (Boston), Nov. 12, 1787.
42 Senate Journals, Nov. 15, 1787, Mar. 14, 31, 1788.
43 Examples are *The Cumberland Gazette* (Falmouth), May 11, 1786; James Warren to John Adams, May 18, 1787, "Warren-Adams Letters," Mass. Hist. Soc., *Collections*, LXXIII (1925), 292.
44 *The Independent Chronicle. And the Universal Advertiser* (Boston), May 1, 1788; *Mass. Centinel*, Sept. 9, 1786; *Hampshire Gazette*, Oct. 4, 1786; *Cumberland Gazette*, Apr. 6, 1787.
45 Henry Jackson to Henry Knox, Apr. 20, 1788, Knox Papers, XXII, 19, Mass. Hist. Soc. See also Senate Journals, Mar. 29, 1788; *American Herald* (Boston), Apr. 18, 1788. The 1787 Senate was almost equally divided between Federalists and Antifederalists, but in 1788 the Federalists had a majority of well over two to one and perhaps three to one.
46 Oscar and Mary F. Handlin, "Radicals and Conservatives in Massachusetts after Independence," *New England Quarterly*, XVII (1944), 343–355; *Mass. Centinel*, Nov. 26, Dec. 3, 1785.
47 See, for example, Senate Journals, May 8, 1781.
48 *Ibid.*, Feb. 21, 1781.
49 *Ibid.*, Oct. 1, 1781.

50 *Ibid.*, Oct. 30, 1781.

51 *Ibid.*, June 19, 1782.

52 George Aldrich, *Walpole as it was and as it is* . . . (Claremont, N.H., 1880), 50–51, 193–196; Nathaniel Bouton *et al.*, eds., *New Hampshire Provincial, Town, and State Papers* (40 vols., Concord and Nashua, 1867–1943), XXI, 781–783 (hereafter referred to as *N.H. State Papers*). As a matter of interest, one-third of the senators are known to have been Federalists, but I have not discovered any Antifederalists.

53 Arthur Gilman, *The Gilman Family* . . . (Albany, 1869), 49, 73; *D.A.B.*, VII, 304–305.

54 Abiel Abbot and Ephraim Abbot, *A Genealogical Register of the Descendants of George Abbot* . . . (Boston, 1847), 131; Abiel Abbot Livermore and Sewall Putnam, *History of the Town of Wilton, Hillsborough County, New Hampshire, with a Genealogical Register* (Lowell, Mass., 1888), 552; *N.H. State Papers*, XXXVII, 122.

55 Louis Bell, *John Bell of Londonderry and his Scottish Ancestry* (n.p., 1920); Edward L. Parker, *The History of Londonderry, comprising the towns of Derry and Londonderry, N.H.* (Boston, 1851), 216–217. He was a Federalist. *The New-Hampshire Gazette, and General Advertiser* (Portsmouth), May 29, 1788.

56 Daniel F. Secomb, *History of the Town of Amherst, Hillsborough County, New Hampshire* . . . (Concord, N.H., 1883), 689, 901; *N.H. State Papers*, XX, 571n.

57 *D.A.B.*, XVIII, 503. Matthew Patten, a surveyor, farmer, carpenter, trader, and justice of the peace, whose long and valuable diary has been published, was also a senator. He came from Ireland with his father, who remains obscure, and settled in Bedford where he became prominent; but he never acquired much property, and died poor. Howard Parker Moore, *The Patten Family* (Ann Arbor, 1939), 13–23.

58 The following table shows the economic status of the New Hampshire legislators (in approximate percentages):

	Senators	Representatives
Wealthy	24%	8%
Well-to-do	58	23
Moderate or less	18	69

59 *N.H. State Papers*, VIII, 930–931, 938, XX, 603–604, 681, XXI, 33, 104.

60 *Ibid.*, VIII, 844–845, XX, 585–587, 744–745, XXI, 27, 341, 373, 376.

61 *Ibid.*, VIII, 887, XX, 170, 175, 601, 605, 661, 679, 681–682, 745–746, XXI, 22, 105.

62 *Ibid.*, XX, 737, 745, 798–800.

63 *Ibid.*, XXI, 215.

64 *Ibid.*, XX, 518–519.

65 One writer, on the contrary, praised the Senate: *New Hampshire Spy*, June 30, 1787.

66 *The Connecticut Journal* (New Haven), Oct. 23, 1776.

67 Timothy Dwight, *Travels in New-England and New-York* (4 vols., New Haven, 1821), I, 262.

68 *The Connecticut Gazette; and the Universal Intelligencer* (New London), Apr. 4, 1777.

69 See, for example, *The Connecticut Courant* (Hartford), Sept. 2, 1783.

70 *The Weekly Monitor* (Litchfield), Feb. 20, 1787; Samuel Wolcott, *Memorial of Henry Wolcott* (New York, 1881), 142–148.

71 *Conn. Courant*, Sept. 2, 9, 1783, Mar. 2, 30, 1784; *Norwich Packet*, Apr. 8, 1784; *Conn. Journal*, Apr. 7, 1784; *Conn. Gazette* (New London), Oct. 31, 1783; *New Haven Gazette and Connecticut Magazine*, May 31, 1787; Peter Colt to Jeremiah Wadsworth, Hartford, Jan. 25, Feb. 28, Mar. 28, 1784, Wadsworth Papers, box 135, Connecticut Historical Society; Jedediah Huntington to Andrew Huntington, Sept. 19, 1783, Conn. Hist. Soc., *Collections*, XX (1923), 466; Jackson T. Main, *The Antifederalists: Critics of the Constitution 1781–1788* (Chapel Hill, 1961), 90–92, 107–109.

72 Benjamin Gale to Erastus Wolcott, Feb. 10, 1787, Conn. Hist. Soc., *Bulletin*, XXVIII (1963), 19.

73 Charles J. Hoadly and Leonard W. Labaree, eds., *The Public Records of the State of Connecticut* (6 vols., Hartford, 1894–1945), V, 323–324.

74 *Conn. Journal*, June 15, 1785. For the sectional alignment on this issue see the vote in *Conn. Gazette* (New London), June 10, 1785.

75 To Henry Knox, Hartford, Apr. 17, 1788, Knox Papers, XXII, 10, Mass. Hist. Soc. James Wadsworth was in fact defeated, as Jeremiah hoped.

76 J. R. Cole, *History of Washington and Kent Counties, Rhode Island* . . . (New York, 1889), 534, 542, 553.

77 Caroline E. Robinson, *The Hazard Family of Rhode Island* (Boston, 1895).

78 "The American Whig, No. IV," *The Providence Gazette*, Apr. 24, 1779.

79 *The United States Chronicle: Political, Commercial, and Historical* (Providence), Feb. 16, 1786.

80 See, for example, Journal of the House of Delegates, Mar. 24, Aug. 23, 1776, July 25, 1780 (hereafter referred to as Journal of the Delegates).

81 See, for example, *ibid.*, Jan. 19, 1779, July 23, Sept. 16, Oct. 29, Dec. 1, 2, 1780.

82 Journal of the House of Magistrates, Oct. 31, 1783 (hereafter referred to as Journal of the Magistrates).

83 *Ibid.*, June 15, 1782, Oct. 29, 1783, May 7, 1785.

84 Journal of the Delegates, May 10, 1777; Journal of the Magistrates, Oct. 29, 1784.

85 The lower house voted six shillings per day; the upper wanted six shillings when members attended in the town where they lived, but nine shillings when they attended away from home. Journal of the Magistrates, May 12, 1783.

86 Journal of the Delegates, July 2, 1778, Jan. 21, 1779.

87 *Ibid.*, Sept. 6 ,1778.

88 *Ibid.*, Mar. 4, 1780.

89 Journal of the Magistrates, Mar. 4, 1783, July 1, 1784.

90 Journal of the Delegates, Mar. 2, 1780; Journal of the Magistrates, Feb. 3, 1782.

91 Journal of the Magistrates, May 6, July 1, 1786. It also concurred with votes to suspend the excise tax, to repeal the act making real and personal estate liable for debts, and to direct the treasurer to receive paper money in payment of continental taxes. *Ibid.*, May 6, July 1, Aug. 25, 1786.

92 *U.S. Chronicle*, May 11, 1786.

93 For example, Journal of the Delegates, Feb. 5, 7, 10, 1777, Oct. 31, 1781; Journal of the Magistrates, June 30, 1785, Aug. 24, 1786, Dec. 4, 1782, Nov. 1, Dec. 26, 1783.

94 Journal of the Delegates, Feb. 28, 1779; Journal of the Magistrates, Mar. 5, 1785.

95 Journal of the Delegates, Mar. 6, 1780; Journal of the Magistrates, Mar. 4, 1783.

96 Journal of the Magistrates, June 13, 16, 1787; *Providence Gazette*, June 23, 1787; *Worcester Magazine*, III, no. 14 (July, 1787), 175; *New Haven Gazette*, May 31, 1787.

97 Journal of the Magistrates, Sept. 14, 1787; *The Newport Herald*, Nov. 8, 1787.

INTRODUCTION TO PART THREE

1 See Stanley Pargellis, "The Theory of Balanced Government," in Conyers Read, ed., *The Constitution Reconsidered* (New York, 1938), 37–49.

2 *William and Mary Quarterly*, 3 ser. XXII (1965), 16.

3 Peter Force, ed., *American Archives*, 4 ser. VI (Washington, 1846), 839–843.

CHAPTER 7
THE UPPER HOUSE IN CONTEMPORARY THOUGHT

1 *Virginia Gazette* (Purdie), May 17, 1776.

2 *The South Carolina Gazette*, Sept. 13, 1773.

3 To Arthur Lee, Dec. 20, 1766, James Curtis Ballagh, ed., *The Letters of Richard Henry Lee* (2 vols., New York, 1911–1914), I, 19.

4 *New York Gazette and Weekly Mercury*, Apr. 23, 1770.

5 *Boston Evening Post*, Sept. 12, 1774.

6 *S.C. Gazette*, May 3, 1764. See the instructions of the Boston town meeting, *Boston Evening Post*, Sept. 26, 1774.

7 William Hand Browne, J. Hall Pleasants, Raphael Semmes, and Elizabeth Merritt, eds., *Archives of Maryland* (65 vols. to date, Baltimore, 1883–1952), LIX, 413; *An Answer . . . by a Friend to Maryland* (Annapolis, 1764), 7–8.

8 John Langdon to Josiah Bartlett, Portsmouth, June 24, 1776, *Historical Magazine*, VI (1862), 240.

9 *The Providence Gazette*, Oct. 26, 1771; *The Connecticut Journal* (New Haven), Mar. 17, 24, 1769; *Newport Mercury*, Nov. 21, 1763, Apr. 23, 1764.

10 *An Answer . . .*, 10.

11 *N.Y. Gazette and Mercury*, Apr. 23, 1770.

12 *S.C. Gazette*, Mar. 6, 1775. See also *ibid.*, Dec. 10, 1772; *Pennsylvania Chronicle*, Feb. 17, 1772; *New York Journal*, supplement, Dec. 7, 1769; Journal of the South Carolina House of Commons, Apr. 10, 1770.

13 *Considerations on the election of Counsellors . . .* (Boston, 1761).

14 *The Connecticut Courant*, Mar. 21, 1768.

15 *The Freeman's Journal, or New-Hampshire Gazette* (Portsmouth), June 15, 29, 1776.

16 *The Independent Chronicle. And the Universal Advertiser* (Boston), July 10, 1777.

17 *Pennsylvania Packet*, Nov. 26, 1776.

18 See also "Massachusettensis," *The New England Chronicle* (Boston), May 2, 1776; *Providence Gazette*, Nov. 23, 1776 (suggesting that an upper house might give advice, but should not have a negative; all authority should be concentrated in a House of Representatives so as to "reserve the power in the hands of the people") ; *The Independent Chronicle* (Boston), Mar. 6, 1770; Nathaniel Bouton *et al.*, eds., *New Hampshire Provincial, Town, and State Papers* (40 vols., Concord and Nashua, 1867–1943), VIII, 421–426; William L. Saunders, ed., *The Colonial Records of North Carolina* (10 vols., Raleigh, 1886–1890), X, 870a–870f; Robert J. Taylor, ed., *Massachusetts, Colony to Commonwealth* (Chapel Hill, 1961), 43, 71; *The People the Best Governors, or, a Plan of Government founded on the Just Principles of Natural Freedom* (1776), reprinted in Frederick Chase, *History of Dartmouth College* (Cambridge, 1891), appendix; Elisha P. Douglass, *Rebels and Democrats* (Chapel Hill, 1955), 177.

19 *Independent Chronicle*, July 24, Aug. 7, 1777.

20 *Pa. Packet*, June 3, 1777.

21 *Maryland Gazette* (Baltimore), Apr. 2, 1776. He felt, too, that "it would add to their importance, and give them more weight in the government, if on all vacancies they were to chuse their own members."

22 Peter Force, ed., *American Archives*, 4 ser. VI (Washington, 1846), 748–754.

23 Julian P. Boyd, ed., *The Papers of Thomas Jefferson* (14 vols., in progress, Princeton, 1950–date), I, 489.

24 Jefferson to Pendleton, Aug. 27, 1776, in *ibid.*, 503–504. A plan similar to those of Pendleton and Jefferson was published in the *Va. Gazette* (Purdie), May 10, 1776. See also *An Essay on a Frame of Government for Pennsylvania* (Philadelphia, 1776).

25 *Col. Rec. N.C.*, X, 870a, 870h.

26 Samuel E. Morison, in Massachusetts Historial Society, *Proceedings*, L (1916–1917), 389.

27 May 12, 1776, "Warren-Adams Letters," Mass. Hist. Soc., *Collections*, LXXIII (1935), I, 243.

28 Charles Francis Adams, ed., *The Works of John Adams . . .* (10 vols., Boston, 1856–1861), IV, 195–196.

29 *The Connecticut Gazette; and the Universal Intelligencer* (New London), Apr. 4, 1777.

30 *At a Meeting of a Number of the Citizens of Philadelphia . . .* (broadside, Nov. 8, 1776).

31 *Independent Chronicle*, Mar. 27, 1777.

32 "Andrew Marvel," in *Pa. Packet*, Nov. 26, 1776; "Scipio," *ibid.*, Oct. 8, 1776; "Demophilus," *The Genuine Principles . . .* (Philadelphia, 1776), 36–37; "Democraticus," *Va. Gazette* (Purdie), June 7, 1776; Thomas Burke to Governor Caswell, Mar. 11, 1777, in Walter Clark, ed., *The State Records of North Carolina* (16 vols., Winston, Goldsboro, Charlotte, 1895–1905), XI, 422; *Independent Chronicle*, July 24, 1777.

33 "Demophilus," *Genuine Principles*, 36–37.

34 William Hooper to the Halifax Convention, Oct. 26, 1776, *State Rec. N.C.*, X, 868.

35 No age limit was set in Massachusetts, New Jersey, New York, and North Carolina. Twenty-five was fixed in Delaware, Maryland, and Virginia, twenty-eight in Georgia, thirty in New Hampshire and South Carolina.

36 *Va. Gazette* (Purdie), May 10, 1776.

37 Marquis de Chastellux, *Travels in North-America, in the Years 1780, 1781, and 1782* (2 vols., London, 1807), I, 272–274.

38 *Massachusetts Gazette*, Aug. 19, 1783; *Falmouth Gazette*, June 4, 11, Aug. 20, 1785.

39 *The Cumberland Gazette* (Falmouth), May 11, 1786.

40 *The Massachusetts Centinel*, Sept. 9, 1786; *The Hampshire Gazette* (Northampton), Oct. 4, 1786; *Cumberland Gazette*, Apr. 6, 1787, May 1, 1788.

41 James Warren to John Adams, Milton, May 18, 1787, "Warren-Adams Letters," II, 292.

42 *The United States Chronicle: Political, Commercial, and Historical* (Providence), Sept. 28, 1786; *Independent Chronicle*, Feb. 15, Mar. 29, 1787.

43 *Conn. Courant,* Sept. 2, 1783.
44 *The Newport Herald,* June 28, July 5, 1787; *Providence Gazette,* June 16, 1787; James M. Varnum to Samuel Holten, 1787, Frederick S. Peck Collection, VIII, #17, Rhode Island Historical Society.
45 *New Jersey Gazette* (Trenton), Mar. 4, 1778, May 12, 1779.
46 Stevens wrote: "But it has been found from experience, that a government by representation, consisting of a single house of representatives, is in some degree liable to the same inconveniences which attend a pure democracy; a few leading men influence the majority to pass laws calculated not for the public good, but to promote some sinister views of their own. To prevent this, another representative branch is added . . ." *Observations on Government . . .* (New York, 1787), 39.
47 Benjamin Rush, *Observations* (Philadelphia, 1777), 7-9.
48 *Pa. Packet,* Mar. 25, 1779.
49 *Ibid.,* Jan. 24, 1784.
50 *Pennsylvania Journal* (Philadelphia), Jan. 31, 1784.
51 *Pa. Packet,* Feb. 12, 1784.
52 *Pennsylvania Gazette* (Philadelphia), Apr. 3, 1784, Sept. 20, 1786, Apr. 1, 15, July 1, 1789; William Bingham to Richard Price, Dec. 1, 1786, "The Price Letters," Mass. Hist. Soc., *Proceedings,* 2 ser. XVII (1903), 361.
53 E.g., Francis Hopkinson to Jefferson, Sept. 28, 1785, Boyd, ed., *Papers of Jefferson,* VIII, 562.
54 *Pa. Packet,* Mar. 24, 1789; *Pa. Gazette,* Apr. 29, 1789.
55 *Independent Gazetteer* (Philadelphia), Apr. 30, 1789.
56 Alexander Graydon, *Memoirs of His Own Times,* John Stockton Littell, ed. (Philadelphia, 1846), 344-346.
57 *Maryland Gazette* (Annapolis), Nov. 26, 1779.
58 *Ibid.,* Mar. 31, 1780.
59 *Ibid.,* Oct. 28, 1784; *Md. Gazette* (Baltimore), Oct. 11, 1785, Jan. 19, May 30, 1786.
60 *Maryland Journal,* Sept. 15, 1786.
61 "Publicola," *Md. Gazette* (Annapolis), Feb. 15, 22, May 10, June 28, 1787.
62 "A Constituent," *ibid.,* Mar. 8, 1787.
63 *Md. Journal,* May 1, 1787; "Aristides," *Md. Gazette* (Annapolis), Apr. 19, June 14, 1787; "A Constituent," *ibid.,* May 3, 1787.
64 Thomas Jefferson, *Notes on the State of Virginia* (London, 1787), 194; Boyd, ed., *Papers of Jefferson,* VI, 280, 296, 308.
65 "A Farmer," *Kentucky Gazette,* Feb. 2, 1788; "A Citizen of Kentucky," *ibid.,* May 10, 1788; Caleb Wallace to James Madison, Lincoln County, July 12, 1785, Madison Papers, Vol. 5, Library of Congress.
66 *Kentucky Gazette,* Feb. 16, 1788. The author is identified on the margin of a Mar. 3 issue as W. Ward.
67 *Conciliatory Hints . . .* (Charleston, 1784), 23. For the identification

of Tucker as the author see the supplement to the *Gazette of the State of South Carolina*, Mar. 3, 1785.

68 *Gazette of the State of Georgia*, Jan. 22, 1784.

69 *Ibid.*, Jan. 29, Feb. 5, 12, 19, 1784.

70 *Ibid.*, Dec. 4, 1788, Feb. 5, 1789. The word "sterling" was dropped, but this made little difference.

71 *Cumberland Gazette*, Apr. 6, 1787.

72 *The New-Hampshire Gazette, and General Advertiser* (Portsmouth), Feb. 22, 1783.

CHAPTER 8

THE UPPER HOUSE AND THE CONSTITUTION

1 Originally published in Philadelphia's *Independent Gazetteer*, June 3, 1786, this nationalistic article was widely reprinted: e.g., *American Herald* (Boston), June 19; *Charleston Morning Post*, July 7; *American Museum*, I (1787), 9–13.

2 Charles Francis Adams, ed., *The Works of John Adams* . . . (10 vols., Boston, 1856–1861), IV, 290.

3 James M. Varnum to Samuel Holten, Aug. 4, 1787, Frederick S. Peck Collection, VIII, Rhode Island Historical Society; Knox Papers, XX, 176, Massachusetts Historical Society; Jay to Washington, Jan. 7, 1787, H. P. Johnston, ed., *Correspondence and Public Papers of John Jay* (4 vols., New York, 1890–1893), III, 226–228. See also Dr. Thomas Shippen to T. L. Shippen, May 7, 1787, Shippen Papers, IV, Library of Congress.

4 Edmund Cody Burnett, ed., *Letters of Members of the Continental Congress* (8 vols., Washington, 1921–1939), VIII, 600.

5 To Nathaniel Gorham, *ibid.*, 603–604.

6 Max Farrand, ed., *Records of the Federal Convention of 1787* (4 vols., New Haven, 1911–1937), I, 20.

7 *Ibid.*, 26–27.

8 *Ibid.*, 48.

9 *Ibid.*, 52–53, 59.

10 *Ibid.*, 123, 132, 152.

11 *Ibid.*, 136, 150.

12 *Ibid.*, 151.

13 *Ibid.*, 151, 154.

14 *Ibid.*, 218–219. The minority included Sherman and at least one other Connecticut delegate, Gerry and Strong of Massachusetts, Pierce of Georgia, and one of the New Yorkers.

15 *Ibid.*, 233.

16 *Ibid.*, 254.

17 *Ibid.*, 289, 299.

18 *Ibid.*, 341–354. See also later remarks by Martin, speaking for one house (II, 4), and King, suggesting three (II, 6).

19 *Ibid.*, I, 409, 423, 425.
20 *Ibid.*, 421–422.
21 *Ibid.*, 424.
22 *Ibid.*, 426, 470–471, 475.
23 *Ibid.*, 426.
24 *Ibid.*, 512–514, II, 52.
25 *Ibid.*, I, 515.
26 *Ibid.*, I, 439. II, 4.
27 Mercer, *ibid.*, II, 205; see also Ellsworth (I, 406).
28 For an exception, see Madison, *ibid.*, II, 8–9. According to Lansing, Mason declared that "The second Branch is intended as a Check to the democratic Spirit." Lansing adds William Johnson of Connecticut to the list of those who made the same observation. Joseph R. Strayer, ed., *The Delegate from New York, or, Proceedings of the Federal Convention of 1787 from the Notes of John Lansing, Jr.* (Princeton, 1939), 86, 76.
29 Farrand, *Records*, II, 273–275, 278–279.
30 *Ibid.*, I, 527, 545, II, 275–277, 279–280, 297.
31 *Ibid.*, II, 286–288.
32 *Ibid.*, 292. See also Dickinson's statement: he "took it for granted that all were convinced of the necessity of making the Genl. Govt. independent of the prejudices, passions, and improper views of the State Legislatures." *Ibid.*
33 *Ibid.*, 632, 638, III, 192.
34 The dangers of election by the people were obvious, but might be avoided, in the opinion of the Nationalists, by longer terms—at least nine years, perhaps for life. The original Virginia Plan had called for indirect election by the House, but the decision that the Senate was to represent the states rather than the people made that method impossible.
35 See the discussion and citations in Jackson T. Main, *Antifederalists: Critics of the Constitution 1781–1788* (Chapel Hill, 1961), 136–139.
36 Richard Henry Lee, *Observations . . . in a Number of Letters from the Federal Farmer to the Republican* (New York, 1787), 9, and *An Additional Number of Letters from the Federal Farmer to the Republican* (New York, 1788, republished Chicago, 1962), 91; Jonathan Elliot, ed., *Debates in the Several State Conventions on the Adoption of the Federal Constitution . . .* (5 vols., Philadelphia, 1861), II, 308–309.
37 See, for example, John B. McMaster and Frederick D. Stone, *Pennsylvania and the Federal Constitution* (Lancaster, 1888), 569, 773.
38 *New York Journal*, Nov. 22, 1787, Apr. 26, 1788.
39 *American Herald*, Nov. 5, 1787.
40 *Pennsylvania Packet*, Dec. 18, 1787.
41 Lee, *Additional Letters*, 92–95.
42 *N.Y. Journal*, Mar. 10, 1788; McMaster and Stone, *Pennsylvania*, 540–541.

43 *N.Y. Journal,* Nov. 22, 1787.
44 *The Independent Chronicle. And the Universal Advertiser* (Boston), Jan. 28, 1788.
45 *Ibid.,* Oct. 18, 1787; Paul Leicester Ford, ed., *Pamphlets on the Constitution of the United States* (Brooklyn, 1888), 140.
46 E.g., Rufus King in Elliot, *Debates,* II, 47; Wilson in Ford, *Pamphlets,* 158; Tench Coxe in *ibid.,* 142; Jay in the "Federalist Papers," no. LXIV.
47 Elliot, *Debates,* III, 376.
48 For example, "Impartial," *American Museum,* II (1787), 376.
49 Fisher Ames in Elliot, *Debates,* II, 46; "The Republican," *The Connecticut Courant,* Jan. 7, 1788.
50 James Iredell in Elliot, *Debates,* IV, 133.
51 For Webster see Ford, *Pamphlets,* 31–41. The most important Federalist Papers on the Senate are nos. LXII and LXIII, both by Madison.
52 Ford, *Pamphlets,* 32.
53 *Ibid.,* 34.
54 The relevant numbers of the Federalist Papers were not published by any newspaper outside of New York, and did not appear in pamphlet form until May 28, 1788, when the contest was nearly over. See Elaine F. Crane, "Publius in the Provinces: . . ." *William and Mary Quarterly,* 3 ser. XXI (1964), 589–592.
55 *Independent Gazetteer,* Nov. 6, 1787.

CHAPTER 9

THE UPPER HOUSE IN REVIEW

1 Julian P. Boyd, ed., *The Papers of Thomas Jefferson* (14 vols., in progress, Princeton, 1950–date), I, 341–370.
2 William L. Saunders, ed., *The Colonial Records of North Carolina* (10 vols., Raleigh, 1886–1890), X, 867.
3 Theophilus Parsons, *Memoir of Theophilus Parsons . . .* (Boston, 1859), 370, 391–393.
4 Jackson Turner Main, "Government by the People: The American Revolution and the Democratization of the Legislature," *William and Mary Quarterly,* 3 ser. XXII (1966), 391–407.
5 See the fuller discussion in Jackson T. Main, "Social Origins of a Political Elite: The Upper House in the Revolutionary Era," *Huntington Library Quarterly,* XXVII (1964), 147–158.
6 "Atticus," in *The Independent Chronicle. And the Universal Advertiser* (Boston), Oct. 18, 1787.

A Note On Sources

The major sources for a study of the upper house during the years 1763–1788 are naturally the legislative records. Many of these have been published in various forms. The well-known colonial and state papers, or archives, contain the complete proceedings of the legislatures of Georgia, North Carolina, and pre-Revolutionary Maryland and New Jersey, and most of those for New Hampshire. Published separately are the records of New York's colonial Council, Delaware's upper house, and some, but not all, of the Virginia journals. Whenever these records were published at the time, they are now available on microcards as part of the "Early American Imprint" series, issued under the auspices of the American Antiquarian Society. See Charles Evans' familiar *American Bibliography* for listings. If the records were never published, they can be obtained on microfilm: see William S. Jenkins and Lillian A. Hamrick, eds., *Guide to the Microfilm Collection of Early State Records* (Washington, 1950). This applies to New Hampshire's Council, the Massachusetts Council and Senate as well as the lower house from 1786 to 1788, all of the Rhode Island records, and all of the South Carolina journals. In addition some Virginia records are available only on microfilm.

Next in importance are the newspapers. Almost all of them were used for this study. Although of very unequal value they are essential. If disputes occurred, as in South Carolina and Maryland, these are excitingly revealed by the press. Relations between the two houses can also be studied through contemporary books and pamphlets, which are especially useful for political ideas. But, curiously, private letters are very disappointing. I have read nearly all of the published collections and a number of the major unpublished ones to very little purpose, though once in a while something of value can be found. The explanation is that the upper house seldom was central in the controversies of the period and was therefore rarely mentioned.

The history of the relationship between the two branches of the legislature became, in some cases, part of the general history of the era. For background I have depended in part upon secondary sources. These include the usual colonial and state histories, together with more general

293

works of which the most important were Jack P. Greene, *The Quest for Power: The Lower Houses of Assembly in the Southern Royal Colonies 1689–1776* (Chapel Hill, 1963), and Leonard Woods Labaree, *Royal Government in America* (New Haven, 1930, New York, 1958). Naturally I drew upon the research done for my own books: *The Antifederalists: Critics of the Constitution 1781–1788* (Chapel Hill, 1961), and *The Social Structure of Revolutionary America* (Princeton, 1965).

Biographical data on the councillors and senators were obtained from genealogies and local histories, where these existed; historical and genealogical magazines; published and unpublished wills; tax records; and other similar sources. These materials are too numerous for individual mention, but some of them are indicated in the notes. The chapter dealing with political thought depends upon primary sources, although secondary works were consulted. The most useful was Elisha P. Douglass, *Rebels and Democrats* (Chapel Hill, 1955).

Index

Abbott, Jacob, Jr., 177
Abbott, Jacob, Sr., 177
Acadians: in Mass., 80
Accomac County, Va., 104
Adams, John, 73, 163, 205–207, 216–217
Adams, Samuel, 163, 208
Agent, colonial: of Ga., 9–10; of Md., 35; of Mass., 78; of N.C., 23–24; of S.C., 14–15, 18; of Va., 46; mentioned, 233
Albany, N.Y., 141
Albany Antifederalists, 225
Albany County, N.Y., 57, 134
Alexander, William, 57, 259–260, 275
Almy, John, 88
Amelia County, Va., 48
Amherst, N.H., 177
Anglican Church: in N.C., 27
Anglican party: of N.Y., 57
Anglicans: in councils, 95, 231, 234; in Md., 31, 102, 111; in Mass., 74; in N.H., 60; in N.J., 51, 143; in N.Y., 55, 59; in N.C., 27, 155; opposed to Presbyterians, 161, 239; in R.I., 183; in senates, 237; in Va., 45, 126. *See also* Episcopalians
Annapolis, Md., 28, 38, 105
Anne Arundel County, Md., 105, 255
Antifederalists: criticize U.S. Senate, 224–226; in Mass. Senate, 167–168; in N.C. Senate, 156, 158; in senates, 240; in S.C. Senate, 118; mentioned, 229, 282, 283, 284
Appointment, power over: in Conn., 85; in councils, 4; in Ga., 8–9; in Md., 33, 37, 233; in Mass., 77, 169–170; in N.H., 64, 66, 178; in N.J., 53; in N.Y., 140; in N.C., 23–25
Apthorpe, Charles Ward, 56, 260
Aristocracy: after the Revolution, 101; in Conn. Assistants, 182; in councils, 94–95, 231–232; decline of, 133; defended, 203–204, 214; in Md., 31, 204, 211, 214; in Mass., 166; in N.J., 148; in N.Y., 142; in N.C. Senate, 155; in senates, 161, 188–189, 214–215; in S.C. Senate, 114–115; in Va. Senate, 126; mentioned, 43, 132, 214
Aristocratic element: in New England councils, 201; in N.H. Senate, 175, 176; in senates, 202, 205; mentioned, 199, 205, 225
Aristocratic function: of New England senates, 187
Aristocratic principle: in Md., 104, 131; in U.S. Senate, 224; mentioned, 96, 129, 131, 190, 195, 238
Aristocratic tradition, 133
Armistead family, 257

295

Johnston, Lewis, 248
Johnston, Samuel, 154
Johnston County, N.C., 158
Johnstone family, 259
Jones, Allen, 156
Jones, John (of Brunswick), 125
Jones, Noble, 248
Jones, Willie, 156
Jones County, N.C., 157
Jordan, Tristram, 282
Jouvencal, Couchet, 24
Judges: in Conn. Council, 83; independence of, 26, 36, 113; in Mass. Council, 70; in Mass. Senate, 165; in New England councils, 92; in N.J. Council, 51; salaries of, 26, 113. *See also* Professional men
Justices of the peace: in Conn., 83; in Md., 113; in Mass., 172; in N.C., 160; in Va., 48

Kearney family, 259
Kemble, Peter, 259
Kent County, Del., 150–151
Kentucky, 125
Kershaw, Joseph, 114
Key, Philip, 29
King, George, 60–61, 175
King, Rufus, 221, 229
Kings County, N.Y., 134, 275
Kingston, N.Y., 141
Kittery, Maine, 69
Knox, Henry, 217
Knox, William, 9

Lancaster, Mass., 74
Land, unimproved, 66, 91
Langdon, John, 175
Langdon, Woodbury, 175
Lansing, John, 225
Large landowners: in Conn., 83; in councils, 95; in Del. 149; in Md., 106; in Mass., 70; in New England, 92; in N.H., 62, 175; in N.J., 50–51, 143; in N.Y., 54–55, 135, 139; and politics, 161; in senates, 189; in Va., 125. *See also* Planters
Laurence, John, 275
Laurens, Henry, 13
Lawrence, John, 51, 259

Lawyers: in Conn., 82–83, 180; in councils, 67, 95; in Del., 149; in Ga., 7; in Md., 30, 36, 102, 104, 106; in Mass., 70, 72, 164; in New England, 92; in N.H., 62, 175–176; in N.J., 50–51, 143; in N.Y., 55, 57, 135, 139; in N.C., 22; as Pa. Republicans, 211; and politics, 161; in senates, 189; in S.C., 114–116; in Va., 45, 125. *See also* Professional men
Leaming, Aaron, 51
Lee, Henry, 125
Lee, Joseph, 75
Lee, Philip Ludwell, 258
Lee, Richard, 30
Lee, Richard Henry, 199, 224–225
Leeds, Va., 48
Lee family, 44, 184, 257
Legal tender clause, 107–108
Legislative Council of N.J. *See* Senate
Leigh, Egerton, 13, 44
Lenoir County, N.C., 158
Leonard, George, Jr., 162
Leonard family, 71
Lexington and Concord, battle of, 21
L'Hommedieu, Benjamin, 136
L'Hommedieu, Ezra, 136
Liberty, personal, 152
Lincoln, Benjamin, Jr., 165
Lincoln, Benjamin, Sr., 69, 165
Lippitt family, 88
Little Compton, R.I., 88
Liverpool, England, 56
Livingston, Robert, Chancellor, 141
Livingston, Robert, Jr., 135
Livingston, Robert R., 136
Livingston family, 57
Livius, Peter, 61
Lloyd, Edward I, 29
Lloyd, Edward II, 29
Lloyd, Edward III, 29, 40, 103
Lloyd, James III, 30
Lloyd, Philemon, 254
Lloyd family, 29–30, 40–44, 50, 103, 184, 254
Logan, James, 50
Londonderry, N.H., 178
Long, Pierse, 176
Long Island, N.Y., 57, 134